WITHDRAWN
COLLEGE OF ALAMEDA LIBRARY

SO-AWB-716

E
183.8
J3
M46

Meyer, Armin
       Assignment Tokyo

DATE DUE

LENDING POLICY

IF YOU DAMAGE OR LOSE LIBRARY
MATERIALS, THEN YOU WILL BE
CHARGED FOR REPLACEMENT. FAIL-
URE TO PAY AFFECTS LIBRARY
PRIVILEGES, GRADES, TRANSCRIPTS,
DIPLOMAS, AND REGISTRATION
PRIVILEGES OR ANY COMBINATION
THEREOF.

Assignment: Tokyo

Assignment: TOKYO

An Ambassador's Journal

by

Armin H. Meyer

UNITED STATES AMBASSADOR TO JAPAN, 1969–1972

The Bobbs-Merrill Company, Inc.

INDIANAPOLIS / NEW YORK

Copyright © 1974 by Armin H. Meyer

All rights reserved, including the right of reproduction
in whole or in part in any form
Published by the Bobbs-Merrill Company, Inc.
Indianapolis   New York

ISBN 0–672–51961–5
Library of Congress catalog card number 74–6526
Designed by Jacques Chazaud
Manufactured in the United States of America

First printing

TO
Kiichi Aichi
who believed in
"mutual trust"

Contents

Foreword

IT HAS BECOME almost a truism that, as communications have speeded up, the role of the Ambassador and his embassy has declined in importance. In the eyes of some, the Ambassador has become little more than a postal clerk and his embassy a letter drop. More apt figures of speech might be to liken the Ambassador to a telegraph operator and his embassy to a hotel and tourist bureau for visiting firemen.

As with most truisms, in this one there is a kernel of truth but also a mountain of misconceptions. No one would dispute that a contemporary American Ambassador, no longer removed by weeks of sailing time from his government, is seldom called upon to make a major decision completely on his own. On the other hand, the decisions in which he does participate are incomparably more numerous and important than were those of the days of sailing vessels. A whole year of trade during that time might not equal one day of commerce now. An international misunderstanding that once might only have ruffled a few feathers in government circles may throw tens of millions into paroxysms of passion today.

It is fortunate that Ambassadors need no longer agonize alone over crucial decisions. But that does not mean that they and their embassies do not play a vital role in the vastly expanded and infinitely more complex international relations of our times. They are a prime source for the information and judgments underlying many important foreign policy decisions; they are a major channel of communication and negotiation; and they help to establish the image of America abroad and to set the tone of her relations with other countries.

Of course embassies and Ambassadors vary greatly in their functions and importance. Some countries are so small or so poor and underdeveloped that their contacts with the United States are limited to a relatively narrow scope. In others, such as the Communist nations, a basically adversary relationship constrains the activities of the Ambassador and his embassy to a limited even if very important field. In still others, such as the major English-speaking countries, relations are so numerous and communication so easy that the work of the Ambassador and his embassy shrinks to a relatively small proportion of the total field of contact.

In a country like Japan, however, the role of the Ambassador and embassy remains very large. High language barriers, sharply different cultural backgrounds, and psychological tensions surviving from clashes and inequalities in the past call for much greater efforts at communication and understanding than are required in our relations with countries of shared Western background. At the same time, our relationship with Japan is much larger and more complex than with either the Communist or the developing nations. Japan is by far our greatest overseas trading partner, second only to Canada in terms of both American exports and imports. Our defense relationship with Japan is the foundation for Japan's security and the basis for our whole strategic position in the Pacific and East Asian third of the world. Cooperation between our two countries, like cooperation between the United States and Europe, has become essential to the world's monetary and trade systems and will become an increasingly crucial element in problems of global ecology, the rational husbanding and allocation of the world's natural resources, and the increasingly urgent need to help close the widening gap between the rich and the poor nations.

Armin Meyer occupied the Ambassador's chair in Tokyo between 1969 and 1972. Having sat there myself not many years earlier, I know what a challenging and fascinating job he faced. He came without previous experience in Japan but with the sound training of a lifetime career in the Foreign Service and ambassadorial posts in the Middle East. As the account of his stewardship clearly shows, he quickly added a deep and broad knowledge of Japan, a sensitivity to Japanese points of view, and a clear understanding of the great importance of Japanese-American relations for both countries and for the world.

During Ambassador Meyer's stay in Tokyo, Japanese-American relations entered a period of difficult transition: Japan came to be recognized as an economic superpower; the Security Treaty between the two countries survived the crisis of 1970; the reversion to Japan of Okinawa with its one million Japanese inhabitants was achieved through careful negotiations and admirable statesmanship; and the relations between the two countries were repeatedly rocked by American "shocks" to the Japanese. Among the latter were President Nixon's sudden announcement of his forthcoming trip to China; the new American economic policy, which resulted in the revaluation of the yen against the dollar; and multiple trade disputes, culminating in a bitter fight over quotas on Japanese textile exports to the United States.

The relations between any two countries can be viewed from a variety of angles, but the Ambassador's chair affords a particularly good vantage point from which to observe them. Ambassador Meyer has given us a very comprehensive and clear account of Japanese-American relations during the crucial three years he was in Tokyo. Perhaps not everyone will agree with all of his interpretations. Differing viewpoints cast different shadows. And not until history provides us with a broader perspective can judgments be made with assurance.

In the meantime, however, it would be hard to write a more authoritative or better balanced account of these three important years in Japanese-American relations than the one Ambassador Meyer has provided us. And on one important aspect of the subject, this book will always remain the definitive source. That is the understanding and attitudes of the American Ambassador himself, which, even in these days of proliferating bureaucracy and instant communication, remain important elements in Japanese-American relations. Ambassador Meyer is to be congratulated on the promptness, thoroughness, and skill with which he has rendered his fascinating account of Japanese-American relations between 1969 and 1972, as seen from the Ambassador's chair in Tokyo.

EDWIN O. REISCHAUER

Assignment: Tokyo

Chapter 1

Mission: Adjustment to the Realities of the 1970's

"COME, MAMIE, SEE what a mess we have gotten ourselves into!"

General Dwight D. Eisenhower reportedly spoke these words in 1952 as he sat in a Chicago hotel, watching via television the roll call vote as the Republican National Convention selected him as its presidential standard bearer.

The Eisenhower exclamation came forcibly to my mind in mid-April of 1969 when a strictly personal telegram arrived in Tehran advising that President Nixon intended to nominate me to be the United States Ambassador to Japan. It was quite a shock.

The experience of one of America's ablest diplomats, Robert Murphy, our first postwar Ambassador to Japan, also flashed across my mind. Shortly after the signing of the

3

San Francisco Peace Treaty in 1951, Ambassador Murphy, then stationed in Brussels, received a telephone call from Secretary of State Dean Acheson suggesting the Tokyo assignment. When the surprised Murphy remonstrated that he knew nothing about Japan or the Far East, and that he had never laid eyes on the Pacific Ocean, Secretary Acheson urbanely asserted that that was precisely the reason why President Truman wished to send him to Tokyo. In Ambassador Murphy's words, his was "an unsullied Far Eastern record."

The Washington telegram to me included the standard question, "Do you know of any reason why the appointment should not be made?" In reply, I quite naturally referred to my lack of Far Eastern experience but hoped that other professional qualifications developed during twenty-six years of service in foreign affairs might provide adequate compensation. However, I was under no illusions. Japan's meteoric growth was astonishing the world. It would be an awesome challenge to represent the United States in Tokyo at such a critical juncture in the relationship between what were now the two strongest economic powers in the Free World.

In ambassadorial assignments, there is usually a stroke of chance. In this case it had occurred when I was in Washington at the end of March, accompanying the Shah of Iran to the Eisenhower funeral. Secretary of State William Rogers, whom I had never met before, greeted me by saying, "You seem to have conned a lot of people. I would like to talk with you." He and other top State Department officials indicated that a number of possibilities for my next assignment were under consideration. It was while describing some of them that Under Secretary U. Alexis Johnson bemoaned the difficulty encountered in trying to fill his previous post, the Ambassadorship to Japan. Suddenly he looked up and said, "We had not thought of you." At the time, it struck me as a most unlikely possibility because of my lifelong specialization in Middle Eastern and South Asian diplomacy.

Another stroke of fortune was that I had had chance encounters with Mr. Nixon when his presidential stock was low. We had met in Beirut in 1963 when he visited for a few days as a Pepsi-Cola representative. Of greater consequence, he had sojourned in Tehran for two days in April of 1967. As former Vice-President he was accorded special courtesies and was a house guest at the Embassy residence. He worked constantly, meeting with Iranian officials, seeking to understand Iran's problems, and asking incisive questions—particularly as to whether there might not be an excessive American presence overseas. His most important engagement was a luncheon with His Majesty, Shah Mohammed Reza Pahlevi.

At the time, the Shahanshah was quite displeased by the prevailing Washington attitude against the supplying of military equipment to developing countries. We at the Embassy were struggling to bridge Washington's negative attitude and the Shah's determination to have an adequate defense capability. Next door, the Iraqis were receiving lavish supplies of Soviet military equipment, and at bargain prices. A MIG-19 could be purchased for around $700,000, with financing at 2½% interest. For a comparable American F-4, the Shah would have to pay $2,000,000, with interest exceeding 5%, if—and it was a big if—Washington would agree to make the aircraft available.

With the unpredictable Iraqis possessed of a military capability more formidable than his own, the Shah was bent on building adequate protection. Noting how the Vietnam war had crystallized, he theorized that Great Power intervention was out of date and in fact undesirable. His Majesty trusted his American friends. But he believed it was in America's interest, as well as Iran's, for Iran to be equipped to handle its own problems in the region. If he were to rely on protection by American armed forces as envisaged in the Dulles pact-building era, the Soviets, he reasoned, would back his Arab neighbors. A protracted guerrilla struggle would take place as in Vietnam, and in the end there would have to be a negotiated settlement. Negotiations, he contended, imply concessions. The battle-field would undoubtedly be the rich oil fields of southern Iran. For Iran and its Shah, yielding territory in that area was an unthinkable prospect. Thus, the Iranian ruler strongly felt the best American course would be to stay out of regional quarrels and let the disputants settle their own problems. It was a view in which, without too much of what we diplomats term "localitis," the Embassy fully concurred.

In other capitals during his world travels the former Vice President was impressed by similar refrains. The essence of the Shah's thesis was what two years later emerged as the "Nixon Doctrine."

Because of what appeared to be a meeting of minds in Tehran, it was my impression that if, in the 1969 reshuffling, my candidacy for a particular post came to his attention, the new President quite probably would have a favorable predisposition. Presumably, that proved true when the proposal for my transfer to Tokyo came to his desk.

Prior to Tokyo, all of my diplomatic experience had been in the Middle East and South Asia: Cairo, Baghdad, Beirut twice, Kabul, Tehran, and two assignments in Washington with the State Department's Bureau of Near Eastern and South Asian Affairs. A key issue in that geographic region, of course, was the Arab-Israeli controversy. It was a tough school of experience, but we took some pride in bearing frus-trations, in forestalling outbreaks of hostility during pe-riods of direct responsibility, and in making progress when possible. Although I had visited the Far East, none of my previous diplomatic experience had directly involved areas east of the Indian subcontinent.

When on April 28, 1969, my appointment to Tokyo was announced, the reaction in Tokyo, according to press reports, was one of "disappointment." My immediate predecessors had been well-known personalities such as Douglas MacArthur II, Dr. Edwin Reischauer, and East Asian career expert U. Alexis Johnson. Following the latter's departure four months earlier, Japanese expectations had been colored by reports that the new American Ambassador would be a celebrity well acquainted with Japan, such as John D. Rockefeller III, or Bank of America President Rudolph Peterson (both were among those who reportedly declined the post). Disappointment at the nomination of a complete stranger was therefore understandable.

When my nomination came before the Senate Foreign Relations Committee on May 20, I anticipated that my lack of familiarity with the Far East would be a major obstacle. To my surprise, Majority Leader Mike Mansfield took a strongly affirmative view, stressing the value of having a fresh mind address itself to the situation. During the hearings, a staff member supplied Chairman J. William Fulbright with the *New York Times* clipping reporting Tokyo's "disappointment." Thereupon, the chairman seconded Senator Mansfield's observations and registered a tinge of annoyance at the Japanese reaction. It was almost as if the Japanese were guilty of intruding on senatorial prerogatives.

Not the least among those surprised on April 28 was the Japanese Ambassador in Tehran, Atsushi Uyama. My good friend and occasional bridge partner, he did his best to assure Tokyo that a worse choice could have been made. Of greater value were his words of counsel to the Ambassador-designate.

A respected and knowledgeable career diplomat, Ambassador Uyama feared there could be no more unpropitious time for any American to be assigned to the Tokyo ambassa-

dorship. First, he cited the question of the return of Okinawa, which would be a highly emotional issue. Even more
volatile would be the tenth anniversary, on June 23, 1970,
of the United States-Japan Treaty of Mutual Cooperation
and Security. Ever since the nationwide uproar in 1960
which forced the cancellation of President Eisenhower's
visit, opposition forces in Japan had been gearing up for
another "anti-treaty struggle" designed to destroy our security agreement at the termination of its original ten-year
life. Finally, Ambassador Uyama pointed out, economic
problems between Japan and the United States were becoming chronic and explosive.

No one could have drawn a more accurate blueprint of
the problems facing the American Ambassador to Japan
during those next three years. It was an assignment not to
be viewed without trepidation. Yet the very magnitude of
the challenge and its historic importance could not but be
stimulating.

Time, unfortunately, was in short supply. The Okinawa
negotiations were ready to move forward, and it would be
desirable for me to be settled into the new post prior to a
Japanese-American joint cabinet meeting scheduled in Tokyo in July. Before leaving Tehran on May 30, following a
ministerial meeting of the Central Treaty Organization, I
had devoured an abundance of material. At my request,
copies of all important telegraphic exchanges between
Washington and the Embassy in Tokyo had been received
in Tehran. Former Ambassador Edwin Reischauer's book
The United States and Japan proved to be an incomparable
cram course. I found highly instructive articles in *Foreign
Affairs*. Kei Wakaizumi, the Kyoto-based intellectual, emphasized in one article that a "relationship based on equality
and close consultation is the only one compatible with the
responsibility and dignity of both nations." Helpful con-

versations were conducted with Korean, British, German and other ambassadorial colleagues, with former Iranian Foreign Minister Abbas Aram, and with Grand Master of Ceremonies Hormuz Gharib, both of whom had served formerly as Iranian Ambassador in Tokyo. *The New York Times*'s Far East veteran Tillman Durdin came for a visit, and I talked with Shinichi Shimizu, the chief of the NHK (Japan broadcasting corporation) Middle East bureau, who came up from Cairo.

In Washington I was beneficiary of the wisdom of as many authorities as time would permit: professional Far East experts such as Under Secretary U. Alexis Johnson, Assistant Secretary for East Asian Affairs Marshall Green, his deputies, Ambassador Winthrop Brown, Robert Barnett and Alfred Jenkins, as well as Richard Finn and his colleagues in the Japan section of the State Department. There were discussions with Secretary Rogers, Under Secretary Elliot Richardson, Dr. Henry Kissinger, Secretary of Commerce Maurice Stans, Agriculture Secretary Clifford Hardin, the Pentagon hierarchy, Treasury Under Secretary Paul Volcker and his associates, former Ambassador Robert Murphy, the AFL-CIO leadership, New York business executives, and members of the Japan Society in New York and the Japan-America Society of Washington. Of particular value was an afternoon and evening with the recognized oracle on Japanese-American relations, former Ambassador Reischauer.

When my wife, our daughter Kathy, and I deplaned at Haneda Airport on June 23, 1969, we realized that we did not enjoy the psychological advantages of our predecessors. We would have to try harder. Soon we were in the swing of Tokyo's arduous activities, grateful for the limitless hospitality accorded us, and trying to make our contribution.

The American press corps, which included a number of

Japan specialists, treated our arrival without much sympathy. Inevitably, the interests of newsmen and diplomats tend to be at variance. For the latter, the objective is the accentuation of the positive. For the Fourth Estate, penetrating vigilance is exercised by a man-bites-dog approach to newsworthiness. Nonetheless, except for a rare acerbic comment (particularly when denied privileged information), American journalists in Tokyo treated the Embassy and our endeavors fairly. Despite the cool initial reception, our relations with them developed in the months ahead into warm friendship.

On July 4, the day after the presentation of my credentials to the Emperor, the Meyers made their debut before the entire American community, which included hundreds of businessmen and their families. They, too, were curious, but warmed up for the duration of our tour when in remarks at the traditional get-together at the American Club I assured them that, when hearing about our appointment, the Meyers were just as shocked as was Tokyo.

On the Japanese side, we quickly developed warm relations with our colleagues in the Foreign Ministry. Most of them had served abroad, could communicate well, and could see problems in perspective. Foreign Minister Kiichi Aichi extended a cordial welcome, as did Prime Minister Sato. Most enheartening of all, however, was the graciousness of Their Majesties, the Emperor and Empress. It was clear, as it was in subsequent encounters, that Emperor Hirohito had a profound friendship and admiration for America and an undying appreciation for America's postwar cooperation.

A few weeks after our arrival, *Mainichi* published an editorial referring to the initial Japanese "disappointment" over my assignment to Japan. It was written by the Japanese diplomat who had startled his fellow countrymen with his book "Japan Unmasked," and it suggested that the time had come for Japan to act like an adult nation. As a mature nation, the editorial said, Japan should not always expect to be favored with a familiar or partisan representative from Uncle Sam.

Although it was not intended as such, the appointment of an American Ambassador unfamiliar to the Japanese was, as the *Mainichi* editorial suggested, symptomatic of the fact that the postwar big and little brother relationship had come to an end. It was an unintended signal that, consonant with the realities of the 1970's, including Japan's new maturity, adjustments in the Japan-America partnership were in the offing.

On the occasion of a White House call by a senior American Ambassador, President Roosevelt once noted that he had received glowing reports regarding the Ambassador's performance and had heard how highly the Ambassador was respected by the people of the country to which he was accredited. The President, however, added that what he would like to know was, "What do you have on your order pad?" What specifically had been achieved?

With the social side of diplomatic life receiving so much publicity, few people, not even the home office, can appreciate the real work which is done by an embassy. Diplomacy is truly a profession. Behind the scenes, untold effort is invested through long, hard, and quiet bargaining before results are achieved. Even then many successes go unadvertised, for if either party claims a negotiating victory, it implies a defeat for the other, thereby jeopardizing the success attained, as well as the long-range negotiating process.

Before embarking on a foreign assignment, it behooves a diplomat to survey the wide range of matters in which his country and the country of his assignment are mutually interested, and to assess the broad challenge before him. A

State Department or a Foreign Office can and does prepare "national estimates" or "country plans," but the diplomatic officer must have a personal sense of what he and his mission are trying to do.

Even in the early days of my Foreign Service career, each posting seemed to have a purpose. In Cairo, with the Office of War Information in 1943 and 1944, it was to assure a favorable Egyptian disposition to the Allied war effort. In Baghdad, 1944–48, it was to "hold the fort," to maintain American interests to the extent possible, despite the furor which predictably was unleashed in the Arab world by the creation of Israel. In Beirut, 1952–55, and in Washington, 1957–61, the mission was to forestall the outbreak of Arab-Israeli hostilities by such flanking movements as the resolution of the Jordan waters problem. In Kabul, 1955–57, the challenge, successfully accomplished, was to secure the reopening of the frontier and the restoration of normalcy to Pak-Afghan relations, thus providing the landlocked Afghans with an alternative to virtually complete dependence on their giant Communist neighbor to the north.

When President Kennedy appointed me Ambassador to Lebanon in 1961, the overriding challenge was to prevent an explosion similar to that which had occurred in 1958, when, in response to a Lebanese request, it became necessary to land an American peacekeeping expedition near Beirut. With another Lebanese Presidential-succession problem looming in 1964, my purpose was to encourage a peaceful solution, without getting personally involved or favoring the candidacy of any individual. Happily, the Lebanese stuck doggedly to their Constitutional processes and achieved the first peaceful Presidential transition since Lebanon gained its independence in 1943. It served as a precedent, which was repeated in 1970.

At the Tehran Embassy, to which President Johnson

appointed me in 1965, the task was largely one of reversing a long standing Washington attitude whereby the Shah of Iran was treated as some sort of school boy, and securing both recognition and support for the progress being made under his leadership. Recovering from a decade of political unrest and economic adversities, Iran by 1965 was proudly standing on its own feet. Some might argue that this mission was too successful, for with the coming of the Nixon administration the pendulum swung in the other direction: e.g., unrestricted, if not enthusiastic, arms sales to Iran.

Both at Beirut and Tehran, it was possible for us formally to terminate United States assistance programs. Not the least of our achievements was assuring in both countries that the cutoff of aid did not provoke bitterness but instead was celebrated as an occasion for congratulation. Never far from my memory had been a remark made in 1961 by Secretary of State Dean Rusk at one of his morning staff meetings that he would award a gold medal to anyone capable of closing down an aid program. More gratifying than the medals, which were never received, was the opportunity to serve at posts where the greater purpose envisaged by Secretary Rusk could be accomplished.

Secretary Rogers described Tokyo as one of the two most important posts in the United States diplomatic service. While the magnitude of the challenge in Japan was beyond comparison, there was a common denominator as far as my two previous posts and my new one were concerned. Between the United States and each of the three there had been since World War II what the psychologists call a "tilt" relationship. Politically, economically, and from the security standpoint, there had existed in varying degrees a dependence on the United States which no longer conformed to realities. A better balance was in order and already well under way. My mission to Japan, therefore, would be to ensure that the United States-Japan relationship would be adjusted to feature greater equality, reciprocity, and partnership. As in Lebanon and Iran, the supreme test would be whether the adjustments, unavoidably painful, could be accomplished without disservice to fundamental bonds of ideology and friendship.

The advice from my Japanese colleague in Tehran included a plea never to suggest in Tokyo any similarities between Japan and my previous posts. A proud and sensitive people, the Japanese would not be flattered.

Ambassador Uyama's advice was sound, and in Tokyo I downplayed my past experience. Privately, however, in addition to finding a common denominator in my missions, I was often struck by behavioral similarities, particularly in terms of a rising tide of nationalistic sentiment. For the overwhelming majority of Japanese, including the government, this sentiment was a justifiable manifestation of national pride in Japan's accomplishments. This prevailing sentiment was, under Prime Minister Sato's leadership, accompanied by mature and responsible behavior. However, when one read the daily newspapers or listened to harangues by representatives of the opposition parties, one could not fail to sense the same sort of excessive nationalism which had plagued some of the nations of the Middle East.

Japan's new sense of national pride was only one of many indications of how the world had changed by the 1970's. Postwar conditions no longer obtained and policies based on them were no longer valid. Devastated nations had made remarkable recovery, none more phenomenal than that of Japan. The nations of Europe were flourishing. The Communist monolith was a faded illusion. Emerging nations were becoming more self-reliant.

Meanwhile, if there had ever been the possibility of a Pax Americana, it, too, was a faded illusion. Taught by two world wars that peace was unattainable without the most powerful nation playing a role, Americans had plunged into world affairs with vigor. Without these American endeavors, the dramatic world changes of the 1950's and 1960's would not have occurred.

Adjusting to these new dramatic realities was the great challenge which faced the United States, Japan, and the world in mid-1969. In Japan, the danger lay in a possible drift toward inordinate nationalism. In the United States, the apprehension was that the pendulum would swing from overinvolvement and overextension in world affairs to a new isolationism. In both nations, while adjustments were necessary, overreaction was to be avoided.

Although there was a certain inevitability about the adjustments needed for 1970's realities, they were first enunciated by President Nixon in Guam on July 25, 1969. It was an unexpected and inauspicious launching site for the President's broad policy thoughts. He shared them informally with the accompanying press corps at the start of a globe-circling journey. Reduced to essentials, the revised American policy assured that the United States would continue to play a key role in world affairs, but at the same time would expect other nations which had gained in strength to assume greater responsibility.

The Embassy in Tokyo was among the first to recognize the importance of the President's discourse, which was well reported in the Japanese press. Also obviously impressed by what later became known as "The Nixon Doctrine" was Senate Majority Leader Mike Mansfield. Within a few weeks, accompanied by the Secretary of the Senate Francis Valeo, he was visiting East Asian capitals to demonstrate his support. Returning through Tokyo, the Senator voiced concern that not all American diplomats in the area seemed to have grasped the significance of the President's policy. He was not even sure it was fully understood in Washington. In Tokyo, however, he found that the new doctrine was already an active ingredient in our diplomatic endeavors.

Even as in mid-1969 the United States was groping for its new and more realistic role in world affairs, so was Japan.

In twenty-five short years, the Japanese nation had risen from the ashes of World War II to become second in the Free World in economic strength. Its Gross National Product had more than quadrupled in the last decade. This economic miracle was accompanied by a resounding recovery of morale, self-confidence, and national pride. As Ambassador Reischauer had observed, the hosting of the 1964 Olympics had provided opportunity for Japan to display its competence to the world, and in so doing to reinforce the new faith which the Japanese had in themselves. Six years later, Japanese self-confidence had turned into exhilaration with the successful staging of Expo 70 in Osaka, and people all over the world became more graphically aware of Japan's progress and prowess.

In assessing Japan's economic upsurge, futurologists like Herman Kahn were predicting that Japan would surpass the Soviet Union, and perhaps even the United States, as an economic power by the end of this century. Not all observers were prepared to agree that Japan's meteoric rise would continue straight upward, but clearly Japan was already in a superpower class economically.

With such a record of growth, the Japanese economic giant could not expect to remain a pygmy in international affairs. Neither was it logical, as Minister of International Trade and Industry Kiichi Miyazawa frequently pointed out, for Japan to continue to be granted the same types of favors and special dispensations which were accorded when Japan was flat on its economic back. Despite their outward exhilaration, most Japanese instinctively still had a lingering sense of insecurity and inferiority. They seemed to lack full comprehension of Japan's new power and the responsibilities which that power bestowed upon them. In short, few

Japanese truly appreciated that their country was groping for its role in international affairs, and fewer still were giving thought to what that role should be.

While there were some similarities between my mission to Iran and that to Japan, there were many more dissimilarities. Probably the most dramatic was in the decision-making process. In Iran, His Majesty, Shah Mohammed Reza Pahlevi, would study any issue intensively and receive advice from his cabinet and other officials. If the Shah were persuaded with regard to a certain course of action, there was little doubt that the course would be promptly pursued. This type of rulership had deep cultural roots throughout the Middle East, where for centuries societies which were essentially tribal in character had tended to follow a strong leader.

In Japan, the system was infinitely more intricate and delicate. The Emperor's role was largely symbolic. The Prime Minister and the Cabinet theoretically governed, but decision-making relied heavily on the generation of a "consensus" among all interested segments of the body politic. These included not only elements of the ruling political party, the bureaucracy, and the business community, but even the opposition parties and the usually critical press had roles to play in this participatory democracy. Long before the phrase "negotiation rather than confrontation" became prominent in American rhetoric, the concept was a fundamental ingredient of Japanese culture. In practice, it was deftly conducted so that no participant need lose face. The process, which could be very time consuming, was employed not only in governmental affairs but in business matters and other sectors of society, including the family. In international dealings, the "consensus" system meant, of course, that quick or dramatic shifts in Japanese policies could not normally be expected. Specifically, it meant that it was not sufficient to persuade a leader or a group of leaders; more widespread agreement among interested parties would be necessary.

Behind Japan's consensus mentality lay a group consciousness that could be attributed to Japan's geographic insularity and to its population, whose homogeneity was unique in the world. In the various sectors of society, there could be many subgroups. The ruling Liberal Democratic Party had its Sato, Maeo, Nakasone, and other factions. A worker considered himself a Mitsubishi-man, or a part of whatever company engaged his allegiance. Beyond the loyalty to the group or subgroup, with the self-discipline and the respect for authority which that inspired, there was an overriding sense of duty to the nation. A most dramatic example of this was the honor which World War II kamikaze pilots felt in being chosen to make the supreme sacrifice. When the brilliant young author Yukio Mishima committed hara-kiri in November 1970, it was his way of appealing to his countrymen to resist the temptations of feckless modernization and to return to the martial samurai spirit of Old Japan.

In the groups and subgroups there were leaders, but they were nondictatorial and tended to serve more like moderators subtly supervising the reconciliation of opinions. There was also strong attachment to hierarchy. Each Japanese knew his "proper place," and this would be reflected even in conversation. It was assumed that those lower on the ladder would show deference to those on higher rungs, and this, for the Japanese, applied to nations as well as to individuals. Yet in each group, every individual, regardless of station, was a part of the whole and a participant in it. What was good for the group, the company, or the country was considered good for the individual. Conversely, what harmed group, company, or country was considered detrimental to the individual. Under the circumstances, group members tended to sublimate independent instincts and heretical tendencies and not get too far out of line. One American observer compared Japanese behavior with a school of fish; leadership was difficult to discern, but tossing a pebble could affect the direction of the whole group.

Japanese children were traditionally taught that if they did wrong, people would laugh at them. Ridicule, shame, pride, and prestige were powerful forces. Such forces carried over into the international arena where, because of the uniqueness and the accomplishments of their civilization, and also perhaps because of some feeling of social inferiority vis-à-vis outsiders, these remarkable people, not without some reason, suspected they were under special scrutiny by the rest of the world community. They were highly sensitive to what others thought of Japan. In this context, the Oriental Exclusion Act passed by the United States Congress in 1924 had been for the Japanese unforgettably offensive.

While masters of stoicism, the Japanese possessed spiritual proclivities not easily definable. Whether busy on an automobile assembly line or meditating over rocks in a garden of carefully raked pebbles at a religious shrine, they were influenced by what Nobel prize winner Yasunari Kawabata extolled as "a universe of the spirit, in which everything communicates freely with everything, transcending bounds, limitless."

Probably the most appropriate word to describe the panoply of forces which motivated Japanese behavior was that suggested by Takashi Oka, Tokyo correspondent for *The New York Times*. That word was "Japanism." No word in the English vocabulary could adequately explain the communal dynamism of the Japanese people. Nor could any other word bring into focus the importance of recognizing that intercourse with Japan and its citizenry was markedly more complicated than dealing with Americans, Iranians, or Europeans.

"Japanism" had deep roots in history. An island civilization, the Japanese had over the centuries preserved themselves as a separate people, dealing sagaciously with alien influences to which their society was exposed. They had been able to remain independent of the neighboring Chinese continent, but had adopted elements of China's culture. Their eighth-century concept had been, "Chinese knowledge, Japanese spirit." In the thirteenth century, the defeat of a Mongol invasion, thanks to a typhoon known in Japan as a "divine wind" or kamikaze, had led to a belief that Japanese territory was inviolable. During two and a half centuries of xenophobic Tokugawa rule, Japan lived virtually in total isolation, but there were a few valuable contacts with the outside world, primarily through the port of Nagasaki. Unlike other Asian nations, Japan did not succumb to European colonialist influences.

In 1853, Commodore Matthew C. Perry had sailed into Tokyo (then Edo) Bay, armed with a letter from President Millard Fillmore requesting that Japan open its doors to American ships, sailors, and trade. But more important, Perry's "Black Ships" were steam propelled and carried cannons, two phenomena which greatly impressed the Japanese. The Commodore's expedition, plus subsequent endeavors by other Western nations, touched off a veritable revolution in Japan. Under a banner of "Honor the Emperor, expel the barbarians," a new regime of collective leadership came to power infused with "a burning desire to catch up" with the accomplishments of the Occident. This was the beginning of the "Meiji era," during which the Japanese combined their national consciousness, sense of purpose, and energies with techniques and technologies studied, borrowed, and assimilated from the West. Thus Japan became the first modernized state in Asia.

Japan also became a power with which to reckon in world affairs. In an age of imperialism, she extended her influence in Okinawa, Taiwan, the Pescadores, and Korea, and vied with the European powers for dominance in Manchuria and significant areas of China. In 1904–1905, the Japanese succeeded in military combat against Russia. In 1919, thanks to a 1902 alliance with England, Japan attended the Versailles peace conference as one of the victorious Big Five and picked up German properties in China and in the islands of the Pacific. As Asia's major power, Japan participated in the 1921–1922 Washington Conferences, which set a 5–5–3 ratio for naval vessel construction by the United States, Britain, and Japan respectively. The terms of the agreement were bitterly resented by Japan's burgeoning military establishment as a "bloodless naval defeat," and were exploited by the militarists in whipping up anti-American sentiment in Japan in the 1930's.

Then came the "Co-Prosperity Sphere," Pearl Harbor, Hiroshima, and General Douglas MacArthur. Nothing in Japanese history could have been more traumatic than the World War II experience, which according to Tokyo's *Asahi Shimbun* had been a "holocaust of blind patriotism." Never before defeated, and never having fought a war on their home territory, a proud people had to face surrender and occupation. Heeding the Emperor's fateful proclamation, they endured the "unendurable." The occupation was not harsh and, with an intensity which only "Japanism" can muster, they buckled down over ensuing years to regain their "proper place" among the leading economic powers of the world. In the process, they clung to their Japaneseness while adopting certain features of the American "democratization" program, such as strengthened parliamentary institutions, reduction of family concentrations of wealth (zaibatsu empires), land reform, educational philosophy, advanced technologies, and profitable collaboration with the leading world power.

Immensely effective though it was, Japanism was not without its drawbacks and its dangers. Consensus mentality and communal action could snowball and, as happened in the 1930's, lead to calamity if the direction in which the group was moving was not responsibly and realistically regulated by the membership. There could also be breakdowns, as in 1960 when polarization over the Japanese-American treaty relationship led to violent confrontation and a threat to internal stability.

It was difficult to escape the impression that Japanism was almost continuously engaged in a tug-of-war within itself, involving such conflicts as looking inward versus looking outward, traditionalism versus modernism, "the seclusive spirit" versus openness, cultural Asianism versus technological Westernism, humility versus self-assertion, pacifism (accentuated by World War II defeat and the horrors of Hiroshima and Nagasaki) versus a concern over military inferiority, craving status as a permanent member of the United Nations Security Council versus reluctance to take positions in international disputes (such as the one in the Middle East), protecting Japanese industries versus support for a liberal international trade and investment system, and, in general, national consciousness versus international collaboration. The tugs were legion, but underlying them all was a gnawing awareness of a contrast between Japan and the outside world. Over the years, as during the Meiji period and the American occupation, mutations in Japanese behavior occurred, but the bedrock of Japanism remained. The crucial question would be what role the resurgent Japan of the 1970's would play in the comity of nations. As the answer to that question unfolded, no country would have more at stake than the United States.

The foreign policy of a nation inevitably reflects the current aspirations of its citizens. In mid-1969, there existed a new and robust national consciousness, enormous economic strength, and an increasing desire for Japan to show mastery of its own fate by assuming responsibilities commensurate with its new status, both at home and abroad. In America, there was welcome recognition that the postwar period, which had demanded an inordinate amount of America's human and material resources, was drawing to successful conclusion and that our friends and allies with their new strength could and should assume greater responsibilities, not only for their own well-being but for the achievement of regional and world peace. Thus, the compulsions in both Japan and the United States in mid-1969 were parallel. (In Japan, caution had to be employed in using the word "parallel" for, since two parallel lines never meet, there could be for the Japanese an implication of disagreement.)

It was within the context of adjusting to the realities of the 1970's and responding to the aspirations of their countrymen, that the governments of Japan and the United States tackled their major diplomatic problems in the 1969–1972 period. For America, it was the Nixon Doctrine in action. For Japan, it was part of a process, sometimes painful, whereby Japan was groping for its role in East Asia and in the world. For both countries, it represented movement toward a more realistic and more durable partnership.

As Japanese Ambassador Uyama had outlined in Tehran, the storm clouds looming on the United States-Japan horizon were: the reversion of Okinawa, the extension of the Treaty of Mutual Cooperation and Security, and the sharply increasing trade imbalances between the two countries. To these bilateral problems would be added a fourth major issue—the thorny question of relations with the People's Republic of China. There would, in addition, be a variety of lesser problems. The work days would be eighteen hours long, and more. During a Tokyo visit to officiate at the opening of the new Imperial Hotel, General Matthew B. Ridgway, who had succeeded General MacArthur, observed that serving as the United States representative to

Japan in 1970 was much more difficult than when he was assigned as Supreme Commander two decades earlier. During that score of years, Japan had moved from the lower to the higher rungs of the international ladder. Problem-solving in 1969–1972 would be via strenuous negotiations between fully sovereign governments.

In grappling with major bilateral problems, Japan and the United States in this period would be required to take the long view. The highly productive postwar relationship must, with undiminished fidelity, be transformed into one manifesting greater equality and reciprocity. The extent of success that could be achieved would determine not only the fruitfulness of their bilateral ties but also the contribution that each, as a dynamic and sovereign nation, would make to a new international equilibrium conducive to peace in East Asia and in the world.

Chapter 2

As Okinawa Goes,
So Goes Japan

ON JUNE 2, 1969, in the oval office of the White House, Japan's Foreign Minister, Kiichi Aichi, discussed with President Nixon Japan's hope for the early return of Okinawa to Japanese political administration. The following three years of negotiations would see the postwar era come to an end and open a new chapter in the United States-Japan relationship.

In presenting what had long been Prime Minister Sato's dream, Foreign Minister Aichi stressed the cruciality of the Okinawa issue. But he placed it in the broader framework of strengthening "mutual trust" between the two nations. The President needed no conversion, for it was his belief that peace for the rest of the century would be heavily dependent on what transpired in East Asia, where nothing was more important than the United States-Japan partnership. Neither the President nor the Foreign Minister underestimated the difficulties, but the President voiced the view that through "hard bargaining" stronger friendship could be forged.

The oval room discussion was a sort of baptism for the new American Ambassador to Japan, who had only two days earlier returned from Tehran. Later in the week, during a supplemental meeting with Secretary Rogers, Foreign Minister Aichi was in attendance when the oath of office was administered. It was the beginning of one of the most treasured friendships of my diplomatic career.

As World War II drew to a close, the Battle of Okinawa was as bloody as it was decisive. More than 12,000 American lives were sacrificed for the capture of the island which was to have been the staging area for the invasion of the Japanese main islands. The war ended earlier, however, and Okinawa became a key bastion in American efforts to secure the peace. To return to former enemies such hard won and valuable real estate willingly was, as Prime Minister Sato later described it, an act "rare in history."

The original American hope was to have the Ryukyu Islands, of which Okinawa was chief, come under permanent United States trusteeship. Since this could only be decided at the United Nations, John Foster Dulles at the time of the 1951 San Francisco peace treaty referred to the Japanese as still having "residual sovereignty." It soon became clear that the United Nations would not grant the trusteeship, and that the Okinawans, unhappy with the American military presence, would increasingly press for reversion to Japanese administration. In the early 1960's, Ambassador Reischauer and others argued that reversion was an eventual necessity. With reluctance, particularly on the part of the military, this became the American government position.

By the late 1960's, it was not a question of whether but when.

With increasing frequency and forthrightness, the Eisenhower, Kennedy, and Johnson administrations had assured Japan's leaders that the Ryukyus (and the Daito Islands, a small neighboring group) would be restored to Japanese control. Meanwhile, other island groups, the Amami Islands in 1953 and the Bonins in 1968, under similar treaty status (Article III) had been returned to Japan. The difference, of course, was that the Ryukyus involved the livelihood of nearly 1,000,000 inhabitants and an investment of more than $800,000,000 in American military facilities.

Two factors inevitably affected the timing of reversion. One was the importance of retaining a healthy relationship with Japan. The other was the need to maintain a hospitable environment in Okinawa.

In Japan, the year 1970 was bound to see the United States-Japan relationship at a crossroads. Inimical forces had for nearly a decade been gearing up for their "anti-treaty struggle." No issue would be more lethal than Okinawa, for it would provide the flag around which anti-U.S. forces would be able to rally Japan-wide support. The subject of a telegram from the Embassy to Washington, three months after the Nixon-Aichi meeting, was "As Okinawa Goes, So Goes Japan." The point was that the fate of our Mutual Security Treaty, the future course of Japanese policy, and without doubt the prospects for peace in Asia depended on the resolution of the Okinawa issue. Meanwhile, it was noted, the assumption of greater responsibilities by Japan, to wit the defense of the Ryukyus, would be fully consistent with the newly enunciated principles of the Nixon Doctrine.

In Okinawa, trouble was on the rise. In 1968 Chobyo Yara, the most zealous pro-reversion candidate, was elected

Chief Executive. His platform was "immediate, unconditional, and complete reversion." Public opinion polls consistently showed 85% of the Ryukyuans wanted the islands
returned to Japan, even though more than 50% thought
reversion would cause them to fare less well economically.
By mid-1969 strikes and incidents were occurring more frequently, and the situation in the Ryukyus was clearly going
to get worse, with increased hostility to the American
presence.

The President, who had visited Japan six times, recognized the political imperatives. Plans went forward, therefore, via the "hard bargaining" process, to compose a joint
communiqué to be issued during a proposed visit by Prime
Minister Sato to Washington in November. It would envisage the transfer of the civil administration of the Ryukyu and Daito Islands to Japan and set a target date.

One frequently heard the contention that in prewar
days Okinawans were treated as second-class citizens and
that if the American administration had invested as much
in the welfare of the Okinawans as it did in its own military
establishment in the islands, the resulting paradise would
have dissuaded the islanders from demanding reversion.
Another school contended that the Okinawans in any case
would have preferred their own independence. Whether or
not such arguments ever had any validity, they were purely
academic by mid-1969. Only one option was open. It was to
proceed with reversion—in the interest of Okinawa, Japan,
and the United States.

Another question frequently asked was why the Japanese did not create as much commotion for the return from
Soviet rule of the "Northern Territories," a group of small
islands off Hokkaido in the southern Kurile chain. The fact
was that the Japanese government was constantly pressing
the Soviets, but hitting a stone wall. A key to Soviet mo-
tives may be found in a personal observation by a Soviet

diplomat, "After you have given Okinawa back, what leverage will you have on the Japanese?"

It should be noted that, unlike Okinawa, the Northern
Territories had virtually no Japanese inhabitants. It also
should be remembered that the normal ringleaders for agitation were leftists. When I asked Chairman Narita why
his Japan Socialist Party never attacked the Soviets as
being "imperialist" for their continued occupation of the
Northern Territories, he eventually came up with the response that what the Soviets were doing was merely "a
mistake." Suffice it to say, even though Japanese agitation
may have been limited, Soviet adamancy regarding the
Northern Territories was an undeniable barrier to conditions of "mutual trust" between Japan and the Soviet
Union.

Two days after presenting my credentials to Emperor
Hirohito, I boarded an Air Force T-39 for Okinawa. The
purpose of the journey was twofold: to acquaint myself
with the situation there and to indicate the seriousness of
American purpose.

Through briefings, inspections, helicopter over-views,
and extensive discussions, I learned what a critical role our
military installations were playing in Far East security
strategy. Scattered over some 350 square kilometers were
the Marines with their Third Division Headquarters, the
Air Force with its huge Kadena air base housing B-52's and
a host of other aircraft, the Army with its massive Second
Logistics Command rehabilitating vehicles and equipment
damaged in Vietnam, and the Navy with its Naha air-sea
complex. For deterrent as well as contingency purposes, it
was considered important to have such capabilities within a
few hundred miles of friendly Asian nations with whom we
had security commitments.

But equally as important as the military panoply was
the substantial economic progress which had been achieved

in Okinawa during the American administration. Press reports from Okinawa usually featured stories of troubles; little if anything had been heard of Okinawa's annual economic growth rate of 18%. Instead of being the poorest of Japanese prefectures, as it once had been, Okinawa was now better off than a number of homeland prefectures. This economic growth, of course, was heavily dependent on American military expenditures, but other factors included United States Government assistance, foreign investment, and development policies generated by the United States Civil Administration of the Ryukyus.

This was my first opportunity to meet Okinawa's Chief Executive Chobyo Yara. Former mathematics teachers, we got along very well personally and this continued over the next three years. Among politicians in so many parts of the world, there tended to be two policies, one which they proclaimed publicly (usually involving the twisting of Uncle Sam's whiskers) and the other which they believed privately (usually admiring American ideals). For publicity purposes, Yara handed me a petition complaining about Okinawa-based B-52's and urging the immediate and unconditional reversion of the Ryukyus. Having carried out this exercise, he listened not without some sympathy as I pointed out that both Japan and Okinawa were thriving thanks to American cooperation, and that, so long as American boys were dying in Vietnam, American attitudes toward Okinawa could be adversely affected by any impairment of their logistic support. The main point was that if Yara wished to see reversion accomplished, it would be best not to rock the boat. Although he did not always find it possible to abide by it, Yara seemed to understand the value of quiet diplomacy.

During my first Okinawa visit I came to know the United States High Commissioner, Lieutenant General James B. Lampert. He, too, had only recently arrived on the scene. Clearly he was the right American for the right job at the right time. Without his leadership, the two-and-a-half-year interlude between the announcement and the reality of reversion would not have gone as smoothly as it did. Inevitably, incidents and tensions occurred which involved GIs and unfriendly elements in the Okinawa community, but he handled them with skill.

From June 1969 until Prime Minister Sato's departure for Washington in mid-November, Japanese and American negotiators buckled down to compose the language for the communiqué which would be issued at the conclusion of the talks with the President. The key issue would be the reversion of Okinawa. Main venue for the intensive negotiations was Tokyo. Given Japanese meticulousness, virtually every word of the proposed communiqué was threshed out exhaustively. After one session, Foreign Minister Aichi likened the procedure to climbing Mount Fuji; we had, he said, reached the eighth of Fujiyama's ten stations.

This turned out to be an exercise of classic diplomacy at its best. The chief negotiators were the Foreign Minister and the American Ambassador. Under our guidance (and staying in touch with our Washington counterparts via daily telephone contact), the numerous complex issues were deliberated by specialist teams from both countries. The United States side was captained by Richard Sneider, aided by Deputy Chief of Mission David Osborn, Political Counselor Richard Ericson, Political-Military Advisor Scott George, and others. The Japanese side was headed by the Director of the Foreign Ministry's American Affairs Bureau, Fumihiko Togo, assisted by his deputy Yoshio Okawara and Kazuo Chiba. Indispensable, of course, were the interpreters: Genichi Akatani on the Japanese side of the table and for the Americans the inimitable James Wickel, whose talents were so unique that he was always flown to Washington for any high-level Japanese-American talks.

Foreign Minister Aichi and I would meet at least once

or twice each month, primarly to ratify the handiwork of our two teams, but also to discuss the broad issues, particularly those which still required resolution. In classic diplomacy of this type, the Ambassador's position is not easy; he must take tough stands. Although knowing what the ultimate fallback position will be, he must often leave the credit for agreement on the key difficult compromises to the Secretary of State, or as in this case with regard to the nuclear weapons issue, to the President himself. It should be noted that, in the main, our method of handling the Okinawa negotiations was highly compatible with the deepseated Japanese decision-making system known as "ringisei." This is the process whereby problems are discussed and a consensus gradually generated at the lower and middle echelons. The participants are conscious of the intentions of their superiors and a mutually agreeable outcome is achieved, with minimal confrontation or "loss of face" for anyone.

Secretary Rogers proved to be a superb negotiator, so described by President Nixon when the new cabinet was announced in December of 1968. In June and September meetings with Foreign Minister Aichi in Washington, and in a brief meeting during the joint cabinet meeting in Tokyo, the Secretary demonstrated a mixture of affability and firmness, keeping the Okinawa negotiations on a mutually satisfactory track. The Japanese were flustered but delighted when he suggested a mixing of negotiators, rather than phalanxes staring at each other across a table. When some of his American associates suggested secret understandings, he insisted that neither he nor the President would be party to any under-the-table agreements. No matter how tough the bargaining, Secretary Rogers believed that everything our two countries had in mind should be set forth publicly in the joint communiqué.

In considering the restoration of Okinawa to Japanese administrative control, a wide range of difficult and complicated problems required attention. The most formidable one was the future of America's vast military establishment, often described as the keystone of our Far Eastern security strategy. There were Americans, particularly those strongly oriented to the military, who feared disaster if we were to give up our freedom of action. There were Japanese, particularly the vocal opposition elements, who feared that American adventures in the Far East, notably vis-à-vis China, would drag Japan into unwanted hostilities.

The task of the American negotiators, therefore, was to assure the continued effectiveness of American military capabilities. It would not be desirable to signal to friend or foe an impairment of American power to cope with or deter threats against those to whom America had given a commitment. Credibility was at stake.

For the Japanese, the fundamental issue was sovereignty. When Okinawa returned to Japanese administration, it must do so as a full-fledged prefecture. This would require that American facilities be treated no differently from those in the Japanese homeland but be governed by the United States-Japan Treaty of Mutual Cooperation and Security, plus related understandings such as the Status of Forces Agreement.

Underneath this central negotiating issue lay, of course, more profound questions as to what roles the United States and Japan envisaged for themselves in Far Eastern security, what each would expect from the other, and the nature and extent of their partnership.

The issue of regional security versus sovereignty had been the crux of the turbulent 1960 treaty revision. It was resolved at that time by an agreement that the United States would consult with Japan before using its Japanese bases for direct combat operations launched from those bases, before making major increases in American forces stationed in Japan, or before stationing nuclear weapons in

Japan. In insisting, therefore, on "homeland level" (in Japanese "hondo-nami") for American bases in Okinawa, the Japanese in the 1969 negotiations were asking for the "prior consultation" formula. This was a logical position with which the United States could not disagree. How the formula would be translated into practice, however, became one of the knottier problems in drafting the proposed Sato-Nixon communiqué.

There was no question of the availability of the facilities for logistic purposes. The ships of the United States Seventh Fleet were by treaty authorized to sail into Japanese ports and would do so in Okinawa. American military aircraft were flying into Yokota in Japan and would continue to fly into Kadena in Okinawa. The Japanese government would continue to make necessary real estate available without cost to the United States.

It was with regard to American combat operations that difficulties arose. There was a fear, particularly among military-oriented Americans, that prior consultations would give the Japanese "veto power" and American effectiveness in emergency situations would be hamstrung. Because of this fear, brief consideration was given to obtaining from the Japanese "advance approval" for future contingencies, but such a "blank check," as Foreign Minister Aichi described it, was unrealistic. To illustrate its unacceptability, I had pointed out to Washington that no American political candidate would conceivably support a platform favoring extraterritorial privileges for foreign forces on American soil . . . not even for purely logistic purposes, let alone using our country as a springboard for military adventures against any nation the foreign tenant might choose to attack.

What the Japanese government was willing to do was to accord "recognition" to the importance of peace and security in the Far East and to affirm that the United States had an effective role to play. Many hours, days and

weeks were devoted to seeking language which would respect Japan's sovereignty and yet assure an effective capability for the United States to honor its defense treaty
obligations in the Far Eastern area.

Finding the language was not easy, but steady progress
was made. Secretary Rogers, during his mid-September
session with Foreign Minister Aichi in Washington, suggested phraseology to the effect that, in light of Japan's
recognition of the importance of Far Eastern security, the
reversion of Okinawa would "contemplate" the effective
discharge of the international obligations assumed by the
United States. "Contemplate" was a good lawyer's term,
with sufficient ambiguity. However, the Japanese, after
lengthy debate, contended the word was untranslatable
into Japanese. Several days went by before mutually agreeable language was found, namely reversion "should not
hinder" the effective discharge of the international obligations assumed by the United States for the defense of
the countries of the Far East, including Japan.

Because the term "Far East" had been somewhat con-
secrated in the Diet deliberations of 1960, it was important
to limit regional security references to that geographic
terminology, rather than using expressions such as Western Pacific, East Asia, et cetera. Nonetheless, there were in
mid-1969 three areas of special concern which inevitably
required attention in the communiqué. They were Korea,
Taiwan, and Vietnam. These were three Far Eastern countries in whose security the United States had an interest.
All three were understandably disturbed by the prospect of
any lessening of American capability to assist in their
defense.

Traditionally, Korea has been considered "a potential
dagger pointed at Japan's heart." It required little persuasion, therefore, to incorporate into the proposed communiqué a declaration that the security of the Republic of Korea
is "essential to Japan's own security." The implication was,

of course, that Japan would be basically sympathetic to such American endeavors as might be needed to maintain security on the Korean peninsula.

Both Japan and the United States had strong ties with Nationalist China and hoped to maintain them. At the same time, both countries were anxious for improved relations with the People's Republic of China. Thus, it was with considerable care that language was chosen for the Sato-Nixon communiqué that would avoid unecessary provocation of Peking's leaders. (This was two years before the announcement of President Nixon's visit to the People's Republic.) Whereas Korea's security was stated as being "essential" to Japan's security, the communiqué would say that the security of the Taiwan area "was a most important factor for the security of Japan."

Vietnam was more difficult. As in America, Japanese opinion was divided. The government in general approved of American policy there. So did most Japanese businessmen, who were reaping millions of dollars in profits and who viewed the American security involvement as a critical factor in the economic well-being of Indo-China. However, clamor against America's Vietnam policies in the Japanese press, in large sectors of public opinion and, of course, among the opposition parties was difficult for the government to ignore.

As a point of fact, Japanese bases, such as the tank rebuilding facility at Sagami, were being used to provide logistic support for our Vietnam military endeavors. The continued logistic use of facilities in Okinawa for similar purposes seemed to offer no problem. With regard to "combat" operations, the only activity to be affected would be Okinawa-based B-52 bombing raids, but these were in any case phasing down (and out by 1972).

In the light of these circumstances, the Sato-Nixon communiqué would express hope that peace would be realized in Vietnam by the time of Okinawa's reversion. If not, the two governments would "fully consult" so that "reversion would be accomplished without affecting the United States efforts to assure the South Vietnamese people the opportunity to determine their own political future without outside interference." Throughout the negotiations, it was stressed that neither the American people nor Congress could be expected to approve Okinawa's reversion if it meant crippling support for our men there.

Discussion of the sensitive "prior consultations" issue did much to remove the narrow nationalistic blinders with which both sides began the negotiations. In preserving both sovereignty for Japan and the potential for effective use of American military strength, the two countries found themselves focusing increasingly on their mutual interests and objectives, their interdependence, their hopes for reduced tensions in the area, and their preference for negotiation over confrontation.

At the same time that negotiations to keep our Okinawa military complex intact after reversion were going on, public opinion in the United States was swinging sharply in the direction of reducing our military presence abroad. Serious questions were arising over whether the United States would again commit its armed forces in situations such as Vietnam and Korea. Thus, when Prime Minister Sato told the Diet that in future crises Japan's answer to prior consultations "could be yes as well as no," it was a position which was less categorically affirmative than the American Okinawa negotiators might have wished, but which also might be more affirmative than would be necessary. Only if both Japan and the United States agreed on taking action in the Far East was it likely that such action would take place. The chances of the United States going it alone were getting slimmer.

Japan's "nuclear allergy" is real and understandable. No Okinawa negotiating session would pass without a

Japanese appeal for the incorporation of clear assurance in the communiqué that no nuclear weapons would be stationed on post-reversion Okinawa. Just as often, the American negotiators would parry the question. Actually a decision had been made within the top levels of the American government some months earlier, but it was to be left to the President to convey the good news to Prime Minister Sato in November. Paragraph 8 of their communiqué would read, "The President expressed his deep understanding (of Japanese sentiment and policy) and assured the Prime Minister that, without prejudice to the position of the United States Government with respect to the prior consultation system under the Treaty of Mutual Cooperation and Security, the reversion of Okinawa would be carried out in a manner consistent with the policy of the Japanese government as described by the Prime Minister."

As American critics never failed to point out, there was a profound contradiction between Japan's wish to be protected by the American nuclear umbrella and its adamant denial to the Americans of any accommodations for their nuclear capability. Paradoxical though they might be, these were the political facts of life in Japan. Banning nuclear weaponry from Okinawa was hard for Americans to accept, but fortunately there were numerous other ways to support America's nuclear deterrent, such as with bases elsewhere, with submarines, and so on. There was also the possibility, albeit extremely remote, that one day in the future a situation might develop where the Japanese, via the prior consultation route, would themselves see value in invoking more manifestly the American nuclear deterrent.

The meaning of Paragraph 8 should have been perfectly obvious, but, because of long-standing American policy neither confirming nor denying the presence of nuclear weapons anywhere, it was deliberately a bit ambiguous. The basic dilemma was that, if disclosure were made with regard to any specific nuclear site, there would be pressures for disclosures elsewhere, particularly in countries which had American nuclear weapons but did not want to give concrete indication of their locations. The Japanese government, of course, needed to allay fears that Okinawa would not be nuclear free. The American intention was clear: there would be no nuclear weapons stationed on Okinawa after reversion day. But not being able to say so explicitly provided grist for Sato's opposition.

Japan's vociferous oppositionists were in an awkward position. Obviously, they could not oppose the cherished concept of having the Ryukyus restored to Japanese rule. So they centered their attacks on the alleged iniquities of the American military presence in Okinawa. They warned that, pursuant to Sato's duplicity and American perfidy, atom bombs, stashed away in the remote recesses of Okinawa, would in one way or another continue to bedevil the peace-loving people of Japan and the world. Their prophecies of gloom were not limited to nuclear matters.

In July 1969 during a routine inspection at an isolated site in Okinawa, several leaky chemical weapons cannisters were discovered. No one was injured, but the incident revealed the storage on Okinawa of chemical munitions. It was a highly exploitable development, grasped with glee by Japan's opposition forces. The uproar was considerably defused, however, when, thanks to some fast footwork by Deputy Chief of Mission David Osborn, Washington speedily agreed to an announcement that the munitions would be removed as soon as possible and in any event before the date of Okinawa's reversion. Explanations that such weaponry is regrettably needed for its deterrent value in this imperfect world fell on deaf ears, as did assurances that every conceivable safety precaution was being exercised.

The removal of the chemical munitions from Okinawa, called Operation Red Hat, was plagued by unavoidable delays. Refusal by the states of Washington and Oregon to accept the weapons for storage only fueled the fires of criticism in Okinawa and Japan. In a crash program, costing $12,000,000 (twice as much as normal), storage facilities were constructed on Johnston Island in the mid-Pacific. Even then, it was a touch-and-go project transporting these lethal arms from their storage site to shipside in Okinawa. A special road had to be built to bypass a protesting village. Everyone breathed a sigh of relief when in September 1971 Operation Red Hat was finally completed without incident.

In December 1970, there was a rash of unpleasant incidents in Okinawa. Angry that an American GI who had been involved in a fatal traffic accident had been acquitted of the charges against him, Okinawans demanded that American military personnel be tried in Okinawan courts. The tensions were such that a spark late one Saturday night ignited a major riot in the Koza area, which, with its "Mother's Bar" and other night clubs, was the hang-out for off-duty GIs. A number of Americans were injured and 87 American cars burned. There had been a series of Okinawan complaints regarding juridical matters, and they were understandable. At the same time, the American military tribunals sought to be fair. The situation calmed somewhat when Okinawan observers were invited to attend the military proceedings. In private conversations, we noted that the youth who in July 1969 had attacked the American Ambassador with a knife at Haneda airport received from the Japanese courts a mere $65 fine.

Another December 1970 incident saw an American Marine chop down the tree in which an imported Japanese protester was perched. The protester was attempting to obstruct a training exercise in northern Okinawa. Fortunately, his injuries were not severe, and under General Lampert's direction he was accorded special treatment at the American military medical center. The training exercise, which was not essential, was called off.

The use of Okinawa as a base for raids on Vietnam by

high-finned B-52 super-bombers was a constant target for attack, both by Japanese oppositionists and Okinawan agitators. Fortunately for all the people affected, as well as for our relations with Okinawa and Japan, these aerial forays from Okinawan bases became unnecessary as our combat role in Vietnam diminished.

The demands of Japan's opposition were reminiscent of the old Cracker Jack slogan, "The more you eat, the more you want." Appeasement on one issue did not deter anti-government politicians from seizing on another, no matter how ridiculous. Two of the most amusing contentions were: a) goats had been observed at the Atsugi Naval Air Station and this was proof positive that, despite American denials, chemical weapons were stationed on mainland Japan; and b) a telephone directory at the Marine base at Iwakuni, which listed a unit whose appellation included reference to the word nuclear, substantiated the presence of nuclear weapons in Japan. As it turned out, the hapless goats were not serving as detectors for chemical weapons leakage but simply as cheap grass cutters at Atsugi. The unit at Iwakuni was conducting normal training exercises to prepare Marines to protect themselves should they someday somewhere be exposed to a nuclear threat; no actual nuclear weaponry was involved in the exercises. Outcries about Iwakuni did not subside until, to put an end to the charges, arrangements were made for a qualified Japanese inspection team to visit the suspected storage sites.

Quite obviously, the opposition's primary aim, as it had been for nine years, was the destruction of the United States-Japan mutual security treaty. Not able to oppose Okinawa's reversion, but keeping an eye on the 1970 "anti-treaty struggle," they sought to exploit circumstances such as the Atsugi goats and the Iwakuni directory to demonstrate that American behavior in Japan was in defiance of the treaty's provisions, and would be so in Okinawa in the future. This was ground where neither we nor the Japanese government had anything to fear. In fact, it was a net gain to have the public debate center on whether "homeland level" would be achieved in Okinawa, rather than on the more fundamental issue, the continued existence of the treaty.

It was probably for the purpose of blunting opposition assaults and generating a Japan-wide consensus that much leakage of confidential information occurred which was traceable to Japanese government sources. For American negotiators, it was annoying to have the substance of secret discussions appear in the newspapers the following day, but for Japan it was no doubt part of an educational process. Disclosures that Japanese representatives were having great trouble securing the establishment of 1972 as the year for reversion; that it was hard for them to cope with American demands for "free use" of the facilities in Okinawa; and that they could not persuade the United States negotiators that the removal of nuclear weapons would not diminish American military effectiveness; all helped to convince Japanese public opinion that the Japanese negotiators were staunchly supporting Japanese interests. Meanwhile, Japan's consensus society was becoming more accustomed to the presumption that the United States-Japan treaty would continue to be operative in the years ahead.

One of the major contributions of Secretary Rogers during his negotiating session with Foreign Minister Aichi in mid-September 1969 was the insertion in the communiqué of the phrase, "subject to the conclusion of specific arrangements with necessary legislative support." Until that time, there was uncertainty concerning the precise form that the reversion documentation would take and how it would be handled legislatively.

As precedents, the return of the Amami Islands in 1953 and the Bonins in 1968 had been handled as simple executive agreements. In both cases, the Japanese government received Diet approval, as it planned to do with the Ryukyus. This was one factor in Secretary Rogers's thinking. However, of greater importance was his desire to bridge the gap which, even prior to the Nixon administration, had been growing between the United States Senate (and especially the Foreign Relations Committee) and the Executive Branch of the United States Government. The Secretary recognized the contribution the Okinawa agreement could make to this objective, provided the administration handled it properly with the Senate.

For history's sake, it should be recorded that Secretary Rogers's injection of the language envisaging appropriate "legislative support" preceded by two months a Senate resolution proposed by Virginia's Senator Harry Byrd which declared that any agreement with regard to Okinawa would not become effective without the advice and consent of the United States Senate. The Byrd resolution, passed by a 63 to 14 vote on November 5, 1969, was not without some value, for by demonstrating Senatorial concern it strengthened the hands of those of us who were doing the negotiating. But its primary objective was already academic, since the communiqué which would be issued on November 21 included Secretary Rogers's mid-September language.

With every word of their communiqué finally determined, the President of the United States and the Prime Minister of Japan on November 21, 1969, following three days of tête-à-tête discussions in Washington, announced their agreement envisaging the "smooth transfer" of Okinawa to Japanese administration in 1972. The importance of the United States's being able to honor its obligations in the Far East was reaffirmed in the communiqué, as was the determination of both governments to continue beyond 1970 the United States-Japan treaty relationship. All of this was within the framework of a mutual rededication to the maintenance and strengthening of "fruitful cooperation in the continuing search for world peace."

Before waiting press and cameramen, the two leaders commented that history would record this communiqué as marking the conclusion of the postwar period of the United States-Japan relationship and the opening of a new era of partnership. "A New Pacific Age" was the title of Prime Minister Sato's subsequent address to the National Press Club, an address in which he also pledged that if the United States sought to use bases to meet an armed attack against the Republic of Korea, the Japanese response to "prior consultations" would be given "promptly and positively." In a separate White House briefing, Under Secretary of State U. Alexis Johnson decribed how United States forces in Okinawa would be governed by the Japanese homeland treaty arrangements, and that in consonance with the Nixon Doctrine there would be a greater mutuality of interest as America's security role and Japan's economic cooperation evolved in the Far East.

Japan's intention to expand and improve its aid programs in Asia commensurate with its economic growth was included in one of two paragraphs dealing with economic matters in the fifteen-paragraph communiqué. The other economic paragraph described in broad terms the steps each country planned to take to improve the health of bilateral as well as international trade. No one was more concerned than the President about textiles and other economic frictions with Japan, but he believed such problems should be fought out on their own merits. Rather than linking Okinawa with such issues, as was advocated by numerous American businessmen, the President was of the opinion that the healthy atmosphere engendered by the Okinawa agreement would be conducive to the resolution of other problems and would encourage constructive Japanese governmental actions. No extraneous issues, in his view, should undermine the character of the Okinawa agreement.

For no one was November 21 a happier day than Foreign Minister Aichi. Following his June 2 meeting with President Nixon, he had vowed not to smoke another cigarette until agreement had been reached on the return of Okinawa. When the President and the Prime Minister called in their top aides at the conclusion of their White House talks, Aichi was overjoyed when to his surprise President Nixon offered him a Japanese cigarette and lighted it. It was a little byplay which our Chief of Protocol Emil Mosbacher had quietly rigged, using a packet of cigarettes which I had brought for the purpose from Tokyo.

It was four years later, almost to the day, that Kiichi Aichi, then serving as Finance Minister for Prime Minister Tanaka, unexpectedly died. With heavy heart and a sense of personal loss, I cabled Mrs. Aichi to express my inability to imagine Japan without Aichi-san. He had demonstrated statesmanship in the face of the most difficult of problems, serenity in times of crisis, love of country, and dedication to what he called "mutual trust" between Japan and America as a cornerstone for a peaceful world.

Aichi had been a superb negotiator. Under intense political pressures from the press and opposition elements in Tokyo, he had acquitted himself with courage and skill. He often called our attention to a Japanese proverb which stressed that by yielding in form, one could gain in substance. For him, as all worthy diplomats realize, a treaty was only a piece of paper, of no greater value than the forces behind it. Repeatedly, he would point out that the development of deep and abiding "mutual trust" between our two countries was infinitely more important than an agreement which could unceremoniously be repudiated if forces hostile to the United States should come to power in Japan. Those indelible words "mutual trust" were Aichi-san's legacy for this colleague and admirer, as they must be for his compatriots and mine if a peaceful post-postwar world is to emerge.

The key question, indeed, was what would be the impact of the Okinawa settlement on the political scene in Japan. Opposition forces had tried to block the agreement by staging major demonstrations designed to prevent Prime Minister Sato's departure for Washington. He had foiled the attempt by using, for the first time, a helicopter to take him to Haneda airport. Aware of this, and concerned that in the communiqué Sato had increased his vulnerability to charges of hitching Japan's fortunes to the American military chariot, two of America's most eminent Japanologists expressed to me their fear that the Prime Minister would not dare to return home.

They were in error. The Prime Minister returned safely, dissolved the Diet, and called for new elections within 30 days. His Liberal Democratic Party's previous platforms had focused on Japan's economic progress, but this time Sato fastened his electoral endeavors to his triumphant achievement in securing the reversion of Okinawa, and to the continuation of close ties with the United States, including the "automatic extension" of the United States-Japan security treaty the following June.

The election results in Japan in December 1969 were almost unbelievable. The Japan Socialist Party, which had most vehemently led the demonstrations against the Okinawa agreement, suffered a stunning drop of 40 seats, from 130 to 90. Sato's party, by securing 300 of the 486 seats in the lower house of the Diet, achieved the largest majority any party had enjoyed since the war. Sato's victory was not without qualifications and extraneous factors, but it perforce had to be considered an affirmation that the people of Japan wished to continue a partnership of "mutual trust" with the United States. More specifically, it took the wind out of the sails of those highly vocal elements who claimed to represent Japanese opinion when they agitated against the Okinawa agreement and the United States-Japan security relationship.

Historic as it was, the November 21 communiqué was only the blueprint. The goal was a "smooth transfer." Translating the communiqué's precepts into "specific arrangements," involving a wide variety of complicated issues, would require many more months of exhaustive negotiating. The machinery would be essentially the same as that previously employed. Overall responsibility was assigned to the United States-Japan Consultative Committee in Tokyo. It would forgather as occasion warranted. Its top representatives, the Foreign Minister and the Ambassador, would meet frequently, but the detailed provisions would be threshed out in almost daily sessions by a greatly expanded American team headed by Deputy Chief of Mission Richard Sneider and a conglomerate of Japanese bureaucrats, coordinated by Bunroku Yoshino and his colleagues in the Foreign Ministry's North American Affairs Bureau.

Someone has described decision making in the Japanese government as the negotiation of a treaty among sovereign bureaucracies. This circumstance proved to be the major hurdle in bringing to conclusion the numerous agreements requisite to Okinawa's reversion. On financial matters, the Finance Ministry was all-powerful; on business problems, the highly protectionist Ministry of International Trade and Industry; on civil aviation matters, the Ministry of Transport with its hard-shell civil aviation bureau; on the Voice of America, the Ministry of Posts and Telegraphs; on court procedures, the Ministry of Justice; et cetera. Each Ministry jealously guarded its prerogatives. Each tended to view its specific aspect of Okinawa reversion in isolation, and each demanded its pound of flesh exclusively on the basis of rules and regulations prevailing in Japan proper.

Federal agencies in Washington are notorious for being slow to act, encumbered with red tape, and, given their vast size and cost, relatively inefficient. These attributes are not unknown in Tokyo, but unlike America, where a certain amount of White House whip cracking can coerce bureaucratic movement and interdepartmental collaboration, government Ministries in Japan wield decisive power which they jealously guard with almost religious zeal.

In the negotiations, we would urge our Japanese friends to look at the big picture, to view details from the perspective of the historic magnitude of Okinawa's reversion. Usually, the Foreign Ministry would understand and try to be helpful in finding a compromise, but it had great difficulties in securing significant concessions from other branches of the government. Time and again, special pleas had to be directed to the Foreign Minister and to Prime Minister Sato himself. On more than one occasion, Aichi or Sato would make an appeal at a cabinet meeting. In some cases, it would be determined that a particularly difficult problem must be resolved "at the political level." With face thus saved, grudging concessions could then be extracted from the bureaucracies. There was no substitute for relentless effort.

In Okinawa, the very extensive range of preparations for the transition from American to Japanese administration was handled by a Preparatory Commission. Prepcom, which was the successor to the former Advisory Commission to the High Commissioner, was under the direction of General Lampert, working with special Japanese Ambassador Jiro Takase and our last Civil Administrator, Robert Fearey. By November 1970 they had worked out a careful plan for the phasing down of the responsibilities of the United States Civil Administration in the Ryukyus and the eventual assumption of these responsibilities by Japanese authorities. Among a host of problems which required their attention were the transfer of United States-owned corporations; the status of state and prefectural land; postal and telecommunications matters; the disposition of American aid projects; automobile and driver registrations; and immigration, quarantine, and customs controls. The list seemed endless, but over the months "smooth transfer" arrangements were accomplished.

By late spring of 1971 most of the knotty reversion problems had been resolved. A draft agreement, whose format resembled that for the Bonin and Amami Islands transfers, was nearing completion. It was a highly technical document which could not have been produced without the expertise of fine legal minds such as that of the young lawyer on the American negotiating team, Charles Schmitz. The agreement, along with a half-dozen or so related documents, covered all aspects of the transaction whereby the United States, under Article III of the Peace Treaty with Japan, would relinquish its rights and interests with respect to the Ryukyu and Daito Islands in favor of Japan, which would assume full governmental authority. Provisions were included granting the United States use of Okinawan military facilities after reversion, in accordance with security treaty arrangements prevailing in Japan.

Setting forth the "metes and bounds" in the documentation became entangled with a dispute which had recently flared up because of bright oil prospects in the Senkaku Island area. The Senkakus were within the geographic region being returned to Japan, but sovereignty over those islands was claimed by both Chinas, as well as Japan. The United States position, carefully reflected in the documentation, was that as custodians we were merely returning administrative power to Japan without prejudice to historic claims. This neat position endeared us to none of the three disputants, but it assured our non-involvement in a controversy which is likely to continue for years.

Other legal matters, patiently negotiated, concerned the transfer of civil and criminal jurisdiction. Japan agreed to recognize court actions taken during the American administration. Japan also, in a separate article, waived all claims against the United States and its nationals arising out of the United States administration of the islands. As far as judicial action against American military personnel was concerned, the well-established procedures would be observed.

With regard to settling financial problems arising from Okinawa's reversion, ball park figures had already been determined prior to the November 1969 communiqué. The detailed settlement, negotiated directly between the Japanese Ministry of Finance and the United States Department of the Treasury, was extremely complicated. Agreement was finally reached that Japan would pay the United States the amount of $320,000,000, which included reimbursement for public utilities and other assets transferred to Japanese control. Other items which had to be taken into account were additional post-reversion labor costs, military relocation expenses, the assumption by Japan of land-rental obligations, and currency conversion. The latter was a tricky matter, for prior to actual reversion the Japanese yen had been revalued and the Japanese government had been compelled to provide special dispensation to the Okinawans, who were complaining loudly that their dollars would net them substantially less yen than previously.

While the $320,000,000 figure was less than the $800,-000,000 which the United States had actually invested in Okinawa, it was a reasonable sum, considering that a major portion of the American investment was for military facilities, the use of which the United States would retain. There were other mitigating factors as well. It was estimated, for example, that as a direct result of reversion the United States would net a savings of $300,000,000 over a five-year period. This would include approximately $35,000,000 annually for defending the Ryukyus, a responsibility henceforth to be shouldered by Japan's Self Defense Forces.

Particularly difficult were problems connected with the private American business community in Okinawa. Under the American regime, its members had been enjoying special privileges which would not be available under Japanese laws and regulations. With investments and livelihoods at stake, American businessmen were understandably worried. To handle their special problems, there was established in Okinawa a Business Advisory Group with which the American negotiating team stayed in close touch. In close cooperation with BAG, as well as with the American Chambers of Commerce in Okinawa and Japan, we sought to convince Japanese authorities that reversion should not cause private Americans established on Okinawa to suffer.

Because the representatives of their firms in Japan were experienced in navigating Tokyo's bureaucratic labyrinth, the five large companies in Okinawa, such as Julian Schon's new Caltex refinery, were able to adjust to post-reversion status quite satisfactorily. It was the small entrepreneurs and professional practitioners, such as doctors and lawyers, who appeared to be in deepest trouble. Most of them would not be able to meet the language and other requirements demanded by Japanese regulations.

It was only after months of meager progress in bucking the respective Japanese ministries that the ice was broken. An important factor no doubt was that time was running dangerously short if all the formalities were to be accomplished to permit reversion in 1972. This was an issue where the American negotiators had dug in their heels, for, aside from the rightness of the cause, there was active Congressional interest. A main theme was that, instead of extending Japan's restrictive practices to Okinawa, Japan's interests would be better served by greater liberalization at home.

As part of the reversion documentation, Foreign Minister Aichi addressed to the American Ambassador a formal letter indicating that after reversion foreign nationals and firms in Okinawa would be treated "in a sympathetic manner." Specific reference was made to the ownership and licensing of business activities, ownership and leasing of private properties, leasing of state and prefectural lands, the remittance of foreign currency, retroactive taxation, reasonable import quotas, and the authorization of lawyers, doctors, dentists and veterinarians, as well as the continuation under Japanese sponsorship of the religiously oriented Far East Broadcasting Company. There was no way that the pre-reversion status quo could remain unaltered. However, all things considered, the Japanese authorities showed understanding. Okinawa's American community wrote us their appreciation. Our impression was that their interests were more than 90% satisfied.

Another tough nut to crack was the continued operation of the Voice of America relay station in Okinawa which was beaming broadcasts to mainland China. Despite the fact that VOA operates relay stations in a number of other countries, there was in Japan a feeling that such activity impinged on Japanese sovereignty (Japanese law precludes radio transmission by foreign nationals). There was also the feeling that VOA would be a stumbling block for Japan's efforts to improve relations with Peking (the negotiations took place before the President's diplomatic breakthrough). In the end, the Japanese government reluctantly agreed to a five-year continuation for VOA, with consultations concerning its future after a two-year period.

In dealing with civil aviation questions, the American negotiators encountered a standard ploy by Ministry of Transport officials, namely, to trade off issues. Japan Air

Lines was avidly seeking to secure landing rights in Chicago; so, inevitably, Japanese authorities linked the continuance of American flying rights in Okinawa to JAL's desire. As in other such cases, the American position was steadfastly against such linkage. After protracted discussion, agreement was reached for a five-year continuation of American traffic rights in Okinawa, with the situation after that period to be determined through consultation.

An American group headed by Vice Admiral Walter Curtis, U.S. Military Representative on the Okinawa Negotiating Team, negotiated military matters with representatives of the Japan Defense Agency. As with civilian matters, there were many details to be discussed in the military domain. Essentially, there were two major areas: a) the United States post-reversion military base structure; and b) defense responsibilities to be assumed by Japan.

The determination of the American base structure in Okinawa after reversion required close coordination. General Lampert and his advisors, being directly interested, provided the most critical advice. Since responsibility would be transferred to United States Forces in Japan, Lieutenant General Gordon Graham, USFJ commander, was directly involved, along with his Chief-of-Staff, Major General Richard Lee.

With an extensive agenda of other matters requiring negotiation, it was not possible to produce a specific agreement for each military facility on Okinawa prior to the signing of the reversion documents. However, three lists were agreed upon and duly recorded in the documentation: a) eighty-eight facilities to be retained for use by United States military forces; b) twelve facilities to be returned to Japan after reversion, the date to depend on their takeover by Japan Self Defense Forces, or on other considerations; and c) thirty-four facilities which were released to Japan on or prior to reversion.

Key installations such as the United States Air Force's Kadena complex, the Army's Second Logistical Command, and accommodations for the Third Marine Division would continue to be available. The Navy's air base at Naha was the subject of much discussion, with the Japanese pressing for its release so that it could become a civil airport. This paralleled Japanese insistence years earlier that, as the gateway to Japan, the Haneda airport at Tokyo should be free of United States military activities. The release of Naha was painful for the Navy, particularly since the other three services passionately contended that there was no space available at their airports. Eventually, the Air Force was induced to make room at Kadena for the Navy's flying activities.

One observer has estimated that American military effectiveness in Okinawa was retained at about 90% of its pre-reversion level. However, if the Nixon Doctrine were to have continuing application, further adjustments and realignments could not be ruled out.

The labors of Vice Admiral Curtis and his cohorts in fabricating the intricate arrangements transferring responsibilities for the defense of the Ryukyus to the Japanese Self Defense Forces were fully consonant with the objectives of the Nixon Doctrine. For America, it meant a tightening of the belt and a reduction of over-exposure. For Japan, the manning of the Nike and Hawk missile sites and other Okinawan defense operations meant the assumption of legitimate responsibility, fully consistent with Japanese sentiment restricting Japan's military activities to the protection of Japanese territory.

Nowhere in the world is a population more captivated by television than in Japan. Atop each of Tokyo's hundreds of thousands of modest dwellings looms a TV antenna, sometimes two or three. The percentage of Japanese viewers of Neil Armstrong's touchdown on the moon exceeded even that in the United States.

It was, therefore, a stroke of genius that prompted Secretary Rogers to suggest that the signing of the agreements returning Okinawa to Japan take place via satellite.

To assure, for legal purposes, that the documents would all bear the same date, the proceedings took place in Tokyo at nine o'clock in the evening of June 17, 1971; it was eight A.M. in Washington. Assembled on the eighth floor of the State Department were Secretary Rogers, Japan's Ambassador Nubuhiko Ushiba, Defense Secretary Laird, JCS Chairman Admiral Moorer, Japan-stalwart Under Secretary U. Alexis Johnson, Senate Foreign Relations Committee representatives, and State Department subordinates who had labored long and hard for this day to arrive.

In Tokyo, it was quite a different drama. For the oppositionists, this was their last chance. With all the powers remaining at their command, they sought to obstruct the solemnities by mobilizing thousands of demonstrators. The Tokyo police were, as ever, their match. It was the showdown.

The American negotiating team assembled at the Embassy residence to proceed to the ceremonies as a group. Shepherded by the Japanese police, we received reports every few minutes on the situation in the streets. About 8:30, our cavalcade, well escorted, headed for the Prime Minister's official residence. Leaving the Embassy area, we had to worm our way through an almost impregnable police bus-barricade. With sirens blaring, our caravan traversed the half mile to Sato's heavily guarded quarters in record time without interruption. Meanwhile, skirmishes between police and demonstrators were taking place in various sectors of Tokyo.

Promptly at the appointed hour, the American delegation was ushered into the ceremonial hall. It was packed with the entire Japanese cabinet, other government officials, Diet members, Okinawan legislators, and press-TV battalions. The occasion was organized with the precision for which the Japanese are renowned.

As the miracle of television brought this episode of history before the eyes of the official assemblages in Washington and Tokyo, and to the citizens of both countries, the Okinawa reversion agreement was signed. In Washington, Secretary Rogers affixed his signature to a copy which already bore Foreign Minister Aichi's signature, while, in Tokyo, Aichi signed a copy which already bore the name of the American Secretary of State. The subsidiary documents were signed by us in Tokyo. There followed remarks appropriate to the occasion by the key participants on both sides of the Pacific.

It was early morning in Washington, so champagne was not appropriate. It being late at night in Tokyo, we were not similarly handicapped. With tears in his eyes, Prime Minister Sato proposed a toast to "the everlasting friendship" between the people of our two countries. Sato's dream had come true. But for him it was more than the reacquisition of a piece of real estate. The whole purpose of Okinawa reversion, he had told me earlier, was to increase the sense of intimacy between Japan and the United States. This broader dream, he had made clear, was shared by the Emperor who had been kept fully informed throughout the negotiations and who with the Prime Minister considered this event "without precedent in history."

Still to be achieved was "the necessary legislative support." The leaders of the Executive Branch of the United States Government might divorce the Okinawa issue from economic problems, such as textiles, but it was by no means certain that political circumstances on their home fronts would allow Senators such statesmanship. Nor was it certain that members of the Armed Services Committee would look with favor on the relinquishment of political jurisdiction over a key military bastion in the Western Pacific. *The New York Times* accused the White House of sending the Okinawa agreement to the Senate in order to make it "hostage to the textile lobby." This charge was unfair and inconsistent with the *Times*'s own oft-repeated complaints of Presidential inadequacies in securing the advice and consent of the Congress.

During his 1969 visit to Washington, Prime Minister Sato was invited by Chairman J. William Fulbright to a tea-discussion with members of the Senate Foreign Relations Committee. Following that meeting, Chairman Fulbright told me that he believed that an Okinawa reversion agreement would be approved by the Senate, even though there might be some strong voices in opposition. He added that it was fortunate that the incumbent in the White House was Republican, for the Democratic side would in any case be reasonably well disposed. Similar estimates were given by Majority Leader Mansfield and other Senators, as well as Senatorial staff members. We tried to keep all of them, as well as interested House members, fully informed as the negotiations progressed.

Many Senators were understandably unhappy about the differences which existed with Japan, particularly in trade matters, but when the votes were counted statesmanship prevailed. There were few Senators who did not appreciate that our whole relationship with Japan was at stake. On November 2, 1971, the Foreign Relations Committee by unanimous vote recommended that the Senate accord its advice and consent to the ratification of the Okinawa reversion treaty. On November 10, the Senate gave its approval by an impressive 84 to 6 vote.

Ratification of the Okinawa agreement by the Japanese Diet took longer. The opposition parties used every parliamentary gambit and exploited any issue, no matter how peripheral, to block passage. Unlike the United States Congress, there is in Japan seldom any crossing over of party lines. The opposition parties vote en bloc, and their aim is only partially related to the merits of the legislation. The overriding consideration seems to be opposition for opposition's sake. In this repect, they are usually abetted by the great Japanese newspapers, which pride themselves on being independent and neutral, even though by tradition and practice they have always tended to be critics of the government in power. The opposition also exploits the fact that Diet debates are nationally televised, thus providing free time for endless interrogating of harried government officials. Since this offers opportunity for making hay in home constituencies, it is an opportunity too good for Diet members to miss.

It should be noted that the Prime Minister and his cabinet must be on hand in person for these Diet inquisitions, which can last weeks and even months. This has a stultifying effect on the bureaucracies, which are forced to function with deputies in charge. Since most of the advantage is with the Diet members, whose questions ramble endlessly, Diet sessions are a heavy, but unavoidable, drain on precious Prime Ministerial time. Reasonably confident as to what the ultimate voting outcome is likely to be, a good Prime Minister adopts what Premier Ikeda had called a "low posture." He confines himself to relatively brief replies, shows due diffidence to his interlocutors, avoids confrontations, and concentrates on generating a maximum amount of consensus. Some aspects of these Diet exchanges take on the semblance of kabuki (Japanese theatre).

Because of the historic nature of the return of Okinawa, Prime Minister Sato called the Diet into Extraordinary Session. Obviously, the opposition parties found it difficult to oppose Okinawa's return to Japan. So their attacks were aimed at the American military presence, which would in effect be ratified by the agreement. In fairness, it must be said that some valid questioning did occur. It focused on the thesis that Japan was being asked via the security treaty and the Okinawa agreement to maintain a posture of Cold War confrontation while President Nixon's forthcoming visit to Peking (announced a month after the Okinawa reversion agreement was signed) offered the United States Government the advantage of appearing to be more progressive and peace-minded. Rebuttals arguing that positions of strength improve negotiating ability were not convincing, for, in the area of China policy, Japan and the United States have perspectives which are not identical.

An added complication was that, besides the Okinawa reversion treaty and its related documents, the Japanese Diet was required to pass nearly two hundred additional pieces of legislation. These would be necessary to implement the various responsibilities which Japan would shoulder as a result of the agreements, such as rental payments for lands occupied by United States facilities. All in all, it was an intricate legislative package which Speaker Naka Funada and the rest of the government leadership were called upon to handle.

Placed somewhat on the defensive, the Liberal Democratic Party government made several efforts to appease the opposition. There was some waffling in interpreting the 1969 communiqué with respect to the availability of American facilities for operations in the Taiwan area. Privately, Japanese government officials appealed to us to relinquish more facilities than had been agreed on in the treaty documents, but these documents, it was pointed out, were now in the concrete of senatorial ratification. Appeals were also received for more categoric language regarding the nonstationment of nuclear weapons.

Despite some of the most intricate Diet maneuvering, including stalling and then repassage of the treaty by the Lower House at the beginning of the normal session, all the legislation was approved prior to Prime Minister Sato's departure on January 4, 1972, for a "summit meeting" with President Nixon at San Clemente.

While the LDP never had any hope of winning the support of the opposition parties, it sought to avoid a complete boycott by all four of them. The government therefore was pleased that, thanks to some minor compromises to which we had agreed, the Komeito and the Democratic Socialist Party split with the Japan Socialist and Communist Parties, the former pair attending but voting negatively, while the latter pair boycotted the decisive session.

While the primary purposes of the San Clemente summit conference, January 6–7, 1972, were to harmonize thinking with respect to China and to discuss economic problems, the subject of Okinawa's reversion was on the agenda. It was discussed primarily in the meetings between Foreign Minister Takeo Fukuda (who had succeeded Aichi the previous July) and Secretary Rogers. In response to appeals from the Japanese representatives, which were based on a desire to secure broader popular support in Japan for the Japanese government position, the following was agreed: a) that although further Okinawa base reductions were not at present feasible, the United States, consistent with standard policy, would keep the base structure there under close scrutiny; b) that at the time of reversion there would be an American pronouncement, probably by Secretary Rogers, affirming that the United States had kept the pledge regarding nuclear weapons made in paragraph 8 of the 1969 Sato-Nixon communiqué; and c) that, despite practical problems, May 15 would be the target date for the transfer of administrative responsibility in Okinawa. Pursuant to a recommendation made by the Embassy, this in effect split the difference between April 1, the date urged by the Japanese, and July 1, the date hitherto envisaged; these mark the start of the fiscal years in Japan and the United States respectively. It was interesting that after the President conveyed to Sato our agreement on May 15 as reversion day, the Prime Minister seemed less sure that it was a good idea from a practical standpoint.

According to the Okinawa treaty provisions, the actual reversion would take place precisely two months after the exchange of ratifications. The latter formality, therefore, took place on March 15 in the Prime Minister's office in Tokyo. After Foreign Minister Fukuda and I exchanged the instruments, Prime Minister Sato proposed a toast with "awamori" liquor produced in Okinawa. With Aichi present as well as others who had been involved in the negotiations, appropriate remarks were made about the indispensability of Japanese-American harmony to world peace. It was my last participation in the Okinawa reversion saga.

Only one act remained. It was the actual transfer of authority on May 15, accompanied by parallel observances in Tokyo and in Okinawa. In Tokyo it was an impressive affair at the large Budokan hall, attended by His Majesty the Emperor and Japan's top officialdom. The United States was represented by Vice President Spiro Agnew, and by the new American Ambassador, Robert Ingersoll. The ceremonies in Okinawa were set for May 16 so as not to conflict with those in Tokyo.

At midnight on May 14, United States High Commissioner James Lampert took formal departure from Okinawa. With his exodus, the Stars and Stripes was hauled down for the last time from the High Commissioner's headquarters; once again the flag of the Rising Sun was waving in authority over the Ryukyu and Daito Islands.

A disappointing irony was the apparent lack of appreciation by the Okinawans. Chief Executive Yara, consistent with the policy of his party which was a counterpart of the Japan Socialist Party in the homeland, refused to attend the Tokyo celebration. He also absented himself from the observances staged by the Japanese government in Okinawa on the morning of May 16, but participated in separately arranged prefectural proceedings that afternoon.

Technically, Yara and his regime favored reversion, but with the immediate and unconditional withdrawal of the American military presence. The most militant supporters of this policy were Okinawa's labor unions. But whenever attempts were made to reduce the American base structure, those same labor unions would stage massive strikes to prevent the dismissal of Okinawan employees. Prime Minister Sato himself frequently drew my attention to this inconsistency.

Aside from the political agitation, the Okinawans were understandably restive over what the future would hold in store for them. Conscious of such anxieties, the Tokyo government went out of its way, both before and after reversion, to make them feel welcome in the homeland. There is good reason to believe that, as normalcy is restored under Japanese administration, Okinawans will look back not without appreciation for the economic, social, and political progress experienced during the period of American administration.

Chapter 3

Mutuality and Mutability
in Security Partnership

MAY AND JUNE 1960 will long be remembered as months marked by massive demonstrations in Japan. Jogging regiments of students snake-danced, day after day, through the streets of Tokyo. Amid public uproar, a harried Japanese government was forced to cancel the scheduled visit of the President of the United States. Subsequently, the government itself resigned.

Triggering this unhappy episode in United States-Japan history was the conclusion of a treaty to replace the security pact which had been signed at the same time as the San Francisco treaty in 1951 and which most Japanese considered lopsided and outdated. In sending the new "Treaty of Mutual Cooperation and Security" to the Senate, President Eisenhower said it would constitute "the foundation for cooperation, a partnership with Japan, based on mutual confidence and sovereign equality, not only in the security field but in the political and economic fields." It was, the President said, "entirely defensive in character and intent," and represented "a threat to no country or people."

In his "fuller explanation," Secretary of State Christian Herter commented on the various articles of the new treaty, as well as the accompanying documentation. In referring to the exchange of notes on January 19, 1960, which set forth United States agreement "to conduct prior consultation with Japan" before staging direct combat operations from Japanese bases, before "major changes" in the deployment of American forces into Japan, and before "major changes" in their equipment, such as the introduction of nuclear weapons, Secretary Herter affirmed assurances which the President had given Prime Minister Nobusuke Kishi that "the United States Government has no intention of acting in a manner contrary to the wishes of the Japanese government."

Neither these words nor the broader vision impressed Japan's opposition leaders in 1960. Exploiting the exhilaration of Japan's national resurgence, and the overpowering anti-war sentiment induced by Japan's humiliating defeat in "The Pacific War," they wanted no treaty. The protest demonstrations were led by leftists, but received support from many non-leftists who shared the distaste for foreign soldiers on Japanese soil, and who feared that association with American defense strategy might drag Japan into unwanted conflict with other Asian nations.

When the opposition forces in the Diet persisted in obstructive tactics, Prime Minister Kishi staged a surprise move. He called the Diet into session in the early hours of the morning of May 20, 1960, and secured the treaty's ratification. This fait accompli sparked an even greater uproar in the streets, with indignant outcries that the treaty had been "rammed through" by Kishi's undemocratic leadership.

With the cancellation of the Eisenhower visit and the resignation of Prime Minister Kishi's government, the tumult gradually subsided. But the opposition leaders were dedicated to the treaty's abandonment. If no earlier opportunity could be found, their strategy called for a repeat performance of the 1960 explosion to climax on June 23, 1970. That would be the date on which the original ten-year life of the new treaty would expire; after that date it would continue automatically until either the United States or Japan gave one year's notice of termination.

As Ambassador Uyama had forecast in Tehran, 1970 was the crisis year for United States-Japan relations. By the time of my arrival in June 1969, the "anti-treaty struggle" was already under way. Almost any pretext was being exploited for taking to the streets, but particularly pretext-worthy were the Okinawa communiqué negotiations then going on. The "strugglers" knew that the Okinawa issue was their best bet. On October 21, the so-called "anti-war day," demonstrations were mounted of a magnitude second only to the do-or-die efforts in November 1969 when the anti-treaty forces sought to prevent Prime Minister Sato from emplaning for Washington and the historic communiqué announcing Okinawa's reversion in 1972.

The October 21 demonstrations were similar to so many held previously and subsequently. They would be well advertised in advance and, when feasible, scheduled for prime television time, like a sports contest. Advance approval had to be obtained from the police, and data had to be provided regarding the expected turnout, the purpose, the assembly point (such as Hibiya Park, where impassioned oratory would provide inspiration), and of course the line of march, which usually included passing the American Embassy or the Embassy Annex. The police effectively stationed their counter-forces to assure that the demonstrators stayed on their appointed course and remained peaceful.

Even riots in Japan seem to be disciplined. Seldom did

the demonstrators deviate from their announced plans. Neither they nor the police, by the rules of the game, employed guns. "Demo" participants would be equipped with gewalt sticks (dull wooden spears) and protected by helmets painted with the insignia of their respective factions. Equal numbers of police would appear in blue battle dress, helmets, visors, arm guards, shields, and their own gewalt sticks. Police contingents would be dispatched to areas of trouble in special armored buses, which served also as temporary on-station housing, as well as, if needed, anti-demonstrator barricades.

For major eruptions, as on October 21, 1969, the various demonstrating factions would coordinate their endeavors. On those occasions the American Embassy compound would be cordoned off by hundreds of police and heavily plated police buses lined up bumper-to-bumper, so that, as Political Secretary Frank McNeil phrased it, "not even a flea could get through." Marooned in the Okura Hotel next door, Chairman Walter Scott of NBC and Julius Stone of the Ford Foundation were invited to join us on the evening of October 21 at the Embassy residence for dinner and the TV performance. Although thousands of bullhorn-barking demonstrators were marching in hour-long files and waving flags (mostly red) just 150 yards away, thanks to Japan's internal security forces we felt safer than anyone else in Tokyo—even though the treaty with America was the target!

No discussion of Japan's effective security procedures could be complete without registering appreciation for the protection accorded the person of the American Ambassador. At Japanese initiative, it was not possible to venture outside the Embassy residence without a bodyguard only a few feet away. Until his replacement for unknown reasons, a gentle, unobtrusive, alert, and tireless officer, Koki Fuchi, had captured our affection and had become in effect a member of our family. Fuchi-san and his gifted associates were welcome companions whether it was eluding the "demos" of Tokyo or enjoying the fresh air and hospitality out in the prefectures.

Parenthetically, it is worth noting that the United States Government is frequently criticized by other nations for its inability to provide protection for foreign diplomats as adequately as American officials are protected abroad. Since we do not have a national police force, it is a difficult problem for our government.

During the entire "anti-treaty struggle," violence and vandalism in Japan were, by most standards, minimal. There were occasions, as on October 21, 1969, when demonstrators resorted to Molotov cocktails, but even the most radical elements usually tried to avoid human injury. Only one death had occurred in the 1960 riots, that of a young girl accidentally trampled by the mobs. No one died in the 1970 "struggle," but subsequently several persons, including policemen, were killed during demonstrations aimed at different issues. It seemed almost as if there were some law to the effect that the extent of violence was inversely proportional to the magnitude of public support for the specific protest. Thus, as Japanese society lost interest in and even turned against extremist politics in the streets, the more radical demo ring-leaders resorted to violence. The Sekigun or Red Army became the most notorious. In early 1972, it seized a woman hostage and engaged in a week-long gunfight with the police at Karuizawa. In the summer of 1972, it reportedly hired itself out to stage the massacre at Lod airport in Israel.

Outside Tokyo, demonstrations were held from time to time in the larger cities, but since they lacked the glare of the national spotlight, they were lackluster affairs. Some efforts were made to harass American bases, but these, too, were not of major significance. At Tachikawa, for example, leftist students had prevented construction of an extension to the runway, and then had installed tall poles flying red flags to hamper landings. Only limited flying activities were based there, however, and by the end of 1969 they had been completely eliminated in the interest of economy.

To a considerable extent, the 1970 "anti-treaty struggle" was an effort to discomfit the Japanese establishment, which had shouldered power in Japan since the war. The Liberal Democratic Party had evolved from the union of two conservative parties whose ancestry dated to prewar times. During his seven years as Prime Minister, Shigeru Yoshida had been largely responsible for setting Japan on its postwar course. He had formerly been a Foreign Ministry official and Ambassador to London. Coming up similarly through the bureaucratic ranks into cabinet positions were Kishi (who was in a wartime cabinet), his brother Sato, and many other LDP leaders.

These conservative forces had led Japan from the dark days of defeat, through the occupation period, and into the era of independence. They had staked their destiny, and that of Japan, on democratic political institutions, economic growth, and close cooperation with the United States. It was an eminently successful formula to which Japan's phenomenal recovery bore testimony. Supporting this conservative LDP political structure were the leaders of industry, the business community, the bureaucracy, and voting strongholds throughout the rural areas. It was the latter upon which the LDP increasingly depended for election victories.

One of the critical problems in postwar Japan has been the lack of philosophical moorings. The old system of values which centered on the position of the Emperor was no longer valid, but no new philosophy had developed to replace it. Reforms introduced by the occupation authorities were premised on American democratic concepts, but only the Japanese people could evolve their own sense of purpose. The government, of course, made a fetish of economic recovery, but while success was impressive it did not fill the ideological gap. Meanwhile, in the intellectual community, the field was left pretty much to the Marxists. Even though progress in the "socialist" countries stood in stark and unfavorable contrast with Japan's own progress, Marxism continued to have appeal to many in Japan. As a major influence in Japan's teaching profession, Marxism inevitably attracted university students, the opposition parties, the newspapers, and the growing urban component of Japanese society.

In order to develop better mutual understanding, various small groups of Japanese opinion-molders were, on a biweekly basis, invited to the Embassy residence for informal discussion of matters of interest. At these gatherings, views would be exchanged with the editorial leadership of the newspapers, with radio-TV commentators, with foreign reporters, with political scientists, and so on. At one seminar with university economics professors, we were told that all the members of their profession could be classified either as "Marxists" or "modernists." While it was not clear in which of these categories he placed himself, one participant took the occasion to inveigh against the iniquities of the United States, the greatest of which, he said, was its failure after the war to hang the Emperor, Sato, Japan Steel Company head Shigeo Nagano, and others of their ilk.

The Marxists' thesis was that, under what they considered to be the wicked capitalist system, greedy Japanese industrialists, supported by the government, would heedlessly expand the capacities of their factories and, when markets were not so readily available as they were in the 1960's, those industrialists, driven by the craze for profits, would force their commercial intentions on Japan's less fortunate neighbors. If the job could not be accomplished through purely commercial means, the industrialists would allegedly press for Japanese military forces to back up their commercial ambitions. All of this was, of course, the classic Marxist theory that capitalism leads inevitably to imperialism.

It was not only Marxist intellectuals who were arrayed against the conservative LDP government in the 1970 "anti-treaty struggle." There was an assortment of opponents. Most of them tended to feel that the LDP government had outlived its usefulness, and that the time was at hand for a change. In past elections, the LDP's popular majority had been eroding, and there were those who wished to give this trend a shove. There seemed to be no better issue than the continuation of a treaty which in their judgment could be denounced as harmful to Japan's interests and incompatible with Japan's resurgent pride. While less scrupulous opponents would not hesitate to indulge in chauvinism and capitalize on deep-seated bitterness over Japan's wartime defeat, there were others, as in 1960, who were sincerely concerned about the propriety of having foreign forces stationed on Japanese soil, and about the danger of being drawn into unwanted Far Eastern conflicts. For some not hungry for power, it would be sufficient to provoke a public crisis which would force the government to repudiate the United States-Japan treaty and adopt what they would consider a more independent stance.

Since being "anti" always gets the headlines, it was easy to get false impressions of the feelings of the Japanese people. In fact, the establishment was on quite solid ground. Polls taken at the height of the 1970 anti-treaty campaign showed that only 14% of the Japanese people favored the immediate dissolution of the treaty. Meanwhile, in polls inquiring who was Japan's best friend, America consistently ranked at or near the top of the list. Statistics of this type prompted Japan's largest newspaper, *Asahi*, to comment, "Such widespread feelings among the Japanese public that friendly relations with the United States are critical only increase the need for well-organized, systematic education through which the next generation can learn to view America objectively."

In the vanguard of the anti-treaty movement, as it had been for a decade, was the Japan Socialist Party. Of the four opposition parties, it was the most militant, spearheading the campaigns both in the Diet and in the streets. As the inveterate rival for political power, and for doctrinal reasons, the JSP was committed to the abolition of the treaty. My suggestion to Chairman Tomomi Narita that less strident anti-Americanism might help the JSP at the polls fell on deaf ears. It should be noted that a moderate wing of the JSP, while opposed to the treaty, was less anti-American.

The Japan Communist Party was also thoroughly opposed to the United States-Japan security relationship. Interestingly, however, it appeared less militant than the JSP. Its demonstrations were periodic, massive, and well disciplined. In its own campaigning, the JCP placed greater emphasis on domestic issues that affected the common man. This low posture and clever technique paid dividends. Although small, the JCP's representation in the Diet continued a steady upward climb.

The Democratic Socialist Party, with some 30 seats in the 486 member Diet, believed in the gradual reduction of the American military presence in Japan, espousing something called "emergency stationing of forces." A moderate group, of the Willy Brandt type in Germany, the DSP participated energetically but non-violently in a campaign to alter the shape of the treaty.

The Komeito, with some 40 seats in the Diet, was the political offshoot of the Soka Gakkai. The latter, a religious revivalist movement, tended to attract those whose value system in the postwar world had lost anchorage, and who were in search of a sense of direction and community feeling. For its part, Komeito offered to those voters who had no use for "socialism" a possible alternative to the long-entrenched Liberal Democratic Party. Komeito's rise was an interesting development, although observers speculated whether its religious connections might not hamper its future electoral fortunes. Energetically and efficiently organized, the party sometimes gave the impression of being an army without a banner. It appealed especially to the young and to the urban lower middle classes, but in charting a course between the LDP and the socialists there was wavering in the formulation of party positions. Komeito opposed the retention of United States bases and favored the gradual dissolution of the United States-Japan security relationship.

Aside from the political parties, Japan's newspapers, with nationwide circulations in the millions, abetted the anti-treaty forces in varying degrees. A main factor was that over the past century, including the prewar period, they prided themselves on their role as critics of the government in power. Furthermore, as in the United States and elsewhere in the Free World, the press had what John Kenneth Galbraith calls "a vested interest in disaster"; the placid status quo is not news. There seemed to be a sort of personal stigma attached to any representative of the Japanese Fourth Estate who might have a few kind words to say about the government or the United States. This was manifestly true in a land where General Douglas MacArthur had removed the shoguns of the publishing world, and where editorial policy was in 1969 determined more by a brain trust of young editors than by the publisher. One Japanese diplomat confided how his nephew, who worked on one of the leading newspapers, was fundamentally conservative, like his family, but followed his herd instinct when the editorial conclaves took place.

Also joining in the "anti-treaty struggle" were Japan's labor unions, whose role had been encouraged by General

MacArthur but which had taken on left-wing coloration. Sohyo, responsive to the Japan Socialist Party, could theoretically muster up to 4,000,000 demonstrators. Domei, with lesser membership, was loosely connected with the Democratic Socialist Party and shared to some extent that party's views. Until 1970, Japan's unions were heavily engaged in political action. By 1970, however, their concerns, particularly those of unions in the private sector, were shifting more directly to the welfare of their memberships. Thus, while the unions constituted an important and indispensable component of the anti-treaty manifestations throughout Japan, there was reason to believe that for most workers it was a duty run.

Seldom in modern history has there been political ferment without students being the torchbearers. The world-renowned Zengakuren had ignited the 1960 explosion, but, as so often happens with such radical elements, the Zengakuren had fractionated. In their stead, there were now numerous student factions, most of them vying with each other. The more radical factions included the Marxist-Leninist League, the Kaku-maru (revolutionary Marxists), the Chukaku (revolutionary nucleus), the Anti-Treaty Joint Struggle, and others. Being irrepressibly restive, young people do not necessarily follow in the footsteps of their predecessors. The majority of Japan's 1970 students were getting bored with the slogans of 1960, according to several American professors in Japan who came in March 1970 to one of my biweekly seminars. This was the first indication to us at the Embassy that students were beginning to view the treaty issue as "threadbare." They were getting more concerned about the issues of the 1970's such as the quality of the environment. Thus, their putting on a full-scale repeat performance of 1960 was subject to doubt.

Aspiring student leaders are never at a loss for resources. The war in Vietnam was a convenient fall-back

issue. In Japan, a student group called Beheiren had organized itself specifically as an anti-Vietnam war movement. With help from visiting Jane Fonda, it found this
cause more profitable from the publicity standpoint than
the timeworn treaty issue. Beheiren mustered as allies a
dozen or so young Americans, who, by notifying the press
and TV in advance that they were going to deliver a note of
protest at the gate of the Embassy, could be assured of wide
publicity. The majority of this handful of young Americans
were no doubt good souls with conscientious intentions, although one could question the propriety of their airing their
complaints so ostentatiously on foreign soil.

In 1969, university students all over the world were
unusually restive, and Japan was no exception. Tokyo University, in effect, had to close its doors, as did other
Japanese universities. In August, the government passed
legislation authorizing police action to restore order on the
campuses. To break up what appeared to be in a number of
cases an unholy alliance between faculty members and their
wards, the law included a provision reducing professorial
salaries 30% at any university which was inoperative. As
in the United States, the "law and order" theme was per-
vading Japan, and this was affirmed by the government's
decisive victory in the December Diet elections. From 1970
onward, the universities functioned more normally.

Earlier, at Fukuoka, the students had received an unexpected boon when a United States Air Force fighter aircraft from nearby Itazuke air base had accidentally crashed
into the top floor of a university building. The students
prevented the police or anyone else from retrieving this
intruder: it provided them with a publicity bonanza. Having this cause célèbre in mind, Lieutenant General Thomas
K. McGehee, Commander of United States Forces in Japan,
stressed to all the units of his command that no effort be
spared to avoid incidents during the crucial period of the
"anti-treaty struggle." Opposition elements sorely needed a

spectacular American military mishap to fan the anti-treaty flames; fortunately, they were in for disappoint-ment. Even the Itazuke aircraft was quietly extracted from its embarrassing plight.

A more amorphous, but yet significant, ingredient in the 1970 anti-treaty movement was the burgeoning urban community. For urbanites, the motivation was not generic leftism, much less an endemic anti-Americanism, but a demand for improved living conditions, particularly in what was termed "the bedroom communities" of the met-ropolitan centers. Their interests focused on such issues as better housing, less pollution, and the reduction of traffic congestion. Blessed with attractive candidates such as Gov-ernor Ryokichi Minobe in Tokyo, Mayor Ichio Asukata in Yokohama, and Governor Torazo Ninagawa in Kyoto, the socialists had already wrested power from the LDP in three of Japan's largest cities. In Osaka, second-largest city in Japan, LDP Governor Yoshiaki Sato in 1971 lost to a social-ist-supported candidate, despite the fact that through his leadership Osaka had gained world attention via Expo 70 and in the process had acquired impressive roads and other public works at the central government's expense. Thus, among the growing urban population there was a visceral dissatisfaction with the LDP government, and such partici-pation as did occur in anti-treaty activities was probably motivated at least as much by the desire for improved do-mestic welfare as it was by foreign policy concerns.

While opposition forces were trying to churn up a crisis in 1970, the ruling Liberal Democratic Party government in Japan stayed steadily on course. In mid-October 1969, its leadership formally decided to continue the United States-Japan Treaty of Mutual Cooperation and Security "for a considerably long period" beyond its original ten-year life. The treaty, according to its provisions, was to remain in force until satisfactory United Nations arrangements were provided for maintaining peace and security in the Japan area. However, after the initial ten years, either party could terminate the treaty upon one year's notice. In deciding on "automatic extension," the LDP was in effect not exercising the termination option. No confirmatory governmental action was required, in the Diet or elsewhere.

In the November 21 communiqué announcing the projected reversion of Okinawa, Prime Minister Sato and President Nixon also affirmed the intention of their two governments "firmly to maintain" the security treaty "on the basis of mutual trust and common evaluation of the international situation." That this position was decisively supported by the people of Japan seemed clear from the Diet election one month later in which Prime Minister Sato's LDP party scored its impressive victory and the militantly anti-treaty Japan Socialist Party sustained a stunning setback.

There was a brief flurry in May 1970 over a remark by the Prime Minister in a press conference, in which he indicated that a change in the international situation was not likely within the next two or three years. This led to speculation that the "considerably long period" for the treaty's extension might be as short as two or three years. Both Foreign Minister Aichi and the Prime Minister hastened to assure us that such an inference was erroneous. The speculation was effectively laid to rest when Chief Cabinet Secretary Shigeru Hori told the press there would be no review of the security treaty until a situation emerges that does not require the treaty, or more specifically "until the time when the United Nations would become strong enough to insure Japan's security." On the treaty's tenth anniversary, the government issued a statement reiterating that the treaty would remain in force for the foreseeable future.

June 23, 1970, may well be recorded in history as the day when the indispensability of a healthy partnership between Japan and the United States was dramatically re-affirmed. Whatever resentments still lingered from World War II, whatever mistakes the two countries may have made in what was a remarkably conciliatory postwar era, whatever undue emphasis there may have been on matters military, and despite conspicuous cultural differences, Japan and the United States had in the postwar period discovered a common dedication to free institutions and to free enterprise. As the Free World's two most dynamic societies, they had so much to gain by working in tandem, and too much to lose by taking divergent courses.

While proponents and opponents had myopically wrangled over the security aspects of the Treaty of Mutual Cooperation and Security, too little attention had been accorded the treaty's broader aspects, or, more important, the forces and spirit behind it. The treaty was, as often described, the cornerstone of the relationship between Japan and the United States. However, not everyone had the vision to see the structure which could be built on foundations so constructively laid in the postwar years. In Japan, there were those who thought the architecture was excessively American and incompatible with Japan's bridge-building to other nations. There were others, however, who felt that America, too, was building bridges, and that the two countries together could play an impressive role in the achievement of a new world equilibrium. The destruction of the United States-Japan treaty relationship was not compatible with that inspiring vision, and most Japanese seemed to sense it.

On June 23, 1970, some 700,000 anti-treaty protestors took to the streets throughout Japan. It was a substantial number, but the zeal of the participants fell far short of the fervor which had characterized the 1960 uprising. To many observers, the performance had almost a ritualistic, if not perfunctory, quality.

A number of sporadic demonstrations in early 1970 having been less than smashing successes, the strategy of the anti-treaty forces was to concentrate on staging a sort of "hell week" just prior to the supreme effort on June 23. The first major demonstration was planned for Sunday, June 14, but the weatherman failed to cooperate. A steady drizzle cut down the numbers and dampened the spirits of the demonstrators. The rains proceeded to fall on most of the succeeding days when demonstrations were scheduled. It was only on June 23 that the skies cleared, but the 700,000 who dutifully turned out seemed lacking in both momentum and enthusiasm. Unlike 1960, popular emotions had failed to ignite. By dawn of the following day, the "anti-treaty struggle" had become history. The people and the streets of Japan enjoyed a tranquillity the like of which they had not known for many months.

Just as in 1960 there had been a conjunction of circumstances which produced an historic uproar in Japan, so in 1970 there was a conjunction of forces which militated against the security issue's catching fire as it had in 1960. They included:

a. INDEPENDENCE. While in 1960 there may still have been doubt in some minds whether Japan was a free agent, in 1970 there could be none. Neither President Nixon, nor Henry Kissinger, nor Secretary Rogers, nor any other American had pressed the Japanese government to continue the treaty. The determination whether the treaty was in its national interest was Japan's free choice, even as it was for the United States.

b. NO FLASH POINT. Unlike 1960, no affirmative Diet action was required in 1970. This deprived opposition elements of a forum for obstructionism and spared the government from flaunting its political power, as Kishi had felt it necessary to do.

c. NO OKINAWA FLAG. No ammunition would have been more surefire for the opposition forces than the demand for the return of Okinawa. This issue had been de-fused by the Sato-Nixon communiqué the previous November.

d. DECEMBER DIET ELECTION. The "automatic extension" of the security treaty, as well as Okinawa reversion, was a prime issue in the December 1969 elections. After Sato's victory and the Japan Socialist Party's set-back, there was no way that the anti-treaty forces could claim to represent majority Japanese opinion.

e. OPPOSITION'S DISARRAY. Internal factionalism and divisiveness over other issues marred the operations of the opposition parties and their confederates. The centrifugal forces exceeded the centripetal. Even the student protesters were hopelessly disunited.

f. JAPANESE MATURITY. No longer beset by the uncertainties and concerns of the postwar years, Japan had regained full self-confidence. It was standing on its own feet. Leftist sloganism, negativism, and the beating of dead horses lacked their former appeal. The majority of the Japanese needed no such anachronistic crutches.

g. ECONOMIC BOOM. As an Embassy-prepared graph demonstrated, no one could say that Japan had experienced hardship during the existence of the 1960 security treaty. On the contrary, Japanese economic upsurgence was almost incredible. Japan's prosperity had benefited from America's involvement with Korea and Vietnam, from the security shield provided Northeast Asia, and from an $11 billion volume of bilateral trade.

h. LAW AND ORDER. The majority of Japanese had developed a revulsion against the constant disruption of normal life by the snake-paraders and other demonstrators. With their 3-C dreams coming true (a car, a cooler and a color TV), they longed for a Japan where orderliness would prevail so they could enjoy their new-found affluence.

i. NATIONAL PRIDE. With the eyes of the world on Expo 70 and its theme of "progress and harmony for mankind," a proud Japan wanted no disturbances that would bring discredit to the country. It is noteworthy that, despite fears based on its vulnerability to incendiary attack, the American Expo 70 pavilion came through unscathed.

j. DE-POLARIZED WORLD. In 1960, association with the United States meant alignment against the "socialist" countries, notably the People's Republic of China and the Union of Soviet Socialist Republics. By 1970, the bipolar world had eroded, the Cold War was extinct, socialism was less belligerent, and negotiation rather than confrontation was the order of the day. These developments substantially undermined the contention that the security treaty would constitute a roadblock to the improvement of Japan's relations with its Communist neighbors.

k. QUIET DIPLOMACY. When things go wrong in world affairs, government officials are the easy targets for condemnation. There seems to be a widely held assumption that all bureaucrats are either disloyal or stupid. While this theory has not been disproved, the possibility remains that they are neither. By its nature, diplomacy does not lend itself to self-applause. Few people, therefore, would be in a position to appreciate fully the quiet missionary work that was done by both Japanese and American officials to reduce misunderstandings and facilitate a satisfactory outcome to what could have been a serious crisis in 1970.

While there were few Americans who would doubt the wisdom of a productive partnership with Japan, enthusiasm for the security aspects of the treaty was not universal.

There were those, particularly in the Senate, who, recognizing this as a different world from the Dulles pact-building era of the 1950's, felt the time had come for America to disengage from military commitments abroad. There were others who contended Japan was getting "a free ride." They noted that the Japanese military budget was less than 1% of the Gross National Product, compared with an 8% figure in the United States. They also pointed out that the United States, according to the treaty, undertook to defend Japan, but not vice versa.

With the unstable conditions prevailing immediately after World War II, there were good reasons why the United States had involved itself in the defense of Japan and in "the maintenance of international peace and security in the Far East." By 1970, however, few people saw a serious or imminent threat to Japan. As an island nation, Japan was unlike Germany, which had to be alert constantly to the threat of invasion across a land frontier. Historically, the Japanese were comforted by the fact that despite the close shave at the end of World War II there had been no invasion on the Japanese main islands since Mongol ships were destroyed by the "kamikaze," or "divine wind," in the thirteenth century.

The Soviet Union, whose ambitions to occupy Japan's large northern island of Hokkaido at the end of the war had been resisted, manifested no aggressive intent in 1970. The Communist Chinese vehemently denounced the Japanese government in their propaganda but had no waterborne capability, nor apparently any intent, to move militarily against Japan. Peking's development of nuclear weaponry was, of course, of great interest to Japan's leadership, but caused no undue trepidation, for there was a general assumption that Peking's purposes were other than the destruction of Japan.

Thus, in terms of Japan's own defense, the "free ride" complaint was not meaningful. The real value of the treaty lay in its contribution to regional security, including its deterrent effect. Without American bases in Japan, the prosecution of the Korean war would have been gravely handicapped, and our ordeal in Vietnam even more difficult. If the American security role in the Far East was to remain credible and effective, the availability of forward facilities such as those in Japan was indispensable. American commitments could not be adequately honored from bases restricted to American soil.

Since Japan had at least an equal stake in the maintenance of peace in the Far East, the contention was often heard that she should shoulder more of the security burden. In some respects Japan was doing so, but to expect the deployment of Japanese armed forces outside Japanese territory was to fly in the face of Constitutional interpretations supported by massive Japanese opposition. It also raised the question whether a major Japanese military buildup was desirable. Even the "free ride" critics paused when asked this question.

While recognizing that the major security value of the United States-Japan treaty was its contribution to the maintenance of peace in the Far Eastern region, it was necessary to bear in mind that the world was changing. The pact-building era of the 1950's and the eyeball-to-eyeball tensions of the 1960's were being replaced, hopefully, by a new structure of world peace. Both Japan and the United States would have critical roles to play. While their basic partnership could go forward as set forth in the Treaty of Mutual Cooperation and Security, adjustments in the manner in which that partnership evolved could be expected.

Given the rising tide of nationalistic sentiment in the Japan of the 1960's, the extension of the United States-Japan treaty without the turbulence that had been anticipated seemed somewhat incongruous. From the date of its birth onward, all banners had been waved against the treaty, none for it. While a solid corps of conservative thinkers truly believed the treaty to be in Japan's national interest, even Liberal Democratic Party spokesmen would frequently defend their support by implying the treaty was an inescapable favor extended to big brother America. Practice bombings by the United States Air Force at Mito and other ranges, and artillery firing exercises by the Marines in potential recreational areas at the foot of scenic Mount Fuji, did not enhance the treaty's popularity ratings. Neither did the wide spectrum of special privileges which the Americans enjoyed under the Status of Forces Agreement.

If it was a miracle that was wrought on June 23, 1970, the credit might well go to an unexpected by-product of the "anti-treaty struggle." The appearance of a unique characteristic in Japan known as "self-reflection" was unanticipated or underestimated. As the fateful June date drew closer, and as tensions increased, Japanese of various walks of life, including some in the opposition, started asking themselves what would happen if the treaty were abrogated. Essentially, the options were only two: a) the road of unarmed pacifism, which to most Japanese was unrealistic; and (b) a go-it-alone defense policy, perhaps in the manner of France under De Gaulle.

At this juncture, Prime Minister Chou En-lai of the People's Republic of China provided an unwitting assist for the treaty's extension by leveling widely publicized charges of a resurgent "militarism" in Japan. The charges were echoed in a Japan trip report by a pair of American Congressmen. A startled Japanese public asked, "Who? Us?"

If there was anything certain in the Japan of early 1970, it was the pertinacity of Japanese revulsion against "militarism." The Japanese socialist parties, being pacifist by profession, were automatically hostile to any military buildup. More saliently, most Japanese retained vivid memories of the humiliation which their nation sustained when the generals and admirals gained control in the 1930's. There was deep determination that there should never be a recurrence.

Article IX of the Japanese Constitution banned war "forever" as an instrument of policy. Despite allegations that this provision was the handiwork of General Mac-Arthur, there was little doubt that it represented the will of the great majority of the Japanese people. It still did so in May 1970, when a poll by the *Yomiuri* newspaper found only 16% of the Japanese people favoring Article IX's revision.

Article IX also banned "land, sea and air forces," but it was determined in the early 1950's that the proscription did not rule out legitimate self-defense. In 1970, Japan's Self Defense Forces numbered under 300,000, all of them volunteers. The prospects for Diet passage of legislation authorizing conscription were nil. The 1970 SDF officers and men were solid citizens, some with professional backgrounds dating from World War II, but socially they were almost outcasts, seldom invited to non-military functions.

The head of the Japan Defense Agency, the counterpart of the United States Secretary of Defense, still in 1970 had only Director General status, even though incumbents of the position were named Ministers of State and attended cabinet meetings. Their tenures in office were fragile. In 1971 an able Director General, Keikichi Masuhara, who had been in office only three weeks was forced to resign because a military aircraft (over which he could have had no conceivable control) was involved in a crash with a civilian aircraft. There was some reason to believe the civilian aircraft was at fault, but the mere involvement of a military aircraft cost the chief of the military establishment his job. The same accident caused the Diet to delay passage of, and eventually cut sharply, the JDA's annual budget.

Aside from domestic constraints, there were potent foreign considerations which helped curb militaristic tendencies in Japan. From Korea to Burma, Asian nations were nervously suspicious that the Japanese economic juggernaut would inevitably take on military trappings. They too had memories of the 1930's, the "Co-Prosperity Sphere," and unstoppable Japanese military cadres. Sensitive as well as shrewd, the Japanese were keenly aware of the fears of their neighbors. Being also pragmatic, they had no intention of jeopardizing Japan's thriving commerce in the Asian region. It may be added that the Japanese also had to take into account that their major ally, the United States, was itself not immune to fears of a resurgent Japanese militarism.

One should not attempt to diagnose the Chinese, but it was difficult to escape the thought that Peking's propaganda about a resurgent Japanese "militarism" sought to alarm Japan's East Asian neighbors and fan their suspicions. If that was the intention, it served to remind the Japanese of the care needed to guard their East Asian image.

Thus, while upsurgent nationalistic sentiment may have been tugging the Japanese away from continuing their security partnership with the United States, they were impelled in the opposite direction by an intense preoccupation to ward off accusations of a "resurgent militarism." Their "self-reflection" helped clarify the options. Whatever its drawbacks, the treaty relationship offered an alternative to either an unrealistic pacifist policy or a military buildup which could be calamitous at home and abroad. Proving that Japan could be a Great Power without a major military establishment continued to be Prime Minister Sato's "grand experiment." It was also an objective which a number of Japan-watchers reflected on with skepticism regarding its long-term feasibility.

That Communist China, with nuclear weaponry and missile programs and millions of men under arms, should accuse Japan of "militarism" was, to say the least, ironic. The manpower of Japan's Self Defense Forces, all volunteer, was at a level under 300,000, and it was projected to remain so under a new five-year Fourth Defense Plan. Even the authorized strength, however, was unattainable due the military's lack of competitiveness in labor-short Japan. Though compact, the Japanese armed forces were an efficient, well-trained organization, theoretically eighth in the world in capability.

Muffled as they were by the anti-militaristic sentiment prevailing in Japan, the Self Defense Forces were content to maintain a low profile. While no doubt envying the advanced weapons systems of the superpowers, they had to follow Andy Jackson's advice at the Battle of New Orleans and "elevate them sights a little lower." Their task was to develop an optimum capability for defending their homeland with conventional weaponry, and with limited manpower. Their equipment was, for the most part, badly out-of-date, but, as U.S. Secretary of Defense Melvin Laird observed during a July 1971 visit, it was maintained in tiptop condition. Their training and technical competence were second to none.

As others of us, Secretary Laird had visited the Japanese Northern Army at its headquarters in Hokkaido, where the Japanese military reflected a remarkable sense of duty and esprit de corps. The commanders utilized standard American military briefing techniques, which by virtue of their boilerplate nature are probably not among the greatest boons ever to have been bequeathed to civilization. What warmed the cockles of the heart was that, despite what is considered to be one of the world's most difficult language barriers, the Japanese gamely conducted the briefings in English.

Idleness is not a word in the Japanese vocabulary. In addition to cultivating its professional capabilities, the Northern Army in Hokkaido was engaged in a variety of civic action programs. Apart from its extensive disaster-relief operations, among the most noteworthy was the key role it played in Sapporo's annual "Snow Festival." Each February, the citizenry of Hokkaido and thousands of visitors would be enchanted by a fairyland of ice-snow sculptures, some of them 10 or 15 meters high. Most had been chiseled by Northern Army men. Another major project was the investment of much of the troops' time and talent in the staging of the 1972 Winter Olympics in Sapporo. This Japanese production was so masterfully handled that scouts from Colorado had grave doubts that Denver's resources would be adequate to host such an affair in 1976. When, on an unforgettable Sunday morning, three Hokkaido-born contestants, before the eyes of their Emperor and the world, scored a grand slam in the 70-meter ski-jump, there was quiet gratification among Northern Army men, for they had helped make this dream come true.

Although haunted by a legion of obstacles caused by bureaucratic and political infighting as well as by the prevalent anti-military attitudes, the Japan Defense Agency painstakingly prepared a Fourth Defense Plan. Covering a five-year period beginning in 1972, it anticipated a budget 220% that of its predecessor. Almost immediately, the top 20% became victim of the air crash in which a military plane was involved, and the whole plan was subjected to many months of harassment in the Diet.

Because of Japan's phenomenal economic growth, even the double rate of defense expenditure would over the five-year time frame represent, as previously, less than 1% of the Gross National Product. No increase in force levels was contemplated in the Fourth Defense Plan. Virtually all of the 100% additional outlay would be for equipment. This aspect precipitated debate over how much of the hardware should be manufactured in Japan and how much might be purchased abroad, primarily from the United States. Already Japan was doing a good share of its own defense production, and this was being expanded with the manufacture of over 100 F-4 Phantom aircraft by Mitsubishi Heavy Industries, with the support of the McDonnell-Douglas Corporation.

Faced with an alarming trade imbalance worldwide, and a bilateral trade deficit soaring from $1 billion to $3 billion, the United States Government was actively interested in boosting its exports to Japan, including military equipment. Items such as fighter-trainers and early-warning aircraft could be delivered to Japan at a much earlier date and at substantially less cost. But there seemed to be a basic Japanese feeling that nothing be purchased abroad if there existed a possibility for its manufacture at home. To this was added pressure from Japanese industrial leaders, who were encountering an economic slowdown and who, incidentally, were a pillar of support for the government.

In the end, a grudging "political decision" was made to purchase a few items from the United States. However, securing Japanese concurrence to a large-scale "offset purchasing" program of the type which had been so helpful in our relations with Germany was clearly out of the question. Japanese leaders were convinced that "offset purchasing" would in effect combine the explosive qualities of both the anti-militarism and the anti-treaty issues to produce some sort of atomic detonation in Japanese domestic politics.

No discussion of Japan's military posture can be complete without reference to nuclear weapons. Through the security treaty, Japan was under the American "nuclear umbrella." With its strong anti-militarism complex, as well as poignant memories of Hiroshima and Nagasaki, there was never a serious move for Japan to develop its own nuclear capability. Technologically, the possibility existed. Estimates were that an A-bomb could be constructed by the Japanese in about two years.

Just as there were skeptics who doubted that Japan would continue to eschew major military rearmament, there were also those who believed she would one day "go nuclear." In recent years, several highly nationalistic voices, such as that of the young author-senator Shintaro Ishihara, publicly advocated that as a Great Power Japan must have a nuclear capability, but the *Yomiuri* poll of May 1970 indicated that only 8% of the Japanese populace favored the development of nuclear weaponry, while 68% were categorically opposed. Other polls revealed that while the percentage of Japanese who were definitely in opposition had not varied significantly, the number of Japanese who surmised that Japan would one day become a nuclear power was increasing steadily.

In 1970, Japan signed the Nuclear Non-Proliferation Treaty. However, the treaty was not presented for Diet ratification, and there were questions if and when it would be. To the skeptics, the conclusion was simple: Japan was keeping its nuclear option open. The position of the government was, however, that the discriminatory nature of the treaty's safeguard provisions, as well as other technicalities, were causing the delay. Japan wished treatment similar to that enjoyed by the EURATOM countries.

Impressed by the strength of "anti-militarism" in Japan, my own estimate was that Japan would not "go nuclear" in the military sense for the "foreseeable future," that is, not for at least five or ten years. A second factor was the pragmatic consideration, frequently voiced by Japanese analysts, that, because of its heavy concentration of population and industry, Japan would have virtually no "second strike" capability and, therefore, the country would be better off by not having a capability which could invite a nuclear attack. It was my view that, if and when Japan should decide to "go nuclear," it would be due to unanticipated but alarming external factors, or a combination of them, such as nuclear aggressiveness on the part of China, threats to Japan's economic survival by quarantines imposed by other nations, or the deterioration in one way or another of the American "nuclear umbrella." Meanwhile, because of its high vulnerability with regard to energy supplies, Japan could be expected to be in the forefront of nations in nuclear power development. It was significant that Japan was building in a northern Japanese port its own nuclear-powered commercial ship, the *Mutsu*, even while outcries by the opposition, echoed in the press, remained shrill against visits by nuclear-powered American warships and while the Japanese government, despite appeals from our Maritime Administration and me personally, steadfastly refused entry of the nuclear-powered American commercial ship *Savannah* to Japanese ports.

In an October 1967 *Foreign Affairs* article Richard M. Nixon referred to the United States-Japan relationship and concluded that it was not logical for one Great Power to be dependent on another Great Power. When, as was unexpected in 1967, he attained the Presidency, his views had progressed into a doctrine which envisaged that America would continue to play its role in world affairs, but would expect, as he said in his 1970 foreign policy report, "a more responsible participation by our foreign friends in their own defense and progress."

In pondering the United States-Japan treaty, as it was being translated into an American security presence in Japan, it struck me from the outset of my tour in Tokyo that a basic assumption must be that United States forces would not be stationed on Japanese soil interminably. The question, however, was not whether the American presence would pull out or be thrown out, but how best to ensure a transformation so that the interests of both countries, and world peace, would be served.

It was noteworthy that as products of their times, the top defense authorities at this juncture in the United States-Japan relationship were both rugged individualists, unhampered by conventional wisdom. A midwesterner, Defense Secretary Melvin Laird represented an America that was realizing that while isolationism was wrong, so also was the myth that somehow the United States could be gendarme for the world. An aspiring leader of the new Japan, Yasuhiro Nakasone, who was appointed head of the Japan Defense Agency in January 1970, was somewhat of a political maverick, particularly vis-à-vis Japan's traditional seniority system, but he sensed that change was inevitable. In addition to politics, he was president of his own bustling university in Tokyo.

Prior to my arrival and his becoming JDA chief, Nakasone had suggested at an academic forum in Hakone that by 1975 consideration might be given to revising the 1960 treaty. With the expected crisis only one year away, Nakasone's observation received wide publicity, to the delight of the treaty's opponents and to the concern of its proponents. Assuming that the American Embassy was among the latter, Nakasone puckishly commented to the press that his views were causing the new Ambassador to "lose sleep."

Prime Minister Sato, with his political sixth sense, saw the value not only of placing Nakasone in a position of responsibility, which tends to restrain free-wheeling critics, but also of placing him in the hot spot as JDA Defense General. Sato admired Nakasone's energy and turned it to good account for a crucial year and a half.

Soon after assuming his defense responsibilities, Director General Nakasone began speaking in private and to newsmen about a time in the future when American bases in Japan would revert to Japanese administration, but under arrangements whereby American forces would be granted "joint use" of the major facilities and "emergency re-entry" possibilities for others which the Americans would relinquish. By the time of the United States-Japan Security Consultative Committee meeting in May 1970, he had coined the phrase "autonomous self-defense" to describe Japan's future policy. In "fireside chats," via a specially constructed Japan-wide communications network, the new Director General sought to instill among the officers and men of the Self Defense Forces a new sense of self-reliance and pride.

All this was heady stuff. The press enjoyed it. Some conservative government leaders were understandably concerned that ammunition was being provided to the anti-treaty forces in their imminent campaign. American military representatives were also disturbed, even though in their conversations with him they were impressed by the JDA Director General's endeavors.

Aside from questions of timing and flamboyance, the thrust of Nakasone's policy formulation was not disastrous. In fact, phased properly, it was highly compatible with the development of American thinking. According to the Nixon Doctrine, nations like Japan which had gained in strength should shoulder more of the peace and security burden, too much of which the United States had shouldered too long. As the first U.S. Secretary of Defense to visit Japan, Secretary Laird enunciated his "total force" concept, whereby other nations, notably Japan, would make their contributions to regional and world security by developing competent conventional forces to assure their own defense in conflicts limited to conventional weaponry.

In Tokyo, the Embassy had sought to make known American gratification that Japan was standing on its own feet and ready to assume responsibilities hitherto borne by the United States. It was often stressed, as in my remarks at an October 3, 1969, symposium at Tachikawa, "It is not the intention of the United States to seek to maintain in Japan more than the minimum facilities necessary for our common purposes, i.e., the security of Japan and the Far East." By coincidence, U.S. Air Force flying activities and a number of other American military functions at Tachikawa were terminated on that date.

The plain fact was that maintaining United States

forces in Japan was costing the United States well over $600 million per year. With severe budget and balance of payment problems at home, we had no reason to spend one dollar more in Japan than was necessary. It should be noted, incidentally, that of the above $600 million figure only 38% was in appropriated funds. The rest of the dollar outflow was caused by the procurement of Japanese products, such as stereos and TV sets, for our military's worldwide post exchange system. The theory was that, unless such items were sold through the PX, American servicemen would buy them on the open market, at an even greater damage to our balance of payments.

Parenthetically, it is worth observing that Japanese products had an irresistible lure for our GI's. On one flying visit to an aircraft carrier, which had the previous day weighed anchor at the Seventh Fleet's main base at Yokosuka, it was fascinating to see the large command center, impressively equipped with the most advanced radar gadgetry, but also heavily laden with cartons of Japanese stereo and TV sets. A previous carrier had reportedly borne away some four hundred motorcycles. Since these cargoes were too much for the sailors' own quarters, the overflow was in desperation stored in operational space. Happily, this booty was safely ferried away without the occurrence of an international crisis!

In late 1969, Secretary Laird ordered a $3 billion retrenchment in the budgets of the military services. Our uniformed colleagues were in great distress. In one of his frequent transits of Tokyo, Admiral John S. McCain, Jr., Commander-in-Chief of United States Forces in the Pacific, confided that retrenchments being proposed by Washington would cut his far-flung command to the bone. In Japan, the surgery would be so extensive as to include giving up the Seventh Fleet's home base at Yokosuka. The Admiral's stature being not much over five feet, his chin was closer to terra firma than it had ever been before.

This book could not be written without a special tribute to the inimitable Admiral whose name became legendary at his headquarters in Hawaii, in Washington, and among hundreds of thousands of officers and men under his authority in Vietnam and elsewhere in the Pacific. The epitome of the old adage that great energy comes in small packages, Admiral McCain commanded instant and unfailing respect. His was a taut ship, with a superb crew.

Salty as any Navy man in history, Admiral McCain was a thoroughbred. His father had been a celebrated carrier admiral during World War II, and the McCain heritage of patriotism was passed on to a son who was shot down in Vietnam, was one of the worst wounded, and refused tenders of repatriation which were obviously based on the position of his father. The Admiral's son toughed it out for five and one-half years, until he with his fellow POW's came home. During those years, the Admiral, traveling indefatigably, regularly visited Tokyo, frequently with his vivacious wife, but they stoically refrained from discussing their son's plight.

While his approach to international affairs unabashedly focused on the Communist "threat," and while with colorful prose he fearlessly let his own views be known, Admiral McCain's sense of discipline was such that whenever the President spoke, he felt it his duty to obey. Similarly, he was keenly aware that Ambassadors were the President's representatives, and that there must be no divergence between civilian and military policies. When Sasebo's Mayor Ichizo Tsuji, who with his voice handicap was a political phenomenon, asked that the tour of Captain Claude Shaw, the Sasebo Navy commander, be extended because of the fine job he was doing in fostering healthy community relations, one word from me to CINCPAC and Captain Shaw stayed on. On Tokyo visits, the Admiral, with microscopic perception, would detect any note of discord and immediately take steps with his military representatives in

Japan to ensure harmony, lacking which he expressed readiness to effect prompt transfers if the Ambassador so recommended.

Dedicated to duty as he was, and when there was clearly no hope for a reconsideration of the 1970 budget slash, Admiral McCain sought to tailor as effectually as possible the cloth which was entrusted to him. The problem was that the scissors were not entirely in his control. Many of the patterns were being cut in Washington, and being cut in a piecemeal fashion, dictated by the special considerations of the individual services.

Concerned that haphazard results would occur from the way the Pentagon budgetary axe was being wielded, the Embassy on August 11, 1970, dispatched a telegram which one Washingtonian dubbed "a blockbuster." My appeal was for a well-coordinated, long-range approach to the problem of base reductions in Japan. Every single action to be taken should be part of a highly efficient and economic package, taking into consideration what the situation might be in the years ahead. There had been several instances where either the American military or the Japanese government, with its responsibility for funding relocations, had invested in facilities which were within a year or two abandoned, like the expenditure of over $2,000,000 on Camp Oji hospital. The telegram suggested lowering American military visibility in the congested Kanto Plain area (Tokyo region) in favor of more reliance on outlying facilities such as Sasebo and Misawa where the political climate was more hospitable. Also suggested was the desirability of moving toward the concepts of "joint use" and "emergency re-entry."

The most important recommendation in the telegram was that whatever base realignments were to be undertaken should be the product of thorough consultation with our Japanese partners, rather than unilateral measures taken on a helter-skelter basis by our financially distressed services. One could expect that the Japanese government and people would be favorably disposed to a reduction of facilities on the scale proposed. So here was an opportunity for discussing the specifics and fusing the best interests of both countries, thereby giving meaning to the word "mutuality" in our security relationship. It would give the lie to contentions that the United States ignored Japan's interests in the furtherance of its own selfish objectives.

Foreign Minister Aichi was informed on August 31 that it was the desire of the United States Government to undertake detailed consultations with the Japanese authorities with a view to coordinating anticipated realignment of American facilities. Describing the United States-Japan partnership as being "of primordial consideration," Aichi heartily endorsed the "mutuality" concept, and a "Base Review Committee" was established. It consisted on the Japanese side of Deputy Vice Foreign Minister Takeshi Yasukawa and Foreign Ministry associates Bunroku Yoshino, Masatada Tachibana, and Wataru Miyakawa. Captaining the American side was Deputy Chief of Mission Richard Sneider, assisted by Major General Richard Lee, Chief-of-Staff of United States Forces in Japan, as well as the Embassy's political-military counselor Howard Meyers and his assistants Stephen Dawkins and later Blaine Porter.

At the time of the 1960 treaty signing, a "Security Consultative Committee" had been established pursuant to a proposal by Prime Minister Kishi in an exchange of notes with Secretary of State Herter. Kishi had suggested that, in addition to serving other specific purposes envisaged in the treaty, the committee "should also consider any matters underlying and related to security affairs which would serve to promote understanding between the two governments and contribute to the strengthening of cooperative relations between the two countries in the field of security." The committee membership would consist of the Japanese Foreign Minister, who would preside, and the Director General of the Japanese Defense Agency, while for the Americans the Ambassador would serve as chairman, the Commander-in-Chief of United States Forces in the Pacific as his principal advisor, and the Commander of United States Forces in Japan as alternate for CINCPAC.

Consonant with SCC's purposes was the ongoing consideration of the United States forces' base structure in Japan. It was, therefore, at the Security Consultative Committee, during its 12th meeting on December 21, 1970, that the major base realignment program, which had been carefully drawn up by the Base Review Committee, was considered and approved. Present for the occasion were Foreign Minister Aichi and JDA chief Nakasone for the Japanese, and for the Americans the Ambassador, Admiral McCain, and Lieutenant General Gordon Graham, who had a few months earlier assumed command of USFJ. It was with a sense of history that the participants were able to announce not only the mutually agreed realignments in the American base structure but also the increased readiness of the Japanese Self Defense Forces to assume responsibilities, specifically at those facilities which were to be relinquished by the American forces.

If one diplomatic success during my Tokyo assignment was the retention of the "Treaty of Mutual Cooperation and Security" as the cornerstone of the partnership between Japan and the United States, of equal, if not greater, importance was adjusting the implementation of that flexible treaty to harmonize with changing conditions and injecting fuller meaning into the word "mutual." Treaties are, indeed, pieces of paper of no greater worth than the forces behind them. Accordingly, the real challenge was to maintain the vitality and growth of the organism for which the treaty was merely the baptismal certificate.

When the peace treaty was signed in 1951, there were 3,848 American military facilities in Japan. That number had quickly plummeted to well under 1,000 with the lifting of the occupation. The decline since that time was less drastic but steady. As to manpower, American force levels had dropped from 260,000 in 1952 to 40,000 at the time of my arrival in mid-1969. Upon my departure the figure was down to 27,000.

Just before his departure from Japan in January 1969, Ambassador U. Alexis Johnson had negotiated with the Japanese (and the American military) an agreement whereby the 150 American facilities then remaining in Japan would be reduced to 100 over a period of months. The status of this reduction program was on the agenda of the July 9, 1969, meeting of the Security Consultative Committee, which was the SCC's tenth and my first. It was noted that 20 of the 50 proposed relinquishments had been completed, but difficulties had arisen in arranging the release of some of the remaining 30, among them Camp Oji hospital, which was caring for Vietnam wounded, the off-coast air bombing practice range at Mito, for which an alternate had not been found, and Itazuke, which was doing double duty by serving also as the civil airport for Fukuoka and which still required satisfactory management arrangements.

Since the American base structure was sure to constitute a chronic problem, it seemed important for me to get to know the remaining 130 facilities if their future were to be discussed intelligently. Given other pressures at the busy Tokyo Embassy, finding the time for this was not easy, but frequent trips outside Tokyo were planned to include visits to outlying American military facilities. For the Tokyo, or Kanto Plain area, my family and I developed a novel practice of serving two interests, religious and professional, with one operation. Our Sundays were organized to visit a different military facility in the Kanto Plain each week, attending the local chapel in the morning, then getting acquainted with the senior officers and their wives at luncheon, following which there would be a thorough tour of the facility under the guidance of its commander.

Those Sunday safaris will always live among our warmest memories.Without exception, the officers and men and their wives were cordial, helpful, and instructive. We felt deeply indebted to them, as we did to Chief of Chaplains Paul Schade, Colonel Arthur Estes, the head of the chaplains' association, and all the Kanto Plain chaplains who, by providing spiritual refreshment, made it easier for us to face another week of the grueling grind in Tokyo. On those weekends when safaris to Tokyo's outlying areas were not feasible, inspiration for the next week's grind was always available at either Tokyo Union or St. Paul's churches, the latter being of my Lutheran denomination.

Unforgettable, also, were our repeated Sunday visits to the seven Kanto Plain military hospitals, which in mid-1969 were caring for more than 2,500 servicemen wounded in Vietnam. Every day huge C-141 aircraft would bring in casualties, sometimes numbering up to 100 or more, many of them litter cases. They would be transferred at the Yokota air base to waiting helicopters to be taken to designated hospitals. The first visit to any of the intensive care units, or to the "burn ward" at Kishine hospital near Yokohama, could tear a person apart. But that same person, steeling himself and passing through ward after ward, chatting with GIs from every corner of our country, could not but be thrilled by the greatness of these young men.

Via the media, Americans and the world heard ad nauseam of anti-Vietnam protesters and draft-card burners. Little did Americans know of these incredibly courageous compatriots, some with limbs blown off by land mines, all of them battle-scarred but almost unanimously chipper, uncomplaining, cheerful, and the majority wanting to go back to their buddies in Vietnam. Three years later Americans could not believe their eyes and ears when prisoners

of war returned blessing America. It was because America's
eyes had not been seeing, nor its ears listening. This inspiring story had been one which the American people apparently did not have the right to know.

As the weeks and months passed, the occupancies in the
hospital wards mercifully decreased. It was like a barom-
eter for the Vietnam conflict. By the time of my 1972 departure from Japan, four of the seven Tokyo-area hospitals
had closed their doors, and the number of Vietnam casualties to be treated in Japan had been reduced to zero. Even
as the spirit of those brave young Americans was never
fully appreciated by their compatriots, so also unsung were
the lifesaving ministrations and miracles wrought by the
men and women in white, serving with the medical units
of our military services.

It was somewhat of a misnomer to describe the 130
American military locations in Japan in mid-1969 as
"bases." Actually, aside from the headquarters for U.S.
Forces in Japan (USFJ) in the Tokyo suburb of Fuchu,
there were only eight military complexes which merited the
"base" label: Yokota, Tachikawa, and Misawa for the Air
Force; Yokosuka, Atsugi, and Sasebo for the Navy; Camp
Zama for the Army; and Iwakuni near Hiroshima for the
Marines. These complexes were supported by a variety of
housing areas such as Yokohama and Kanta Mura, plus bits
and pieces of real estate scattered throughout Japan which
served as sites for communications facilities, supply depots,
et cetera.

The major base realignment announced by the Security
Consultative Committee on December 21, 1970, envisaged
reducing the number of American military personnel in
Japan by 12,000. The U.S. Air Force would withdraw both
of its F-4 fighter squadrons hitherto stationed in Japan.
Yokota Air Base near Tokyo would continue to be a major
Far East logistics center, but Misawa Air Base in northern

Honshu would be converted into a facility for "joint use" with the Japanese Air Self Defense Forces. The Navy planned to shift Seventh Fleet headquarters from Yokosuka to Sasebo in southern Japan and release much of the Atsugi Naval Air Station near Tokyo. At Itazuke, Japan would assume responsibility for operating the civil airport, but with some limited American flying activities. For the U.S. Army, already pared down, there would be further belt tightening which would allow for the stationing of some Japanese Ground Self Defense Force elements at the Camp Zama headquarters complex. There would be no changes at the Marine base at Iwakuni.

While the consolidation of the American military structure in Japan had political, as well as military, advantages, it took place not without some anguish in Japan. Some 8,400 Japanese employees would be dismissed. A few months earlier, pursuant to the 50-base reduction program, some 2,300 Japanese had received reduction-in-force notices which led to a plea to us from Foreign Minister Aichi that they be given "humane treatment." In Japan's paternalistic system, an employee normally works for life with a single organization. He does not try to skip rungs on the ladder, nor does he switch to some other firm. Most of the Japanese working with the American forces had started in their youth; now in mid-life they were faced with the formidable task of achieving lateral entry into another organization. Presumably, the facilities relinquished by the Americans would continue to operate, but there were many uncertainties and much unhappiness for those subjected to the reduction.

The ink was scarcely dry on the December 21, 1970, base realignment agreement when modifications in the agreement were attempted. They were prompted by what appeared to be an unexpected budgetary windfall, coupled with second thoughts by our military authorities about the wisdom of some of the proposed changes. This was particularly true for the Navy. Within two months, we were back at the Base Review Committee seeking to reverse the transfer of Seventh Fleet headquarters from Yokosuka to Sasebo, the turnover to the Japanese of Yokosuka's Ship Repair Facility, and some of the relinquishment at Atsugi Naval Air Station. In mid-January, Prime Minister Sato had told Chairman of the Joint Chiefs of Staff Admiral Thomas Moorer that relinquished facilities such as those at Yokosuka should retain their operational capability, but he did not indicate under whose auspices. Working in favor of the Navy was the reduction-in-force backlash. By the end of March 1971, following reluctant agreement by the Japanese authorities, the Navy's operations at Yokosuka were extended and reduction notices for several thousand Japanese workers rescinded.

With the American armed services moving toward voluntary recruitment, the Navy was understandably eager to boost its reenlistment rate, which had been exceedingly small. To do this, the concept of home-porting was developed, whereby families would accompany officers and men to base stations overseas. For the Navy in Japan, this meant retaining much of the Yokohama housing complex which had previously been slated for release.

Despite the frequent zigzagging, the number of American military facilities in Japan proper (excluding Okinawa) was down to 116 by the time of my departure in 1972. American military expenditures in Japan in 1971 had been cut by $50,000,000. Real progress had been made in "joint use" arrangements at Fuchu, Zama, Yokosuka, Misawa, Chitose, Itazuke, and elsewhere.

The two trends were continuing, American retrenchment and the assumption of greater responsibilities by the Japanese. On the drawing boards was yet another major realignment plan, initiated by the Air Force, but to be worked out in the spirit of mutuality with the Japanese. Its aim would be to relinquish nearly a dozen sites totaling some 3,600 acres and to consolidate Air Force activities in the Tokyo region at Yokota Air Base, where some additional construction would be needed, such as a small hospital to replace the larger one at Tachikawa. When completed, this Kanto Plain Consolidation Plan would permit a reduction in personnel of 9,500 and would effect an annual savings of $73,000,000.

From all of these exercises in translating the Nixon Doctrine into a befitting American military presence abroad, four themes seemed to me to be emerging: a) extravagances in American military expenditures could no longer be tolerated; financial retrenchment was imperative; b) in playing its role, at least in the Far East, the American military presence was apt to be skewed toward the Navy, away from the Army, with the Marines as back-up, and with the Air Force assigned selected but restricted functions; c) since any military man worth his salt could advance seemingly irrefutable arguments against the modification of any specific facility or the abolition of any personal position, the civilian administration's most efficient control was via the power of the purse, i.e., subject to political parameters, the military establishment should be responsible for determining where the limited resources available could most effectively be invested; and d) for the Nixon Doctrine to be productive, there could be no substitute for communication, consultation, and mutuality in the relationships with our friends and allies. The Nixon Doctrine should be more than a unilateral proposition.

"Mr. Ambassador, who really won the war?" That question was put to me one morning on Capitol Hill during a briefing of some 50 members of the House of Representatives. What rankled the questioner, as it did many Americans, was that Japan's defense outlays totaled only $1.8 billion annually while Amerian boys were dying in Vietnam and American taxpayers were burdened with $80 billion per year in defense expenditures. Presumably, a world was being preserved in which Japan, free of enormous defense burdens such as ours, could devote its resources and energies to reaping vast profits—often, as in Indo-China, at the expense of the United States, which was in serious economic trouble. This was a broader concept of the "free ride" than merely the American commitment to defend territorial Japan.

While such rancor was understandable, most Americans, haunted by painful memories of Pearl Harbor, would have viewed with equal displeasure the resurgence of Japan as a military superpower. Here was a real dilemma with no easy answer. No one was more deeply troubled by it than Prime Minister Sato. Under a crossfire of sniping on this and other issues by American critics on one side and the domestic opposition on the other, Sato was particularly depressed during my farewell call on March 21, 1972, to the point of confiding that memories of the 1930's were occasionally passing through his mind.

Sato's response to the "free ride" versus "militarism" dilemma was governed by the overwhelming sentiment of his people against any major military buildup and against any military involvement outside Japan's borders. At the same time, his government realized the need for Japan to assume increased international responsibilities. Although inadequate in the eyes of some Americans, the Japanese sought to make their contribution to Far East security in alternate ways:

a. SELF DEFENSE. That the Japanese Self Defense Forces were increasingly capable of assuring the security of Japan in conventional warfare (Secretary Laird's "total force" concept) was substantiated by the fact that the United States was able to remove completely its Army and Air Force combat units from homeland Japan. Also indicative was the doubling of the SDF budget over a five-year time span, and the acquisition of F-4 Phantom aircraft, Hawk and Nike missiles, and other modern weapons systems. All this meant that Japan was assuming costs previously borne by the United States. In Okinawa, Japan's assumption of defense responsibilities eased the American taxpayer's burden by at least $35,000,000 annually.

b. BUDGETARY SUPPORT FOR U.S. FORCES. True to its treaty obligations, Japan faithfully defrayed the rental expenses and assumed other obligations, upward of $110,-000,000 annually, for properties occupied by American forces in Japan. Similarly, millions of dollars were expended to finance such relocations of American facilities as were needed, to pay certain extra labor costs, and for the acquisition of properties. To these outlays were added expenditures assumed with the reversion of Okinawa, including rental payments for 20% of the land area of Okinawa, at least $60,000,000 per annum, plus the cost differentials in raising military base wages in Okinawa up to the Japan level. Earlier, in quiet transactions, the Japanese had tried to help us with our balance of payments problems through Export-Import Bank investments. Unlike some European countries, the Japanese made no raids on Fort Knox, but kept their mounting financial reserves in dollars despite the prospect of devaluation.

c. LOGISTIC SUPPORT. Japan's logistic contributions were invaluable to the United States in the fulfillment of its Far Eastern commitments. The home base for the United States Seventh Fleet was at Yokosuka. The headquarters of the United States Fifth Air Force was at Fuchu; the Commander of U.S. Forces in Japan (USFJ) doubled as the Fifth Air Force Commander. The finest Far East tank and personnel carrier repair facility, working full time during the Vietnam war, was the U.S. Army depot at Sagami. A substantial program for repairing Navy aircraft was based at Atsugi. The Military Sea Lift command, with its headquarters at Yokohama, conducted LST transport missions to Vietnam, manned by Japanese. There were reserve ammunition, petroleum, and spare parts depots in Japan, and also a variety of major and minor communications facilities. Finally, many young Americans owed their restoration to health, even their lives, to the fine hospital facilities available in Japan during the Vietnam conflict.

d. MILITARY PURCHASING. While "offset purchasing" was not possible as in Germany, the Japanese did in fact purchase a considerable amount of military equipment from the United States, at the cost of about $120,000,000 per year. Despite pressures for local production, there remained the prospect that, under the Fourth Defense Plan, nearly $1 billion of military hardware might be purchased in the United States. The reasons were more practical than political: if the Japanese wished the advantage of the most sophisticated equipment available, the United States was the best source.

e. REGIONAL AID. Highly sensitive to the suspicions of their neighbors, the Japanese scrupulously avoided any transactions which could be considered as having a militaristic tinge. Sometimes they were too scrupulous, such as in their reluctance to provide trucks to Korea. Nonetheless, the Japanese government placed great emphasis on regional economic assistance, an emphasis which Americans vigorously encouraged. Totaling $800 million, Japan's aid to Asian countries on concessional terms in 1971 was 50% greater than the previous year. In 1971, Indonesia received $155 million and Korea $200 million in "soft" loans from Japan (3% interest, 25-year repayment period, and an initial seven-year grace interval). Modest amounts of assistance were also provided quietly to Cambodia, Laos, and Vietnam.

f. REGIONAL POLITICAL ROLE. Mindful of their neighbors' sensitivities, the Japanese were reluctant to exercise political leadership in the East Asian region. Nevertheless, with its burgeoning economic strength Japan could not avoid responsibility. When there was widespread Asian reaction to President Nixon's decision in April 1970 to move militarily against Communist sanctuaries in Cambodia, Japan agreed to join with eleven other nations to confer at Djakarta. Foreign Minister Aichi represented Japan and Deputy Foreign Minister Shinsaku Hogen served on a three-nation post-Djakarta diplomatic team. It was a timid step in the political-security arena, but was possible because Japan could share the leadership role with other Asian nations, notably Indonesia and Australia. While the outcome of the May 15 Djakarta conference was not impressive from the substantive point of view, it did foreshadow greater collaboration among Asian nations in seeking solutions to Asian problems. Such collaboration, with Japan playing an indispensable role, was highly welcome. Indeed it was essential, if a durable peace was to be forged in Asia and in the world.

While falling short of full-fledged membership in a regional defense organization, taken as a whole Japan's contributions to the maintenance of peace and security in the Far East were, as enumerated, above, quite considerable. Moreover, the world was changing, and the directions in which Japan was moving as it assumed increasing responsibilities were consistent with the hoped-for new structure of peace.

If treaties are no better than the forces which underlie them, those forces can be no better than the people who shape them. During the crucial 1969–1972 time frame, when the Treaty of Mutual Cooperation and Security was being extended and its implementation adjusted, the Japanese people as a whole and their representatives stood firmly for what they considered to be right. The electorate ignored the sound and fury of demagoguery to register its confidence in the Japan-United States partnership. Prime Minister Sato, his Foreign Ministers, the JDA Directors General, and their colleagues in government remained unflappable. The oppositionist parties themselves showed reasonableness, as did most of their allies, in that they confined their vehemence to the issues and stopped well short of Samsonian efforts to destroy Japan's institutions or the basic relationship of friendship with the United States.

Unsung heroes were the uniformed representatives of both countries. They were soldiers in a non-military combat. The Chairmen of the Joint Staff of the Japanese Self Defense Forces, Admiral Takaichi Itaya and General Hayao Kinugasa, were sincere and dedicated men. However, because of their profession, they were harangued in the Diet, unrevered by the press, and in effect quarantined socially. American military men were not much better off. Primarily because of Vietnam, they enjoyed no beds of roses on Capitol Hill or in the American press. For both Japanese and American servicemen, a kind word or a smile was rare, but, therefore, all the more appreciated. It was not surprising that between the services of the two countries a special comradeship developed.

With the American presence in Japan diminishing, it was important to maintain the warm friendship and cooperation between the services of both countries through personal relationships. This view was shared by General William Westmoreland who, as Chief of Staff of the U.S. Army, visited Japan in September 1970. Plans were, therefore, developed for exchanges of visits by servicepeople of all ranks, for technology consultations, for training exercises as in Alaska and Hokkaido, and for other opportunities to nurture ties of friendship.

From 1969 to 1972, countless Japanese and American man-hours were devoted to organizing the reversion of Okinawa, surmounting the "anti-treaty struggle," extending the Treaty of Mutual Cooperation and Security, revamping the American military presence, and welcoming the assumption by Japan of responsibilities commensurate with its new strength. None of these endeavors was an end in itself. Each was viewed as a contribution to a larger goal. It was the building of a new structure of world peace. While the ultimate architecture was still visionary, it was increasingly clear that the structure could not be built without a sound basis for effective cooperation.

One of the difficulties was that there had long been a belief that world peace depended virtually entirely on one or two superpowers. Now it was clear that nations like Japan had important resources, architectural technology, and human talent which must be brought to bear if successful construction were to take place.

Chapter 4

Detente with Mainland China: Nixon's Billiard Shot

FOR THE AMERICAN AMBASSADOR in Japan, no commodity was in shorter supply than time. Thus, when early in the morning of July 16, 1971, news bulletins were proclaiming that President Nixon would be making a major foreign policy pronouncement just before noon Japan time (evening of July 15 in the United States), I arranged for a long overdue haircut during which to listen. The President's remarks were to be broadcast by our armed forces radio station, known locally as the Far East Network (FEN).

When the President began by stating that he had sent Dr. Henry Kissinger to Peking, my instant reaction was that it was a slip of the tongue, that he had meant to say Vietnam (which had figured so prominently in Dr. Kissinger's most recent journey). The illusion vanished quickly, however, as the President of the United States disclosed his acceptance of an invitation to visit the People's Republic of China. In a brief three and a half minutes, it became clear that one of the most astonishing diplomatic developments in a generation was being announced. It was also immediately clear that a seismic impact could be expected in Japan.

Quickly dispensing with the barber, I directed urgent telephone calls to Washington. One top State Department official was at San Clemente. A second, upon hearing the President's announcement, had rushed to the residence of the Under Secretary of State, where I could ask them both whether any country had been given advance notification, stressing that if Japan had not we were in for real difficulty. By way of explaining the move to our Japanese friends, I suggested we say that it was consistent with public statements which had been made by the President and the Secretary of State, and consistent also with the tenor of our close bilateral consultations which had envisaged the development of improved relations with Peking for both Japan and the United States. We should also stress the President's pledge that his bold diplomatic breakthrough "would not be at the expense of old friends."

My Washington colleagues cited firm instructions from San Clemente, which at that moment were being telegraphed to all our diplomatic posts abroad, that no United States Government official should comment in any way on the President's announcement. They agreed, however, that my proposed rationale to the Japanese would be appropriate. Just before we concluded our conversation, my colleagues on the other end of the line received word that Secretary Rogers had in fact informed Japanese Ambassador Nobuhiko Ushiba by telephone in advance of the announcement. Due to difficulties in locating the Ambassador, who was out to dinner, the notification was less than the three hours in advance which had been intended. The information reached Sato only a few minutes before the President's announcement.

No nation has for so long been of more profound interest to Japan than China. Since World War II, policy toward China had been among the most important items on the United States-Japan diplomatic agenda. It was understandable, therefore, that the President's surprise announcement produced what the Japanese described as a "shokku." The problem was not so much the substance of the President's endeavors, for Japan, too, favored the de-isolation of mainland China. Prime Minister Sato, during a private conversation with General Motors Board Chairman James Roche, heartily endorsed the President's move, and a public statement of approbation was issued by the Japanese government. For their part, the opposition political parties and the press were pleased, for they had long been hammering at Sato and his predecessors to normalize relations with China.

If the Richter ratings in Japan were higher than anywhere else, it was, as we pointed out in our telegrams from Tokyo, because the tremors from the tactical aspects of the President's action were bound to have dramatic impact both on the domestic political scene in Japan and on the critical ingredient of trust in the relationship between Japan and the United States.

Ambassador Koichiro Asakai, who served in Washington from 1957 to 1963, had become famous in Japan for telling of a "nightmare" he once had that he would wake up one morning and read in *The Washington Post* that the United States had recognized Peking and was negotiating diplomatic relations. Now, all Tokyo was saying that "Asakai's nightmare" had in effect come true. In reporting this, we noted that even before the President's announcement the "China mood" had become a fever in Japan, that Sato had already suffered dissension within his own party on

China policy which affected his control of the Diet, and that the erosion of Sato's premiership might well be hastened. What concerned us most of all was the chorus of outcries, in the press and in official circles, that the United States had "jumped over Japan's head." Such accusations could call into question the special relationship between Japan and the United States which Prime Minister Sato and his predecessors had made the hallmark of Japan's postwar policy.

To repair the damage which was likely to occur, the Embassy urged, as we had on numerous occasions prior to July 15, that steps be taken to shore up the feeling of mutual trust, particularly through high-level consultations of as intimate a nature as circumstances would permit. Opportunities in the future would include the joint cabinet sessions in Washington in September, and, of greater urgency, the coordination of our positions on the question of Chinese representation at the United Nations. Ever since the preceding General Assembly, the Japanese authorities had urged the development of a new common position and, in recent weeks, they had become understandably impatient, arguing that virtually every day that was lost was costing the vote of a friendly nation at the United Nations. (Washington's unresponsiveness was no doubt related to the imminence of the July 15 announcement.)

Washington was not unmindful of our problems in Tokyo. Some hours after his announcement, the President himself sent a personal message to Prime Minister Sato. Secretary Rogers provided further explanations to Japanese Ambassador Ushiba. Aside from the Embassy's assessments, Washington could not ignore American public criticism to the effect that our most important East Asian ally had not been properly consulted. With characteristic serenity, Prime Minister Sato replied to the President's message without rancor, pledging cooperation in the fashioning of peace in Asia, and expressing his eagerness for close consultation in the development of policies with respect to China.

To understand why the President's announcement caused consternation in Japan, one had to appreciate the depth of the Japanese psychological complex with respect to China. Japan's relationship with its other massive neighbor, the Soviet Union, was rather cold and matter-of-fact. But with regard to China, emotions were involved. It was a love-hate syndrome, with a number of contributing factors:

a. CULTURAL MOTHER. Ever since the sixth century, and undoubtedly before, Japan was indebted to mainland China for most of its cultural heritage. Its language, its religion, its ruling concepts were greatly influenced by the Tang and subsequent Chinese dynasties. Its history in many ways was parallel, if not interlocked, with that of China. In Japanese culture, no force was more compulsive than one called "on," which is a deep sense of obligation to those who have been benefactors.

b. PROPINQUITY. With territory many times larger than that of the Japanese islands, and with a population at least seven times that of Japan, the neighboring Chinese mainland perforce commanded deference. Japan's dynamic society had no cause to feel inferior, but subconsciously it was difficult to disregard living next door to the legendary Chinese dragon. Propinquity was inevitably a strong force.

c. ATONEMENT. When they were overrunning China in the 1930's it was possible for the Japanese, consistent with their hierarchical philosophy, to rationalize the action to themselves as a virtuous endeavor. It may not have been an American Point Four program, but, in many Japanese eyes at that time, it was at least as honorable as Western imperialism's shouldering the so-called "white man's burden." When the "Co-Prosperity Sphere" ended in disaster, apology and redress were as natural for the hierarchically disciplined Japanese as were the sacrifices made two centuries earlier by the legendary forty-seven "ronin" who committed hara-kiri as atonement for having taken lives to redeem their master's honor. Some 10,000,000 Chinese perished during the fourteen years when Japanese authority held sway over China, and the Japanese of 1971 retained a deeply felt sense of guilt. Certainly, the guilt was not expiated by the 1952 peace treaty with Chiang Kai-shek's government.

d. ECONOMIC OPPORTUNITY. Economically, the Japanese believed that three-quarters of a billion Chinese could provide an enormous market for Japanese transistors, automobiles, and other manufactured products. During the 1930's, China trade accounted for about one-third of Japan's total external trade, but this was largely due to a distortion of natural economic patterns brought about by Japan's empire building in Manchuria and North China. In many ways, the nations were complementary, China with raw materials, Japan with industry. However, China was short of foreign exchange, and there were few indications that she would be any more willing than Japan to import competitive products or to purchase abroad any more than would be minimally necessary. In 1971, trade between the two countries was nearing the $1 billion level and there were prospects for expansion, but it was likely to be more gradual than many Japanese hoped.

e. DEMONSTRATION OF INDEPENDENCE. The common assumption in Japan was that Japan's postwar China policy had been heavily influenced by Washington. It was an assumption not without validity. John Foster Dulles had warned Prime Minister Yoshida that the Japanese Peace Treaty (and with it the termination of American occupation) would not be approved by the United States Senate unless Japan would conclude a separate peace treaty with Generalissimo Chiang Kai-shek's government at Taipei. That such influence on Japan's China policy still existed in 1971 was a myth. For a variety of reasons, including a level of trade exceeding that with mainland China, Japan's leadership saw wisdom in maintaining its ties with Taiwan, even while courting favor with Peking. Foreign Ministry officials, however, complained of "grappling with the ghost of Dulles," and even Foreign Minister Aichi was heard to say that in China policy, Japan tended to play "second fiddle" to the United States. If in light of the resurgence of strong nationalistic sentiment Japan should wish to demonstrate its independence, nothing would be more dramatic than Japanese initiatives in China policy. Conversely, following in America's wake would tend to confirm that Japan was still not unshackled.

f. BRIDGE-BUILDING ASPIRATIONS. Not only did most Japanese wish to build Japan's own road to Peking, but there were many, including government leaders, past and present, who envisioned Tokyo playing the key role in bringing Washington and Peking together. They based this ambition on Japan's "unique position"—history, proximity, and superior comprehension—in dealing with the Chinese. They considered the Taiwan issue an insurmountable roadblock for the Americans but were confident that they could find a way around it for the United States as well as for themselves. If the bridge could be built, it would emancipate Japan from the dread of becoming embroiled in any hostilities that might develop between its valued ally and its massive neighbor. Among those who were pressing for Japan to play the role of mediator was Dietman Tokuma Utsonomiya, who helped organized a conclave of American and Japanese parliamentarians at Santa Barbara in January 1969 and who strove vigorously to follow it up with a conference expanded to include Peking representatives. His efforts were overtaken by the President's breakthrough signaling that the good offices of Japan were unneeded.

g. ANXIETIES ABOUT SINO-AMERICAN AFFINITY. While welcoming Sino-American rapprochement, the Japanese would, of course, not wish it to be at Japan's expense. Traditionally, Americans had had warm affection for the Chinese people, and, according to *Asahi*, the Pacific War was in essence a "clash of China policies." Such considerations caused some Japanese anxiety that a Washington-Peking reconciliation might result in a shift in American-Asian policy away from the postwar emphasis on partnership with Japan in order to focus on China. To allay Japanese uneasiness, repeated assurances were given, both publicly and privately, that no American relationship was more important than that with Japan. Nonetheless, the Japanese could be expected to be continually on guard to assure that in any Sino-American settlement, or in any deliberations regarding the future shape of political relations in Asia, Japan's legitimate interests would be taken into account. This underscored the importance of close consultations, specifically with regard to China policy.

h. ASIA FOR THE ASIANS. The special United States-Japan postwar relationship notwithstanding, Japan was also tugged by regional imperatives. A common bond among the nations of the Orient was their past resistance to Western domination. That Asian hands should shape Asia's destiny was, therefore, a call with undeniable appeal. It was being clarioned frequently by Philippine Foreign Minister Carlos Romulo. The concept, as President Nixon himself emphasized, was fully compatible with the Nixon Doctrine. But its full potential as a cohesive force in drawing China and Japan closer together had not yet been tested.

What was known in Japan as the "China mood" had by mid-1971 become a fever. Those registering the highest temperatures were, of course, the opposition political parties, the newspapers, and the intellectuals. To their ranks were added some leaders of the business community and a significant faction in Prime Minister Sato's Liberal Democratic Party. Public psychology was such that making the pilgrimage to Peking and being received there were regarded as marks of distinction, progressivism, independence, and patriotism. The Japanese populace was in full support, but was not stampeded. In a Yomiuri poll, 54% favored Peking's admission to the United Nations and only 8% opposed. However, only 20% opted for diplomatic relations with Peking, a husky 52% considering that economic ties would be adequate.

Among the newspapers crusading for normalized relations with the People's Republic of China, *Asahi*, with its 6,000,000 circulation throughout Japan, was in the forefront. A constant concern at the Embassy was that in order to ingratiate themselves with Peking, some Japanese felt it necessary to prove their credentials by lambasting the United States. This was the focal point of an unforgettable three-hour luncheon tête-à-tête with *Asahi*'s distinguished publisher Tomoo Hirooka. Hirooka-san was an ardent advocate for the normalization of Japan's relations with the People's Republic of China, but in our conversation he left no doubt of the sincerity of his conviction, which was not always reflected in the reports and editorials of the *Asahi* staff, that it should not be at the expense of Japan's mutually valuable relations with the United States.

Parenthetically, it should be noted that if a Japanese newspaper wished to maintain representation in Peking it had to toe the Peking line. *Mainichi* newspaper and the Kyodo News Agency declined to pay this price and their news bureaus were ousted. The China mood being as feverish as it was, other Japanese news services in Peking tailored their dispatches to avoid ouster, and even Kyodo and *Mainichi* by evidencing appropriate penitence were eventually restored to grace. Thereafter, all Japanese press coverage out of Peking dutifully avoided anything which might irritate the Chinese authorities.

In the political arena, the real crunch was within Prime Minister Sato's own Liberal Democratic Party. There was a group willing, if not eager, to defy the party's policy of caution in pushing for ties with Peking. During the Diet session in early 1971, as many as fifty-four LDP members were at one point ready to desert and vote for the opposition's unrestrainedly pro-Peking resolution. If sixty members had swung over, the LDP policy would have suffered defeat. Strong pressure was brought to bear, including suggestions that the party's formidable campaign financing resources might be suspended. Eventually, the number of rebels was reduced to thirty. The opposition's pro-Peking resolution was forestalled, but it was a harrowing experience for the LDP leadership. It tended to confirm that erosion was taking place in Sato's mastery of his party and in the party's cohesiveness. Predictions were being heard that the China issue could cause the breakup of the LDP and that, in any case, it would be a decisive factor in the Sato succession struggle. For us at the Embassy, it did not matter who succeeded Sato, but the important thing was to avoid the China issue's being exploited to damage the Japan-United States partnership.

On the other end of the LDP spectrum on China policy was a group of Diet members who, while agreeing on moves for improving relations with Peking, opposed Japan's abandonment of the Republic of China. It was their contention that Japan was indebted to Generalissimo Chiang Kai-shek, who in the postwar period had been a staunch and non-vindictive friend. He had, for example, not demanded reparations (which he could well have used), and he had opposed the dethronement of the Emperor (which in his view could have led to political chaos in Japan). For many Japanese there was in addition a sentimental attachment to Taiwan which had for fifty years been under Japanese rule. Beyond that there were, of course, Japan-Taiwan economic ties and even some consideration of Taiwan's importance from the security standpoint, particularly after the nearby Ryukyu Islands would revert to Japanese administration.

The crux of the China issue for the LDP was, therefore, not whether to normalize relations with Peking but what to do about Taipei. Those who wished to maintain connections with Chiang, at least until he passed from the scene, were being challenged by those wanting to dump the Generalissimo and establish diplomatic relations with Peking at almost any price.

With all the fervor to get to Peking, few Japanese calculated with normal Japanese precision what the net gains would be in practical terms; for example, only a modest increment in trade would result from ties with mainland China. For the Peking-or-bust crusaders, it appeared to be a case of previously forbidden fruit being tastier.

Despite Japan's China fever, Prime Minister Sato remained remarkably coolheaded. He and his government were being unceasingly importuned not to "miss the bus" to Peking, but as Foreign Minister Aichi told Secretary Rogers in July 1969 it was first necessary to know the destination. While other nations, one by one, were submitting to Peking's inflexible proviso (the severance of relations with the Republic of China), Japan was demonstrating greater self-respect.

Fundamentally, Japan and the United States had identical objectives: a) to bring mainland China, with its quarter of the world's population, into a constructive relationship with the international community; and b) not to turn our backs on our loyal friends in Taiwan. Neither country needed to hop on a bandwagon; nor was either so attached to the other as to preclude its own initiatives. In sharp contrast to the Dulles days, the partnership was one of equals. Yet it was a fruitful partnership featuring close consultations at every opportunity.

In our initial "tour d'horizon" on July 14, 1969, Prime Minister Sato stressed to me that Japan and the United States must stay in close touch regarding both the People's Republic of China and the Soviet Union, keeping "doors open," as well as "our eyes." Two weeks later Foreign Minister Aichi told Secretary Rogers that our policies with respect to China must inevitably change, but not before Peking became more realistic. In drafting the Okinawa communiqué, we carefully tried, at the particular insistence of Prime Minister Sato, to avoid language which might be provocative to Peking (a not entirely successful attempt). Aichi noted this to Senator Charles Percy in a September 1969 conversation.

Peking did not make it easy for Japan. Its propaganda was exceedingly hostile, concentrating on Prime Minister Sato. In excoriating the November 1969 Sato-Nixon communiqué, exploiting Japan's China fever, and agitating Japanese-American economic tensions, Peking seemed bent on exacerbating Sato's domestic political troubles and driving a wedge in the United States-Japan relationship. The effect, however, was to strengthen our resolve, at least in Tokyo, to consult closely and to avoid divergences.

Much of our bilateral dialogue centered on the perennial issue of Chinese representation in the United Nations. In July of 1970, Aichi and Rogers agreed that our policies would remain unaltered unless the United Nations outlook should change, which was not expected that year. However, a speech at the United Nations on November 15 by the United States Ambassador Christopher Phillips and subsequent comment by Ron Ziegler to White House newsmen caused concern in Tokyo that the United States had shifted to a position more favorable than previously to the entry of the People's Republic of China. With approval from Washington, we assured the Japanese that American policy remained unchanged, that it opposed admission if it were to be at the expense of Taiwan. We also pledged further consultations after the General Assembly. China again failed to gain entry, but just by a whisker.

In my 1970 year-end review of our relations with Japan, emphasis was placed on the rising tide of nationalist sentiment in Japan, and it was noted that unless issues like China were properly handled our partnership could be damaged. In the prognosis for 1971, a coordinated approach with regard to the China issue was strongly recommended, including providing information in advance of any maneuvers we might contemplate. The State Department was in concurrence. A series of unpublicized working-level consultations took place, followed by Deputy Assistant Secretary Winthrop Brown's Tokyo visit in mid-March specifically to confer about China. Meanwhile, during brief Tokyo stops, Senators Hugh Scott and Jacob Javits responded to inevitable questions about China along standard American government lines. Prime Minister Sato, in my talk with him on June 2, 1971, reiterated that close Japan-United States consultations on the subject of China were "of utmost importance" and he was assured that such were America's intentions. Japanese concerns had been heightened by the political overtones of a visit to China by an American ping-pong team.

Ten days before the President's July 15, 1971, announcement, Defense Secretary Melvin Laird was closely interrogated in Tokyo by Japan's Defense Director General Yasuhiro Nakasone about possible changes in America's China policy. Laird assured Nakasone that the United States was proceeding cautiously and that there was no basic change. Laird cited China's development of ballistic missile and nuclear capabilities as causing concern.

Denying that any policy change is taking place is probably the most unalterable of all policies in the field of foreign affairs. The automatic answer to a newsman concerning almost any development is that it represents no change from established wisdom. From the occasion in 1954 when John Foster Dulles spurned a handshake with Chou En-lai in Geneva, until the day when the Chinese Premier and President Nixon greeted each other with smiles at Peking airport, it is doubtful that at any single moment did any official respond affirmatively to questions suggesting that a shift in "basic policy" was occurring.

In retrospect, an article published in the May 9, 1971, issue of *Asahi Shimbun* makes interesting reading. It was titled, "The Bus to Peking," and it was part of a series exhaustively studying what one of the *Asahi* reporters described as "the pervasive American postwar influence in Japan." (The series was subsequently published in book form as *The Pacific Rivals*.) Leading off with a reference to "Asakai's nightmare," the article reported that Japan's current Ambassador in Washington was not having sleepless nights, quoting him as saying that America "has neither the power nor the inclination to recognize China right now." A highly placed State Department official was reported to have said, "Japan is far ahead of the United States in relations with China. Our policy is to follow a half step behind the situation." Former Ambassador Edwin Reischauer was confident that "the United States and Japan had far too much invested in one another for Washington to adjust its relations with China without any consideration for the position of Japan." Under Secretary of State U. Alexis Johnson suggested, "Americans and others should not be overly optimistic about the improvement of the American-Chinese atmosphere." The concluding quotation was from a "member of the White House staff," who laughed and stated, "You don't have to worry about missing the American bus. Even if you're waiting for it, it won't come by for a long time yet." A parenthetical insertion in *Pacific Rivals* notes that the President's announcement just over two months later and the subsequent admission of Peking to the United

Nations "dramatically altered the complexion of Chinese-Japanese-American relations."

After his defeat in the California gubernatorial race in 1962, Richard Nixon's political fortunes had reached their nadir. During a Tokyo visit by the top management of *The Los Angeles Times*, Mrs. Norman Chandler, benefactress for the *Times* and for Los Angeles, recalled vividly the former Whittier College performer avowing, after the 1962 defeat, that once having been on the stage, the urge to attain the center-stage spotlight continues and is irresistible. Such determination won out in 1968.

For the Japanese audience, center stage in the July 15, 1971, "shokku" was occupied by Richard Nixon, brilliantly supported by Dr. Kissinger. But the spotlight was not exclusively theirs; it had to be shared with China's clever leadership. According to Foreign Minister Aichi, "China shock" would have been a more apt appellation than "Nixon shock." In dealing with Peking, Japan and the United States had identical objectives. Neither sought to mislead the other. On the contrary, they were in close consultation. It was no secret that each had been making its own overtures to the Peking regime. Where the trouble lay was that Peking was responding differently to each country, apparently to stimulate frictions between them. Brisk commerce was allowed with Japan, but American business interests, handicapped by earlier American embargoes, were frozen out. Peking was not unresponsive to American political gestures, but it brusquely rejected government-level talks with the Japanese. With skill, the Chinese leaders were working the economic side of the street with the Japanese and the political side of the street with the Americans.

By mid-1971, Japan had become China's leading trading partner, with an annual bilateral volume near $900 million. Representing only 3% of Japan's total foreign trade, it was less than one-tenth of Japan's trade volume with the United States, a perspective usually beclouded in Japan by political and psychological factors. America's trade with China was, of course, a mere trickle, perhaps $2 or $3 million via Hong Kong. At the Canton Trade Fair in October 1971, 2,300 Japanese representatives participated, but no American businessmen were allowed entry.

Theoretically, Sino-Japanese trade relationships had developed on a basis of "separation of economic from political affairs." It was a useful smoke screen for China's engaging in such trade as it deemed beneficial, such as importing steel, fertilizers, agricultural chemicals, and machinery in return for coal, iron ore, corn, soybeans, salt, and tin. At the same time, the theory did not preclude exerting pressures for political purposes. During Kishi's premiership, for example, a dispute about flying the Chinese flag prompted Peking to cut back the modest trade volume by two-thirds. It dropped to .5% of Japan's total trade in each of three years.

During the premiership of Ikeda in 1963, Peking had agreed to semi-official trade arrangements, which five years later were covered by an annual Memorandum Trade Agreement. Each spring a Japanese delegation would trek to Peking to negotiate. By 1971, this had become a ritual in which the Chinese authorities would make the Japanese sweat for a week or so on the political section of the communiqué before expeditiously agreeing to the economic content. Even though the Japanese delegation included members of Sato's LDP, the political declarations which they were forced to sign included denunciations of their own government and, in particular, of Prime Minister Sato. The Japanese negotiators passed this off as justifiable duty, and publicly Sato bore these annual humiliations serenely. Privately they invoked his disgust, but not a loss of his sense of humor.

The fact was that trade covered by the Memorandum represented only about 10% of the total volume between the two countries. The remaining 90% was conducted by what were determined by Peking to be "friendly firms." Such companies had either a clear record of no commercial dealings with Taiwan, or they had been able to arrange "dummy companies" with clear records, or they dealt in advanced electronics equipment or other products which were of such acute interest to the People's Republic that sinful transactions with Taiwan could be overlooked.

As the China fever became more elevated and Japanese commercial appetites more whetted, Peking became more demanding. It imposed "Four Principles" on all Japanese seeking to do business in China. The first two principles forbade business ventures in Taiwan and Korea. The third was aimed at Japanese firms which were in any way connected with "imperialist" American activities in Vietnam. The fourth principle was perhaps the most insidious. It prohibited Japanese firms from doing business in China if they were involved in any sort of joint venture with an American company. Given our intensive efforts to open Japan's doors wider for American investment, this Peking ploy inevitably discouraged Japanese-American commercial ventures, some of which had already been planned. The first two principles, of course, deterred the Japanese from proceeding with investments which were greatly needed in Korea and Taiwan.

The enunciation of the "Four Principles" created quite a stir. A few companies, such as Nippon Steel, resisted the blatant injection of politics into commerce, and we were so informed by their top representatives, who were obviously concerned that their submission to the Chinese conditions might affect their enormous American market. One sensed that Japanese ingenuity was at work as usual and that inter-company arrangements would be worked out compensating one another for losses set in train by the "Four Principles." As time passed, however, and it became clear that major American retaliation would not be forthcoming, most Japanese companies took the Peking-required pledge.

With such mastery of economic relationships, there was no reason for the Chinese Communists to manifest civility to Premier Sato who, in any case, was already on the political defensive because of Japan's China fever. The Sato government sought contact with Peking's diplomatic representatives in various third-country capitals, but met only rebuffs. From Peking itself came the response. As preconditions for inter-governmental talks, Japan must jump through three hoops: a) recognize that Taiwan is part of China; b) recognize the People's Republic of China as the sole legitimate government of China; and c) abrogate the Japan-Republic of China peace treaty which Prime Minister Yoshida had concluded. Earnestly wishing to normalize relations with Peking, and despite treaty-based noncommittal positions taken in earlier years, the Sato government had no trouble with the first condition, for Sato himself had stated as standard Japanese policy that "China is one." (He contended that over the centuries, regardless of the configurations of Chinese suzerainty, the Chinese people considered themselves one people. To this proposition, he pointed out, even Chiang Kai-shek would agree.) The second condition was also not too difficult, although the adjective "sole" was a stumbling block. With regard to the third condition, the Sato government, anxious to demonstrate faithfulness to its commitments, considered as unacceptable the abrogation of Japan's treaty with Taiwan as a pre-condition for talks with Peking. In order to keep the door open, however, Japanese authorities made clear that once inter-governmental discussions commenced, the status of Taiwan could be included on the agenda.

Turning a deaf ear to Sato's emissaries, Peking was enjoying the fact that its maneuvers were increasing the Sato government's domestic difficulties. With an increasing number of ambitious Japanese politicians beating a path to his door, Premier Chou En-lai became selective, letting it be known that the welcome mat would be out for specific individuals. Among these were several potential successors to Sato. According to press reports, one of them declined the invitation, facetiously observing that apparently Peking wished to select Japan's next Prime Minister. To outsiders, Peking's aim appeared to be to secure a pliable government after Sato's departure, which Peking well knew would take place in 1972. Tokyo's Socialist Governor Minobe, who in early 1972 failed in and was criticized for his attempt to play a sort of Kissinger role in China, received the impression that Prime Minister Chou En-lai, who attached great importance to "summitry," looked forward to dealing directly with Sato's successor whoever he might be.

Peking asked President Nixon to jump through no such hoops as Prime Minister Sato. The disavowal of America's defense commitment to Taiwan, for example, was not exacted, even though in significance it must have been an issue at least as critical for the Chinese leaders as the tribute that was being required from Japan. Clearly, criteria for political contacts with the Americans differed from those for Japan.

Governor Minobe, whose landslide electoral victories in Tokyo were more attributable to his distinguished personality than to his affiliation with the Japan Socialist Party, asked Chou En-lai during one Peking visit why there was such discrepancy in Peking's treatment of Japan compared with that accorded the United States. Premier Chou explained that no conditions were attached to inter-governmental contacts with the United States because the way had been paved by the Geneva and Warsaw talks. Undoubt-edly, there were additional and more deep-rooted consid-erations.

The Ambassadorial-level discussions, more than one hundred of which were held between Chinese Communist and American representatives in Geneva and Warsaw in the 1950's and 1960's, were sporadic and inconclusive. Nev-ertheless, they provided a channel for the verification of the views of each country and gave indication of a desire to lessen Cold War tensions. It was President Kennedy who quoted a Chinese proverb that he who would make a thou-sand-mile journey must take the first step. With the end of the bipolar world, the loosening of Sino-Soviet ties, and the resolution of serious Chinese internal problems, as well as the new American emphasis on negotiation rather than confrontation, hope glimmered for altering the adversary Sino-American relationship.

Coming to grips with the reality that if a new structure of peace were to be achieved continental China must parti-cipate, the Nixon administration moved throughout 1969 and 1970 on three fronts to develop a dialogue with the People's Republic of China. Publicly, signals were transmit-ted conveying America's preparedness for a constructive relationship with Peking. Such signals were expressly in-cluded in the President's annual foreign policy reports and in a speech delivered by Secretary Rogers in Australia in August 1969. The words were backed up by deeds. Without much fanfare, a series of about six specific steps were unilaterally taken relaxing American trade and travel re-strictions vis-à-vis China. They were gestures of our earn-estness. Finally, approaches were made to Peking through private channels and with the aid of well-wishing third-country intermediaries. By the end of 1970, highly secret communication between the White House and Peking was becoming a reality.

On March 15, 1971, the United States announced that

American passports no longer needed special validation for China. Less than a month later, during an international tournament at Nagoya, Japan, representatives of the Chinese table tennis team startled the American participants with an informal invitation to visit mainland China. G. B. Steenhoven, manager of the American team, promptly telephoned the Embassy in Tokyo for advice. Without hesitation, the Embassy's China specialist William Cunningham suggested an affirmative response and Steenhoven was subsequently briefed in Tokyo on what we knew about contemporary China. It is worth noting that in encouraging Steenhoven the Embassy was, of course, unaware of the super-secret channel evolving between the White House and Peking but was fully conscious of the other indications of Washington's desire to improve relations with the People's Republic of China. It may be added that the Embassy's uninstructed handling of the table tennis exercise was endorsed by the State Department, and Cunningham was accorded full marks for the role which he had played.

As might be expected, "ping-pong diplomacy" had a tremendous impact on public opinion in Japan. The fact that America's paddle wielders were not in the same league professionally as China's table tennis virtuosos was immaterial. Infinitely more important were the political overtones. Chou En-lai told the Americans their visit had "opened a new page in the relations of the Chinese and American people," and the State Department welcomed it as an "encouraging development." Upon his return to the United States, Steenhoven was personally received by the President.

Not knowing the full implications, our tendency at the Embassy was to concur with our Japanese counterparts in assuming that, while it was no doubt a carefully measured response to the carefully measured steps which the President had taken to reduce barriers to trade and travel, the invitation to the American ping-pong team was only one of

a number of signs of a general, albeit gradual, turning outward by the People's Republic after the Cultural Revolution, and in the wake of the Sino-Soviet tensions which
flared up in the spring of 1969. Ambassadors were being
sent out to posts which had long been manned only by
Chargés d'Affaires. Six other Nagoya ping-pong teams, including the Japanese, were invited to China, and the Chinese
team toured Japan. Even the Chinese participation at Nagoya was construed as part of this evolutionary reemer-
gence. Under the circumstances, our China-watchers at the
Embassy shared the belief of Japanese analysts that there
was no reason for the Japanese government to get unduly
excited. It was perhaps to test American reaction to such an
assessment that a senior Foreign Ministry official twice informed me that the Japanese government did not plan to be
"rushed" by ping-pong diplomacy into dramatic initiatives
of its own.

Less than a month after the ping-pong flurry, the Communist Chinese in a circuitous manner approached the
Japanese with a view to strengthening their respective
trade offices in Tokyo and Peking, plus authorizing the use
of cryptography for the messages of those offices. Whether
the Chinese purpose was to throw a few crumbs to the Sato
government in atonement for its persistent hostility and in
anticipation of the July 15 announcement is not known. Not
wishing to miss opportunities, but also staying in tune with
their friends, the Japanese responded decorously to the Chinese probe by inquiring further into its authenticity. All
these developments were reported to Washington, from
which there was no reaction.

As a direct response to the hospitality accorded the
American ping-pongers, President Nixon announced a
series of further steps to facilitate trade and travel with
China. Meanwhile, private channel diplomacy was apparently making substantial progress, specifically with respect
to possible Peking visits by Dr. Kissinger and eventually
the President of the United States.

During the precise period, July 9 to 11, when Dr. Kissinger was secretly in Peking, Defense Secretary Laird was in Tokyo. In a background briefing for the American press corps, Defense spokesman Jerry Friedheim stressed the belief that Japan could shoulder more security responsibilities. In further discussion with *Washington Post* correspondent Selig Harrison, the subject arose of Japan's possibly becoming a nuclear power in the future. Presumably a false impression was conveyed, for the next day *The Washington Post* ran a front-page story saying in effect that the United States was pushing Japan to build up a larger military establishment, not excepting an eventual nuclear capability. The State Department categorically denied the thrust of the *Post* story, and dispatched hot telegrams to Tokyo demanding explanations.

It is doubtful that those drafting the Washington telegrams were fully aware of all the unhappy repercussions which the erroneous *Post* story might have precipitated. Reports that America was pushing Japanese militarism could conceivably have been sufficient to derail the delicate negotiations in which Dr. Kissinger was engaged in Peking. Fortunately, this did not occur, and plans went forward culminating in the July 15 announcement.

The President's July 15 broadcast was brief: Dr. Kissinger had held talks in Peking: knowing of the President's "expressed desire" to visit the People's Republic, Premier Chou En-lai had extended an invitation which the President had accepted; the purpose of the Peking meeting would be to "seek the normalization of relations between the two countries" and "to exchange views on questions of concern to the two sides."

Neither Japanese nor Americans could but marvel at this diplomatic triumph, but it hit Tokyo with typhonic force; and from Americans at the vortex, the immediate reactions were almost as bitter as those of most Japanese. It seemed incredible that on a matter of such critical consequence to our most important ally in Asia, we appeared to be dealing behind the back. We were honeying up to our adversaries and neglecting our friends. Insensitive to the destructive potential of the China fever in Japan, we were undermining those who for a generation had hinged Japanese policy on a deep and abiding trust in the United States. We had reneged on our repeated pledges to engage in intimate consultation and coordinated action. "Asakai's nightmare" had come true—if not literally, at least psychologically. Outcries that America had "jumped over Japan's head" were difficult to refute. It seemed in effect like a diplomatic Pearl Harbor. (One of our European diplomatic colleagues told the Japanese they had no right to complain, for they had taught the Americans this tactic in 1941!)

Given the emotions of the hour, all these reactions were normal. In varying degrees, they would continue to be held by many observers. But after days and weeks of reflection, my own conclusion was that this historic action was so delicate and so precarious that the President and his Assistant for National Security Affairs could not have handled it in an intrinsically different manner if its accomplishment was to be assured. This conclusion was prompted by the following considerations:

a. BASIC ACCORD. The July 15 announcement was fully in accord with the desire of both Japan and the United States for improved relations with Peking. It was a technical application of mutually agreed policy. The Japanese were far ahead of us in their economic intercourse with Communist China, which was also a tactical application of policy; they should understand the value to our common interest of our capitalizing on Peking's responsiveness to make progress in the political field.

b. TIP-OFF. That the United States was not insensitive to the fact that the Presidential announcement would have a major impact on Japan was demonstrated by Secretary

Rogers's advising Ambassador Ushiba in advance. Admittedly, it was short notice and could not forestall the shock, but it was clear indication that Washington appreciated Japan's problems.

c. PROBABILITY OF LEAKAGE. Premature disclosure of the American diplomatic breakthrough to China would undoubtedly have wrecked the aircraft before it got off the ground. So important was this factor that, according to Dr. Kissinger, the only officials besides himself in the United States Government who had been fully aware of the project were the President, Secretary Rogers, and a few communications technicians. With respect to the Japanese government, there had in the immediately preceding months been unfortunate leakages of highly secret information pertaining to Japanese-American affairs. In mid-June in Paris, Secretary Rogers, consistent with an appeal made to me two weeks earlier by Prime Minister Sato, confided our views concerning the Chinese representation question to Foreign Minister Aichi. Two days later, this information, which had been shared with no other non-American, appeared on the front page of Tokyo's *Asahi Shimbun*. Remedial action for such chronic leakages was discussed during the last week in June with Foreign Minister Aichi, his senior assistants, and even Prime Minister Sato. Too many eyes were seeing highly sensitive papers. (A Deputy Vice Foreign Minister a short time later was forced to resign because his secretary was leaking documents to a news reporter.) On this score, American skirts were far from clean. Day after day, columnist Jack Anderson was publishing excerpts from classified American government communications. Thus, had the President sent any messages for us to convey in Tokyo, there would have been an additional risk of leakage.

d. WHY NOT OTHERS? If the United States had undertaken to confer with Japan in advance of the July 15 announcement, the question would have arisen as to what other

countries must be consulted. Certainly, the Republic of
China, which was more directly affected, would have a justifiable claim. So would Korea. Then what about our Australian and New Zealand allies, the Philippines, Thailand,
and our NATO partners? It would have been exceedingly
difficult to draw the line, and with each additional consultation the probability of leakage would mount.

e. PRESSURES AND INFLATED EXPECTATIONS. As the
President pointed out in his 1972 foreign policy report, risking advance public disclosure might have risked disillusion-
ment by inflated expectations. At the same time, pressures
would have been created on both the Chinese and American
sides, forcing both to take public positions which could only
have frozen discussions before they began.

f. SHOCK NO MATTER HOW HANDLED. Whatever
method might have been conceived for disclosing the Nixon-
Kissinger breakthrough, the hard fact was that the change
in the United States-Chinese relationship after twenty years
of animosity could not but produce major repercussions, particularly in Japan. It was in this context that Prime Minister Sato a month later told *The New York Times*'s James
Reston that even had he known of this development weeks in
advance it would have made little substantial difference.

g. LONG RANGE BENEFITS. Despite the initial shocks,
the opening of a new Sino-American dialogue set into motion a whole series of repercussions beneficial to Japan and
other nations. It furthered the spirit of detente and opened
opportunity for a new structure of peace. As the months
wore on after July 15, 1971, this new vista unfolded around
the world, including in Japan. Once again adjustment to
new realities had been a painful experience, but it was
essential if a healthier and more durable international
equilibrium were to be achieved.

In retrospect, it was safe to say that the July 15 announcement had produced an overreaction in Japan. There was, to be sure, an entirely normal emotional reflex. But there were also vested interests who seized on the "Nixon shokku" to voice more shrilly their customary denunciations of the United States, the Japan-United States partnership, and the Sato government. There may also have been a few Japanese officials who found the President's surprise action a convenient scapegoat for other troubles currently besetting Japan. After our own speedy recovery at the Embassy, we did our best to persuade our Japanese friends to manifest a constructive long-range outlook. Defensiveness could serve the interests only of ill-wishers by implying a mutual alienation of Japanese-American affections. To say the least, such implications were premature.

Even though a shock was unavoidable, it would, nonetheless, have been extremely helpful if the American Ambassador to Japan could have been given at least a clue that something sensational was about to happen. We could have conditioned the psychological climate for Japan's top officialdom, if not beforehand, certainly as soon as the news broke. With the matter being so tightly held in Washington, this was probably too much to ask. There were, however, in my judgment, minor variations in the adopted procedures which would have been feasible. Given Japan's supreme interest in this development, Prime Minister Sato could have been informed from 12 to 24 hours in advance, with the President's personal message being delivered at the same time. Secret word to Sato via the Embassy was unlikely to leak during that brief period. As it was, he received notification via Ambassador Ushiba only minutes before the rest of the world heard the news. Other countries which received pre-announcement notification would not have been likely to raise objections, and this special treatment would have highlighted the importance of our relationship with Japan.

Less comprehensible than our performance on July 15 was the American government's subsequent behavior with respect to the Chinese representation issue at the United Nations. Each year the United States position, faithfully supported by Japan, had been eroding. In 1970, we had by a 66 to 52 vote succeeded with the "Important Question" strategem, which had been initiated as a rearguard action by the Kennedy administration. This procedural exercise established as a requirement that Peking's admission must be approved by a two-thirds majority of UN members. However, the perennial "Albanian resolution," which provided for the seating of Peking and the ouster of Nationalist China, had in 1970 for the very first time received an affirmative simple majority, 51 to 49. Seven countries had deserted our ranks since the 1969 voting when the Albanian resolution had been rejected 48 to 56. That we would lose in 1971 seemed virtually certain, even before the death knell was sounded on July 15.

Unfortunately, the issue of China's representation at the United Nations had long since been transformed from a debate on the merits of the case to a roll call on whether a nation was in effect a lackey of the United States or truly independent. This was in large measure the result of the inordinate amount of diplomatic capital which the United States had invested year after year to persuade friendly nations to vote against Peking's entry. One by one, other nations were boarding the Peking bandwagon. Those still supporting our position, the core of which had been reduced to favoring retention of a seat for Taipei, were getting increasingly restive.

Fully conscious of the gravity of this situation, Japanese authorities during the spring of 1971 were extremely anxious to coordinate strategy for the autumn General Assembly. Dating back to the previous November, frequent consultations had taken place and the various options had been exhaustively explored. However, aside from repeating the standard line about opposing Peking's entry at the expense of Taiwan, Washington remained silent over strategy and tactics, and registered annoyance at the Embassy's persistent requests for guidance. In the Japanese view, precious time was being wasted.

Then came July 15. The immediate reaction in Tokyo was that the props had been knocked out from under the Japanese-American position at the United Nations. With a Washington-Peking rapprochement in the offing, our remaining allies were likely to abandon the Taiwan ship in order to assure their own future standing in Peking. Two weeks later, however, Washington proposed that our two countries press for "dual representation." We would agree to the "seating" of Red China provided Taiwan was not expelled, and we would leave the question of which one would occupy China's seat on the Security Council to be determined by the General Assembly. In essence, China would have two seats, the three UN seats occupied by the Soviet Union being somewhat of a precedent. Peking, of course, had consistently stipulated that Taiwan's ouster would be a sine qua non for its acceptance of UN membership. The Japanese went along with the Washington proposal but were reluctant to be co-sponsors. For some time there had been a body of official Japanese opinion contending that Japan's best course would be to stick unalterably to previous strategy, for any change—and, in particular, anything smacking of the "two China" concept—would only succeed in antagonizing to a greater degree both Peking and Taipei as well as their respective advocates on Japan's volatile domestic scene.

In a memorable joint press conference following the Japanese-American joint cabinet meeting in Washington in September, Foreign Minister Fukuda differed publicly with Secretary Rogers on strategy concerning the Chinese representation issue. With Fukuda reserving his position, the Secretary stressed that Japanese co-sponsorship would be indispensable if our mutually agreed "dual representation" formula were to muster the needed support. Privately, the Japanese were perplexed. They were being pressured by Secretary Rogers to undertake a role which would widen the political gulf between Tokyo and Peking while the President and Dr. Kissinger were carrying on a secret liaison with Peking's leaders. No direct indications were obtainable from the White House that the President was as insistent as Secretary Rogers about Japan's co-sponsorship. This led to a suspicion that Japan was being caught in a nutcracker between the State Department and the White House, with the former eager to improve its prestige by proving its capabilities. America's behavior was described by Japan's former Ambassador to the United Nations, Toshikazu Kase, as being "very much like feeding poisoned cakes to member nations and then passing out antidotes." He speculated that the American government, with an eye toward countering criticisms for Nationalist China's ouster, wanted to be able to say that it "did everything it could."

Upon Fukuda's return to Tokyo, Prime Minister Sato made the decision that Japan would co-sponsor the "dual representation" resolution. Aside from wishing to continue close cooperation with the United States, it was for Sato a question of not impairing "the trust of the international community in Japan's faith and sincerity." Furthermore, he shared our view that the substance of the resolution was reasonable. The Republic of China did exist, and it had faithfully participated in the United Nations since its inception. However the Taiwan issue would ultimately be resolved, it was not in the interest of the United Nations to undertake the expulsion of any loyal member of that organization pursuant to the dictates of another member, actual or aspiring; neither was it a healthy precedent for the UN, and particularly its smaller nations, to allow the bullying tactics of a larger power to prevail.

Whatever impressions might have been conveyed by the Japanese newspapers, Sato was not without some support as far as the sympathies of the Japanese people were concerned. Polls showed that while 80% might favor the normalization of relations with the People's Republic of China, a hardy 70% retained favorable disposition toward Taiwan. Nonetheless, in political circles the predictions were that if the Japanese-American strategy would fail, and after July 15 that seemed highly probable, the Sato government would be toppled. In pondering the prospects, Sato's lieutenants arrived at a conclusion that the government's fate would hinge not so much on defeat but on the margin of defeat. Thus, accepting Rogers's thesis that an unequivocal role by Japan was crucial to maintaining the support of wavering nations, the Japanese government not only agreed to co-sponsorship but with the United States launched an impressive diplomatic offensive. Our two foreign offices stayed in close touch, maintaining an up-to-the-minute tabulation of the attitudes of each member of the United Nations. Since more than 130 countries were involved, the daily stack of telegrams from capitals throughout the world was high. Our efforts included enlisting the help of diplomatic colleagues whose countries might be supportive.

With Foreign Minister Fukuda, who had recently recovered from a gall bladder operation, holding the fort in Tokyo, Prime Minister Sato commissioned ex-Foreign Minister Aichi to take command of operations at the General Assembly in New York. His mission received a significant boost when former Foreign Minister Ohira, an outspoken advocate for Peking's admission to the United Nations, authorized a distinguished member of his political faction, Kenji Fukunaga, to join Aichi's team in New York.

In early October, following an initial round of soundings, Aichi returned to Tokyo in a pessimistic mood. We
sought to encourage him by citing American UN Ambassador George Bush's confidence that our cause was
"winnable," and stressed to him, Fukuda and others, the
importance not only of hard work but also of psychology.
If we could win the initial procedural vote to secure "priority" for a proposal that any expulsion from the United
Nations must be considered an "Important Question" requiring a two-thirds vote, the momentum could carry us
through. (The opposing forces had already gained tactical
advantage for their "Albanian resolution" through tabling
it, by most intriguing coincidence, on July 15.) Aichi remained gloomy. He foresaw the loss of the China contest as
a body blow to all the principles for which Japan and the
United States had stood. He was particularly bitter that
America's European allies failed to understand these implications. Privately, the Japanese felt that the announcement
of Dr. Kissinger's second visit to Peking, which would coin-
cide precisely with the General Assembly's voting on China,
dashed our last hopes.

The grand finale took place at the United Nations on
October 25, 1971. With unanticipated suddenness, Peking's
supporters brought the issue to a vote. The representative
of Saudi Arabia, whose king had no fondness for Communists, appealed for a one-day delay, but was voted down
56 to 53. The procedural proposal for giving priority to our
resolution that the expulsion of any member should be
considered an "Important Question" secured a 61 to 53
majority. There was a flicker of hope. However, when the
"Important Question" resolution itself was put to a vote,
eight nations which had previously indicated to the Japanese
or us that they would lend support unaccountably shifted
to "abstention." The resolution went down to defeat, 55
yeas and 59 nays, with 15 abstentions. After that, wavering friends hastened to clamber aboard the Peking
bandwagon. "The Albanian resolution," which had been

repeatedly forestalled in previous years, scored a victory, even greater than the unrequired two-thirds, 76 in favor, 35 against, and 17 abstentions. Before the final vote, but with the handwriting on the wall, the delegation of the Republic of China had with dignity departed the UN corridors. Within days, the representatives of the People's Republic of China were welcomed.

The outcome for those on the losing side was, of course, a tremendous disappointment. But there were silver linings. At long last, the annual ordeal of China-representation arm-twisting was past history. On the domestic political front in Japan, the dire predictions that Sato's government would be toppled failed to materialize. The Diet turned back a no-confidence motion by a 274 to 169 vote. In short, the battle had been lost and there would be scars, including the one resulting from America's undue influence on Japan's China policy, but not lost was the campaign for a better world in which even our opponents had a stake.

It was not only in Tokyo and at the United Nations where the President's diplomatic breakthrough with China had impact. There were few capitals in the world where continuing repercussions would not be felt, but key centers included Moscow, Saigon, Hanoi, Taipei, Seoul, Pyongyang, Canberra, New Delhi, Islamabad, Cairo, Berlin, London, Paris, and, coming full circle, Peking itself. There would, of course, also be reverberations on the domestic political scene in the United States, not the least being a powerful boost for the President's reelection chances the following year.

To me, the China breakthrough resembled the opening shot in a game of pool, the billiard balls flying off in various directions, caroming off the sides of the table and off each other, and dropping into pockets previously unimaginable.

No ball seemed to bounce around the billiard table more briskly than the one with the hammer-and-sickle insignia.

This despite the fact that the President's July 15 revelation rated only straight news coverage on page 5 in Moscow's *Pravda*. Ten days elapsed before *Pravda* devised a commentary: "The true intent of the United States and China is hidden and not known, but it smacks of an anti-Soviet alliance." *Izvestia* referred to a "strange alliance." The United States, of course, had consistently declared its aloofness from the Sino-Soviet rift.

Propaganda notwithstanding, the Soviet Union in ensuing months engaged in an extraordinary amount of diplomatic activity. On August 9 a Soviet treaty of peace and friendship, with defense overtones, was signed with India, which for years had preened itself in its pristine nonalignment. In September the four-power Berlin agreement was signed. Progress was being made in the Strategic Arms Limitation Talks at Vienna and later at Helsinki. On October 12 an announcement was made that President Nixon would be visiting Moscow, a visit which produced an impressive array of bilateral agreements the following May. It would be an exaggeration to describe such developments as direct reactions to July 15; at the same time, there could be little doubt that their evolvement was in accord with the Soviets' view of the emerging international system, particularly after the July 15 perturbation.

In Tokyo, business picked up precipitously at the Soviet Embassy. By August 20, the press was reporting that suggestions were being made by the Soviets to the Japanese for bilateral discussions on matters of mutual interest. Shigeo Nagano, the super-capitalist head of the Nippon Steel Corporation and President of the Japan Chamber of Commerce, had reportedly been invited to visit Moscow, as had Zentaro Kosaka, former Foreign Minister and Chairman of the LDP's Political Affairs Council. By mid-October, Semyon Tsarapkin, a deputy in the Soviet Foreign Ministry, had already had quiet talks at the Japanese Foreign Ministry, Alexander Shelepin was in town, and the

Japanese Minister of Agriculture, Munenori Akagi, was on an official visit to Moscow. There had been low-level suggestions of a Sato visit to the Soviet capital, but the Prime Minister had long made clear that such a visit could only take place if there were signs of progress on the "Northern Territories" issue. In reporting these developments, the American Embassy described them as Soviet "flirtation" with Japan.

Moscow's man in Tokyo was Ambassador Oleg Troyanovsky. In the 1950's, he had become a TV celebrity in the United States, having served as interpreter for the ebullient Premier Khrushchev. The son of a diplomat, Troyanovsky had spent his early years in Japan where he picked up some language fluency. When President Roosevelt extended recognition to the Soviet Union, his father was transferred from Tokyo to become the first Soviet Ambassador to Washington. Troyanovsky had studied at Sidwell Friends School in Washington, and shared alumni status in Tokyo with the sister-in-law of the Emperor, Princess Chichibu. Japanese political observers were never quite sure where Troyanovsky stood in the Communist Party hierarchy, but there was common consensus that with his attractive personality, and that of his wife Tania, the U.S.S.R. was well represented. My wife and I will not forget the farewell buffet dinner in late March 1972 when the Troyanovskys joined lustily with a hundred other good friends in Sing-Along-With-Mitch renditions. The decibels far surpassed the tonal quality, particularly when the Mitch Miller record got to the State Department's fight song, "I Wonder Who's Kissing Her Now."

Despite the impetus of July 15, Soviet-Japanese rapprochement was a slow process. Ambassador Troyanovsky had to cope with a legacy of distrust dating back many years, including what some Japanese still considered a Soviet stab in the back at the conclusion of World War II. Then, too, thousands of Japanese families mourned relatives who had become prisoners of war in Soviet hands and never returned. There were also recent problems caused by Soviet capture and harsh treatment of fishermen in the waters north of Japan. The major stumbling block, of course, was Japanese insistence on the return of four small islands just off the coast of the northern Japanese island of Hokkaido. In Japan's view, they were an integral part of Japanese territory, not relinquished with the other islands of the Kurile chain at the termination of World War II. Except for one brief period in the 1950's when the Soviets during a period of "smiling diplomacy" appeared to be using two of the islands as bait for wrecking the United States-Japan security relationship, the Soviet position was categoric that all postwar territorial matters were settled (no doubt this position was taken with one eye on Sino-Soviet border disputes) and the return to Japan of Habomai, Shikotan, Kunashiri, and Etorofu was not a matter for discussion.

Even in trying to get together in the more attractive economic area, words tended to outpace actions. The volume of trade was not impressive. In 1970, Japan's bilateral total with the Soviets was $650 million, compared with $800 million with Communist China, $825 million with Taiwan, over $1 billion with Korea, and $10.6 billion with the United States. As part of the "flirtation" in 1972, a Japanese trade mission was scheduled to go to Moscow, but most ado centered on Siberia. There, vast resources were waiting to be developed, but the Soviets lacked capital and technology. Japan had both, and the prospects for joint development were, as they had been for years, exciting. Interest was urgently renewed in late 1971. Siberian development ranked high on any Soviet-Japanese agenda.

The most gigantic project envisaged collecting oil (and gas) resources, estimated by one Soviet diplomat as being in trillions of barrels, and piping them from as far away as Tyumen on the eastern slopes of the Ural Mountains to a port on the Japan Sea. Politically, moving oil eastward across Siberia risked the hostility of the Chinese Communists, who no doubt would understand arrangements for Japanese offtakes, but who would be more concerned that such a project was designed to provide fuel for the Soviet's million-man army on the north China frontier. For their part, the Japanese had to worry whether their allotted offtakes would be sufficient to make Japan's participation economic but not so large that excessive dependence vulnerable to Soviet political manipulation would be created. It was not surprising that for political reasons, as well as for additional capital technology, the Japanese wanted American participation.

One of America's most reputable international contractors became actively interested in the trans-Siberian project. The way it was shaping up, the Soviets would construct a pipeline to a junction at Tomsk, less than half the 3,500 miles or so to the Vladivostok area. The Japanese would provide the pipe from that point onward, with the Soviets doing the construction. The Americans would provide the know-how. Without referral to Washington, we at the Embassy expressed the strong belief that, if the American contractor was anticipating American government support, his participation would have to include the supply of American steel and other manufactured products. There might be some hope, according to the contractor, for America's supplying the terminal facilities and the compressors for at least part of the line. Obviously, a project of such Herculean proportions and ramifications would be under deliberation many months, probably many years.

From the Tokyo vantage point, the improvement of Soviet-American relations seemed to be proceeding without impairment. Upon returning from a Moscow visit in late 1971, Ambassador Troyanovsky affirmed that his superiors were looking forward to President Nixon's visit. Soviet-American problems, he noted, were primarily of a nature other than bilateral, such as in Vietnam (where Hanoi was independent-minded), China (where, as with Japan, the Soviets did not wish American moves to be made at their expense), the Middle East (where the Soviets' control of the Arabs was as tenuous as American control of the Israelis), and the subcontinent (where alleged Pakistani brutality was inflaming the Indians). As far as China was concerned, there apparently was some Soviet thought that the President risked coming back from Peking empty-handed because of the Taiwan issue. There were also opinions that Mao was fully in charge in the People's Republic, and even Chou En-lai was not invulnerable.

By mid-December 1971, it had become clear, although the Soviet Embassy was as usual noncommunicative, that Foreign Minister Andrei Gromyko would be visiting Japan. In the mid-60's, parallel with the Sino-Soviet estrangement, the Soviets and the Japanese had agreed to hold annual Foreign Minister consultations. The first meeting had been held in 1967 when Foreign Minister Takeo Miki had journeyed to Moscow. That was also the last such regular conference, primarily because of the unpleasant Japanese habit of raising the "Northern Territories" demand. Now, in late 1971, both countries wanted to resume the talks. Dates proposed by Moscow were inconvenient to Tokyo. Thus, even though it meant missing a Warsaw Pact conference, Foreign Minister Gromyko turned up in Tokyo in late January 1972 to confer with Foreign Minister Fukuda.

The communiqué issued at the conclusion of Gromyko's sojourn reflected, as one Foreign Ministry official phrased it, more form than substance. Like most such communiqués, it extolled the virtues of nearly everything except motherhood: exchanges of persons, culture, science and technology, trade and economic cooperation, discussions of international problems, mutual equality, non-interference, et cetera. The knotty "Northern Territories" issue was cleverly finessed, with the Japanese taking comfort from the fact that the Soviets did not, as was customary, gruffly declare publicly that the subject was not discussable. The communiqué envisaged meetings within the year to negotiate at long last a Soviet-Japanese Peace Treaty (the best that had previously been accomplished was a "peace declaration" and the establishment of Embassies in 1955). Privately, few Japanese expected much progress. Realistically, they had no basis for hope that there would be any Soviet flexibility on the northern islands issue, which would be a sine qua non for Japan. Two years later the peace treaty negotiations were still wishful thinking. Obviously, the communiqué had been an exercise in atmospherics, with the Peking audience very much in mind.

Fuzzy though the communiqué was, the fact remained that, despite well-known frigidities, Japan and the Soviet Union were speaking to each other. Neither Ambassador Troyanovsky nor our friends in the Japanese government minded my twitting them that the communiqué was lacking a paragraph that should have read, "Both parties wish to express their appreciation to the President of the United States for having made this resumption of Ministerial discussions possible."

During an official visit to Afghanistan fifteen years earlier, Chinese Premier Chou En-lai had impressed Afghan leaders with his comments about the United States. Noting that educated Chinese like himself had not forgotten American educational and medical missionary work in China, and that the Chinese people were in America's debt for decisive support against the Japanese invaders, Premier Chou had said he was puzzled why the Americans, by spurning China's desires for friendship, were allowing their great reservoir of goodwill in China to be replaced by the inbred hostility of a whole new generation. Persuaded of Chou's sincerity, the Afghans had conveyed his observations to us at Embassy Kabul for relay to Washington.

Unfortunately, the same sentiment had not been shown

in the uncompromising, often acrimonious, positions adopted by the Chinese Communists at the Warsaw talks and elsewhere. The then Assistant Secretary of State for Far Eastern Affairs, Governor Averill Harriman, has commented that the Kennedy administration submitted proposals to the Chinese, not too dissimilar from those which were eventually incorporated in the 1972 Shanghai Sino-American communiqué, but had received in response only an insulting rejection.

The impression of Tokyo observers was that by 1969 the time was ripe; Peking's leadership was responsive to the Nixon-Kissinger secret approaches because of "family problems" at home, and for pragmatic foreign policy considerations, such as Sino-Soviet rivalry. With the Cultural Revolution under control, the internal political situation was stabilizing. Meanwhile, the Great Leap Forward had been a flop. According to Japanese observers, there was a growing Chinese awareness that the buildup of China's economy was imperative and, to achieve it, increased contacts with the outside world would be indispensable.

In the international sphere, the Chinese Communists in the 1950's and 1960's had unremittingly castigated "American imperialism" as China's Public Enemy No. 1. By the 1970's, however, priorities had shifted. Gough Whitlam, then the leader of the opposition in Australia, came away from Peking in early July 1971, convinced that in the "devil competition" the United States was now running a poor third, having been replaced in first position by "Japanese militarism," followed in second place by "Soviet revisionism." With grim recollections of the "Co-Prosperity Sphere," the Chinese feared that Japan's economic expansion would inevitably bring about military expansion. When *New York Times* correspondent James Reston visited Peking in mid-August, no acupuncture needles could divert him from concluding that Japan's resurgence had become a "nightmare" in Peking, "an anxiety amounting almost to an aberration." So aberrant was Peking's outlook that facts were being supplanted by imagination. Chou had even told Reston that the Japanese would take over America's nuclear bases in Japan (there were none).

Some China-watchers, including French diplomatic associates, were confident that China's leaders were well aware that Japan posed no credible military threat to them for the foreseeable future. According to these observers, the immediate purpose of Peking's lambasting "Japanese militarism" was to alarm Japan's neighbors and thereby thwart the powerful influence which Japan was gaining from its economic inroads, including the development of a sort of "Marshall Plan" for assisting East and Southeast Asian nations. In any case, there could be no doubt that it was because of its concerns vis-à-vis both Japan and the Soviet Union that Peking considered the opening of a Sino-American dialogue as useful. It took this course even though minor shocks might occur on the internal political scene, as well as "jumping over the head" problems with its allies, notably Hanoi.

If the time was ripe in Peking for Sino-American rapprochement, no less was true in Washington. Gone were the days when the "China lobby" had monopolized American Far Eastern policy and had as its allies such anti-Communist warriors as John Foster Dulles, his redoubtable Far Eastern Assistant Secretary Walter Robertson, Senator Joseph McCarthy, and California Congressman Richard Nixon. Vietnam had put a damper on confrontation diplomacy. As Senator Fulbright had observed about Okinawa, the long overdue change in America's China policy was made easier because of the anti-Communist credentials of the incumbent in the White House.

After the billiard ball effect of July 15, one of Tokyo's most astute Asian observers sketched a thesis that, in the light of Pakistan's defeat by India and Moscow's new treaty with New Delhi, Peking could rightly be concerned over the presence of Soviet power in the Indian Ocean area, whence it might without much difficulty flow around into the South China Sea region. It could not be ruled out, according to this observer, that Taiwan might in desperation shake hands with the devil, and the fact that the Generalissimo's son-in-law and heir apparent, Chiang Ching-kuo, was not without previous contacts with the Russians was noted. Under the circumstances, Peking might not be so anxious to see the United States Seventh Fleet leave the Taiwan area, nor the American presence liquidated in Taipei. It could open up the region to the Soviets by default, for the Chinese People's Republic had no adequate navy to fill any vacuums. All this, according to this analysis, brightened the prospects for the success of President Nixon's China visit.

Meanwhile, Peking had also to reckon with the growing coziness between the revisionist Soviets and the primary opponent, the Japanese "militarism." Almost overnight, the Peking propaganda attacks against Japan took on less shrillness. Criticism of Prime Minister Sato continued (it was known he would soon be leaving office), but this did not forestall Japanese initiatives in order to "catch up" with the Americans. Quietly, Japanese and Chinese trade missions were expanded, even to the point of the authorized use of cryptography. Cultural contacts increased, as did visits each way by political leaders. The way was being paved for full "normalization" of relations, with Sato's upcoming exit providing the Chinese with a pretext.

It was not necessary to be privy to the intricacies of the Vietnam negotiations to appreciate that July 15 gave a boost to moves toward peace in Indo-China. Naturally, the principal combatants, Hanoi and Saigon, were somewhat miffed, but it was not news to them that their supporters on both sides were wearying of having significant portions of their resources drained interminably. This was true of the Soviets and the Chinese, as well as the Americans. In February 1972, as one of several post-July 15 initiatives of its own, the Japanese government sent a secret mission to Hanoi. Upon its return, we were informed that it had received two distinct impressions: a) possibly to make clear that it was no stooge of Peking's, Hanoi would insist that it would be the party with whom any Vietnam settlement would have to be negotiated; and b) the mood in Hanoi was that "peace was not too far off." It would be difficult to guess when the protracted negotiations for a cease-fire in Vietnam would have reached their conclusions had it not been for Nixon's July 15 billiard shot.

In a broader context, July 15 signaled the passing of an era when participants in neighborhood quarrels, or even in civil dissidence, could blithely rely on outside superforces to be subject to their beck and call. Some years previously, a President of the United Nations General Assembly, Afghanistan's Abdul Rahmann Pazhwak, had expressed to me his pessimism about the UN's effectiveness so long as the Cold War existed and virtually every international dispute got caught up in it, the Communist bloc rushing to the support of one side and the Americans protecting the other. This situation was now becoming unfrozen as disputants found incentives, if not compulsions, to come to grips more directly with their immediate problems. Almost unbelievably, the North and South Koreans, who were also keeping an eye on Japan, instituted stuttering conversations. On the Indian subcontinent, Pakistani and Indian leaders at Simla agreed to resolve their differences through direct negotiations and without involvement of outside powers. A half-world away, the two Germanies were negotiating rather than confronting. And even in the Middle East, the impression was that Arab leaders were not getting push-button responses from their Communist arms suppliers. All these were healthy developments.

Ironically, the sharpest billiard impact occurred in the internal politics of America's staunchest ally, Australia. Prime Minister William McMahon, holding a slim parliamentary majority, was facing problems. Apparently to show displeasure at Australia's support of American policies, Peking had stopped purchasing Australian wheat. This move was a blow to the splinter agricultural party whose backing was essential to keeping the Conservatives in power. At this juncture in early July 1971, the leader of the opposition, Gough Whitlam, journeyed to Peking where he pledged to the Chinese leadership that when he came to power he would promptly withdraw Australian forces from Vietnam, recognize Red China, and sever relations with Taipei. Prime Minister McMahon's widely publicized comment was that the Chinese had played Whitlam like a trout on the hook. Unfortunately for that solid and loyal friend of the United States, his statement was made a day or so before July 15.

After his Peking conversations, Whitlam visited Japan. At the time, Deputy Assistant Secretary of State Winthrop Brown was in Tokyo to confer again with the Japanese about China, so the two of us called on the tall Australian opposition leader who shared with us his Peking impressions. He was particularly hopeful that a Vietnam peace could be achieved, based on his estimate that Peking was much less distrustful of the United States than it was of Japan and the Soviet Union. When on the following day President Nixon's announcement was made, Whitlam was in clover. At a dinner hosted by the Australian Ambassador, Gordon Freeth, Whitlam told our transiting Ambassador to Australia, Walter Rice, and me that he was very pleased to be President Nixon's "pathfinder." Needless to say, Whitlam won the upcoming election. He proceeded to carry out his pre-July 15 pledges to Peking, but happily realized that it was in Australia's interest to maintain productive ties with the United States.

The July 15 announcement was a bitter blow for the government and people of the Republic of China. They had over the years suffered the slings and arrows of fortune with courage and pride and by dint of ingenuity and hard work achieved economic success. But history had been against them in their ambition to regain the mainland. It had been an illusion, as July 15 painfully pointed out to them. If there was any solace, it was that the United States was able to accomplish what no other nation had the courage or ability to do, namely, to establish contact with the government on the mainland without repudiating its ties with Taipei.

Over the years, the Japanese government had also been a proven friend of Nationalist China. However, as Tokyo's China fever intensified, a schizophrenia developed in Japan's body politic. One high Foreign Ministry official noted that many politicians were gaining cheap mileage by beating the drums for relations with Peking, but slyly avoiding taking a public attitude toward the former Formosa, which still retained the affection of a significant portion of the Japanese people. Meanwhile, skittish businessmen were reducing their trade and curtailing investments in Taiwan. One reason was Peking's pressure, such as the so-called "Four Principles." Another was a fear that if one day Taiwan should come under mainland China's control, Japanese investments there would be confiscated under the pretext of World War II "reparations." Some Japanese suspected Peking was really not averse to assistance for Taiwan's industrial development, for, like Manchuria, it would be that much more of a prize when the takeover did eventuate.

The problem which Japan would inevitably face would be what to do with its peace treaty with Nationalist China. Prime Minister Sato favored "normalization" with the People's Republic, and believed that it should take place soon after a decision by the United Nations favoring Peking's entry. At the same time, he also believed the treaty with the Republic of China must be dealt with "fairly." The Foreign Ministry was moving to a position whereby the formal recognition of the People's Republic of China would be considered as superseding the Republic of China-Japan treaty relationship, thus avoiding a formal abrogation. Peking, of course, was permitting no options. In anticipation of an awkward period ahead, the Japanese in December 1971 installed a new Ambassador in Taipei so as not to be confronted with credentials presentation problems in the years immediately ahead.

During the postwar years, close personal ties had developed between the leaders of Nationalist China and Japan. It was through these channels that Japan appealed to the Generalissimo not to withdraw from the United Nations if approval could be obtained for the "dual representation" formula. The appeal was academic, however, and in walking out before the fatal vote on the "Albanian resolution," Taipei's representatives maintained their self-respect.

The real question was Taiwan's future. Some Japanese in mid-1971 professed seeing a drawing together of the ruling mainlanders and the native Taiwanese, and conceivably this would give impetus to a hitherto unimpressive "Taiwan Independence Movement." More likely, however, was the prospect, mentioned during a December 1971 conversation between New York's Mayor John Lindsay and Prime Minister Sato, that when the present aging leadership passed from the scene in both Taipei and Peking there ought to be a possibility for Taiwan and mainland China to work out a modus vivendi. The official United States position, quite correctly, was that a peaceful settlement of the Taiwan question must be left for resolution to the Chinese people themselves.

Even without the Embassy's persistent coaching, Washington recognized the need for measures to refurbish the tarnished trust between Japan and the United States, a need which doubled after the second bombshell, the President's surprise economic moves of August 15, 1971. Communications from the inner sanctums of the White House, to the State Department as well as to embassies abroad, were not such as to provide much guidance. We had to play by ear, discounting, for example, such rumors as the report that Henry Kissinger had a personal dislike for the Japanese, and that President Nixon was getting even with Prime Minister Sato for the latter's failure to impose voluntary restraints on Japanese textile exports. Fortunately, evidence was soon forthcoming that the administration meant what it said in its subsequent annual foreign policy report: "It would be shortsighted indeed to exchange strong ties with a crucial ally for some mitigation of the hostility of a dedicated opponent."

Aside from the close comradeship developed by our two governments on the Chinese representation issue, even in defeat, Washington opened a new chapter in high-level communication. Advance word would be sent to Tokyo concerning a variety of initiatives being undertaken by the President, so that Prime Minister Sato could be notified and, in some cases, asked his personal reactions. On one occasion, the Prime Minister was 600 miles away in southern Japan. Even though the subject was of minor interest to Japan, the news was delivered in person within a few hours thanks to the prompt cooperation of the United States Air Force in making a T-39 jet available.

Most dramatic of all was President Nixon's flying from Washington to greet Emperor Hirohito during the latter's brief plane refueling stop at Anchorage, Alaska, on September 26, 1971. It had been my impression that His Majesty, grateful for America's postwar friendship, would have liked nothing better than to visit the United States. However, his advisors wanted no sullying of the imperial image, and they judged a visit to Europe would be less apt to come under attack by unscrupulous elements in the opposition political parties. Publicly, the defensible position was taken that His Majesty was returning the visits of Chiefs of State who had come to Japan. The visit to England was rationalized as a return "in advance" of a projected visit by Queen Elizabeth, plus a return by His Majesty to haunts remembered from his youth.

After registering some personal unhappiness to representatives of the Imperial Court that European countries were being given precedence over Japan's staunchest friend, we reported to Washington on July 31 that this would be the first time in history that a Japanese Emperor would be leaving Japanese territory, and that, while Anchorage would only be a fuel stop enroute to Europe, the fact was that the first foreign soil on which the foot of a reigning Japanese monarch would tread would be American. Under the assumption that the President would not be interested in making a 7,000 mile round trip for such a brief encounter, we, nevertheless, urged special official representation up to the Vice Presidential level. On August 9, Prime Minister Sato was informed via his Embassy in Washington that President Nixon himself would be at the bottom of the ramp when on the evening of September 26 the Emperor deplaned at Anchorage. The news was released publicly on August 24, with an overwhelmingly favorable impact in Japan.

With all the spit and polish for which the military are famous (they had even painted most of the buildings), Elmendorf Air Force Base, just outside Anchorage, was beautifully organized when in 37° weather the Emperor's Japan Air Lines plane taxied up to the hangar. At the end of a red carpet, the President and Mrs. Nixon were waiting, along with top American government officials, bands, banners, and several thousand excited Alaskans. Haltingly, 70-year-old Emperor Hirohito descended, followed by the Empress, Foreign Minister Fukuda, the Grand Master of

Ceremonies Shigenobu Shima, and others. The President in his podium remarks noted Anchorage was equidistant between Tokyo and Washington. Both he and the Emperor pledged unbreakable ties of friendship and cooperation. After a half-hour of discussion at the quarters of Elmendorf's Commanding General Robert Ruegg, the two Chiefs of State returned to the airport for bon voyage ceremonies. As the Emperor's plane soared off into the night sky, there was an exceptional display of the aurora borealis. For Alaska, it had been an unforgettable evening. With pages full of pictures, *The Anchorage Daily News* proudly headlined, "History in Hangar Five."

Top level visits were very much a part of the trust rehabilitation program. In mid-September, American cabinet members had met in Washington in joint session with their Japanese counterparts, but at that juncture the Japanese were still recoiling from the August 15 economic "shock." The Japanese Ministerial delegation, led by Foreign Minister Fukuda, was visibly cheered when President Nixon hosted a White House dinner in its honor. In October, the President sent California Governor Ronald Reagan to the Far East to give assurances that despite the forthcoming Peking visit the United States would remain faithful to its friends and allies. In November, Treasury Secretary John Connally (although the main subject was trade and economic problems) carried a commission from the President to reassure our friends and allies of America's faithfulness.

On October 12, instructions arrived to tip off Prime Minister Sato that a Presidential visit to Moscow was about to be announced. As it turned out, Sato had already received the information from the Soviet Embassy, one full day before the time which had theoretically been agreed upon by Washington and Moscow. On November 24, instructions arrived to inform the Prime Minister in secret of the President's plans to meet, before his Peking and

Moscow visits, with Britain's Prime Minister Edward
Heath in Bermuda, with France's President Georges
Pompidou in the Azores, and with Germany's Chancellor
Willy Brandt at Key Biscayne. Somewhat horrified that the
Prime Minister of Japan was ignored, I telephoned Washington and, not being able to reach Secretary Rogers, spoke
to a senior aide, from whom I could glean only that the
possibility of a meeting with Sato had been given consideration but there would be no harm in my making a
recommendation. As a diplomatic gambit, I sought dis-
creetly during our conversation to obtain from Prime Minister Sato a quote that he would like to meet with the
President, but his only comments were that the proposed
summits would no doubt deal with world economic problems and he had full trust in President Nixon. In reporting
the conversation, I added a strong personal appeal urging
a Presidential meeting with Sato either in Hawaii or San
Clemente, pointing out that the inclusion of Sato in the
summitry would underscore the President's expressed determination that nothing should mar the United States-
Japan partnership. Two days later, word was received that,
via Ambassador Ushiba in Washington, Sato was being invited to a summit meeting at San Clemente on January 6–7.
Once again, we in Tokyo were deprived the pleasure of conveying good news, but the important point was that another calamity was averted.

Announcement on November 29, 1971, that Prime Minister Sato would be holding summit discussions with President Nixon at San Clemente in early January was ac-
claimed throughout Japan, but particularly by those whose
faith in the United States had been shaken on July 15. For
them, the mere fact that the meeting was taking place was
almost as important as what would be said. Obviously, a
wide range of matters of mutual interest would be re-
viewed, and in particular growing economic frictions, but a

coordinated policy with respect to China was Japan's greatest concern.

Former Prime Minister Nobusuke Kishi, Sato's elder brother who deserved much appreciation for his postwar efforts on behalf of Japanese-American friendship, had shortly after July 15 observed that the sooner the President's Peking expedition would become past history, the better it would be for Japanese-American relations. Fear of the unknown was making Japan jittery. From Japan's deep-seated "China complex," emotions were stirring. What had happened to Sino-Japanese cultural affinity? Was the Japanese personality inferior to that of the Chinese? Was America jilting Japan for China? Did the Americans truly consider Japan "a doubtful ally" requiring the development of China as a counterweight? Were Japan and America heading for another "clash of China policies" of the type which had led to Pearl Harbor? Were the Americans trying to preempt Japan's natural market with its prodigious potential? Was Japan's postwar faith in America misplaced? Such anxieties seemed confirmed by the fact that the President of the most powerful nation in the world was making a pilgrimage to the capital of China in apparent conformity with historic Chinese expectations that such homage was due from rulers in the outlying world. In a December 22 speech at the Japan-America Society, former Foreign Minister Aichi lamented that by keeping Japan in the dark, the American administration had "cast a long shadow over the future relationship between our two countries."

During a full evening's discussion on December 6 as to what might be achieved at San Clemente, Foreign Minister Fukuda's plea was for a "fundamental meeting of minds." He thought the question which needed clarification was, "How far is the United States ahead of Japan?" Meanwhile, Japanese intellectuals such as Kei Wakaizumi were concerned that miscues might occur in Peking, such as

American attempts to persuade the Chinese that the United States-Japan security relationship had a restraining effect on Japanese "militarism." The Chinese would undoubtedly let the Japanese know that this was what the Americans were saying, and Japanese-American frictions would be exacerbated. Regrettably, an Embassy telegram reporting this conversation was printed textually by columnist Jack Anderson during the San Clemente summit. It seemed incredible that the same newsmen who demanded as a sacred right that their sources be protected could not appreciate that similar constraints should apply to conversations affecting the interests of their country and its friends.

In pre-San Clemente recommendations to Washington, the Embassy stressed that Sato would need assurances that the United States was not forsaking Japan for China, and above all that the Sato government would not be embarrassed by further dramatic developments, such as announcements during the President's Peking visit of diplomatic recognition of the Peking regime, the breaking of ties with Taiwan, or the withdrawal of the American military presence in the Taiwan area. American credibility and reliability would be indispensable to the preservation of Japan's favorable orientation to the United States. What had been the keystone of Sato's policies and those of his postwar predecessors could be damaged, for example, if the China issue, and America's neglect of Japan's interests, were to become a political football in the Sato succession contest. That contest was already evident in the jockeying for position as to who would accompany Sato to California. Foreign Minister Fukuda, the front-running candidate, was saddled with the China problem. His chief rival, Minister of International Trade and Industry Kakuei Tanaka, could not be excluded, because economic issues, also offering no great political bonanzas, were to be discussed by Treasury Secretary Connally, Commerce Secretary Maurice Stans, and former Treasury Secretary David Kennedy, who two months earlier had extracted from Tanaka a textile agreement.

There were three levels of discussion at San Clemente. Sato had his customary tête-à-tête with the President, who had Kissinger at his side, but this time the Japanese insisted that Sato must have a companion, Ambassador Ushiba. Ushiba's presence may have been prompted by a desire to protect Sato from the repetition of a previous occasion when a major controversy had developed in Japan over precisely what he had promised President Nixon with regard to textiles. As usual, the American interpreter was sworn to secrecy. Thus, the State Department or other American officials would have no way of knowing what was said, except from helpful tidbits gathered from Japanese associates. The second level concerned economics. There was much verbal table-thumping, presentation of respective positions, and dedication to high ideals, but, as customary, it was largely a dialogue of the deaf. Diplomatic discussions composed the third level, the agenda including the reversion of Okinawa, which was to take place shortly, and the primary subject, China.

In the discussions with Secretary Rogers, Foreign Minister Fukuda was assured that the improvement of American relations with Peking was apt to be a lengthy process, that there was no thought of abandoning our friends on Taiwan, and that the results of the President's February visit were certain to be modest, such as opening the way for cultural exchanges and for further political discussions, with each side recognizing the differences in their respective positions. Having had visions of more dramatic moves, the Japanese were relieved. At luncheon beside the swimming pool, President Nixon pointed out that his residence overlooking the ocean was named Casa Pacifica, a concept which should give assurance to our Japanese neighbors that because of our mutual dedication to peace in the Pacific our ties were firm and lasting.

The spirit of San Clemente was reassuring for Prime Minister Sato and his associates. In Japan, however, suspicions still lurked. The Tokyo press, and a good portion of the Japanese bureaucracy, were convinced that dramatic breakthroughs would result from the President's trek to Peking. According to some Tokyo newspapers, a naïve Sato had once again been deceived by the Americans.

When President Nixon's plane landed at Peking on February 21, 1972, millions of Japanese eyes were glued to television screens. The warm exchange of greetings, and the smiles which continued through the visit, evoked, as *The New York Times*'s John Lee reported, Japanese "feelings of apprehension and even petulance." One official was quoted, "We feel we have been left behind." Another: "Watching television, I realize this is an historic turnaround after all. I am shocked." That this was, as President Nixon phrased it, "a major event of the century" was a difficult pill to swallow, even reportedly for Prime Minister Sato.

As to outcome, the real results, aside from atmospherics, were essentially as had been indicated to the Japanese at San Clemente: no instant diplomatic recognition, no turning of the back on Taiwan. Japan's officialdom breathed a sigh of relief. To some extent there was a restoration of confidence in the United States. Nonetheless, on the blackboard of Japanese domestic politics, it was not possible to erase the impressions that Sato's China policy had been too cautious and that Japan had been upstaged by its most trusted friend.

Within ten days of the mid-July announcement of the President's China visit, a telegram had gone in from the Tokyo Embassy suggesting that, if it could be accomplished without damaging the primary purpose of the mission, there were cogent reasons, which were outlined, why the President should stop in Tokyo either en route to or returning from Peking. No reply was received, but perhaps that suggestion had been a factor in the decision a fortnight later for the President to greet Emperor Hirohito at Anchorage. The concept of providing the Japanese with a first-hand account obviously had merit. For this purpose, therefore, Assistant Secretary of State for East Asian Affairs, Marshall Green, and John Holdridge of Kissinger's National Security Council staff made Tokyo their first stop in a Far Eastern tour following their sojourn in Peking with the President. It was not the same as hearing directly from the President or Dr. Kissinger (who made his first Tokyo visit some weeks later), but Prime Minister Sato and other Japanese officials appreciated the Green-Holdridge explanation of the Shanghai communiqué, and the general background which was provided.

Eisaku Sato had served a record four terms (each of two years duration) as head of Japan's majority party, the LDP, and therefore as Prime Minister of Japan. With his principal objective accomplished, the reversion of Okinawa on May 15, 1972, he relinquished his post in June. At times, in the view of some critics, he could have taken firmer stands. One highly placed Washingtonian, after explaining that the textile issue was really a political issue for the President, left Sato's office wondering about his leadership ability. To some of us, Sato's apparent submissiveness under fire in the Diet often seemed disappointing. But Japan was not the United States, and in its consensus atmosphere Sato was, in the opinion of most of his peers, a wily fox. Profiting from the tragedy which had befallen his brother, he exercised the LDP's decisive political power judiciously, preferring patiently to zig and zag until the desired result could be achieved without the spilling of blood. These political refinements were not always understood nor appreciated in a White House dominated by bright young captains of industry, advertising executives, and action-oriented anti-bureaucratic law school graduates. Yet, Sato would rank with his brother Kishi, and the incomparable Yoshida, as a true friend of the United States in postwar Japan, and one who took no little abuse because of his conviction that Japanese-American cooperation was of vital importance to both countries.

To succeed Sato, the Liberal Democratic Party on July 5, 1972, elected Kakuei Tanaka. If traditional hierarchical seniority had been followed, the shrewd Foreign and ex-Finance Minister Takeo Fukuda would have been chosen. To what extent Fukuda's candidacy had been affected by the China issue, and in particular by the President's "jumping over Japan's head," would be difficult to assess. Without doubt, the LDP's primary objective was to arrest what had been a slow but steady erosion of the party's nationwide popularity. In electing Tanaka to the party's presidency and the Premiership, the LDP appeared to be seeking a "new look" of progressivism, and to reveal itself as no longer hidebound by tradition. Tanaka, 54 (Fukuda was 67), was the youngest Prime Minister since the war. He was a self-made man from peasant stock rather than the product of an affluent family and Tokyo University; a so-called human bulldozer rather than a polished lifelong bureaucrat; a construction contractor, more in tune with growing demands for better living conditions; a self-assertive politico not inhibited by Sato's cautious conservatism, particularly with regard to China, but also a realist who would state publicly that Japan's ties with the United States were vital to Japan's existence. As Foreign Minister, Tanaka chose Masayoshi Ohira, himself Prime Ministerial timber and the leader of an LDP faction strongly advocating rapprochement with the People's Republic of China.

The road to Peking was quickly opened. The Tanaka government upon assumption of duty publicly expressed its desire for expeditious normalization of relations and within three weeks, as had been expected, an invitation was extended to Prime Minister Tanaka by Premier Chou En-lai.

It was promptly accepted, along with public insinuations that the treaty with Taiwan would be invalidated when diplomatic relations with the People's Republic became a reality. Also accepted by the new Prime Minister was an invitation from President Nixon for a pre-Peking conclave in Hawaii on August 31 and September 1. *The New York Times* described the Hawaiian summit as the President's "declaration of peace." Three weeks later, Prime Minister Tanaka made his pilgrimage to the capital of China. For a six day period, September 24 to 30, affability abounded, and at the conclusion of Tanaka's sojourn it was announced that diplomatic relations had been established between Japan and the People's Republic of China. In Tokyo, the Nationalist Chinese Ambassador was notified by the Foreign Ministry that diplomatic ties between Tokyo and Taipei were to be considered severed.

Thus, despite the Nixon "shokku," and probably assisted by it, Japan managed to outdistance the United States in terms of formal diplomatic relations and the establishment of a full-fledged Embassy in Peking. As an interesting footnote, it was only a year later that Tokyo political pundits were ascribing a marked decline in Tanaka's popularity ratings to his having played his ace card too hastily.

In retrospect, neither Japan nor the United States had hopped on a bandwagon. The Nixon "shokku" notwithstanding, both countries had with renewed confidence resumed their inspection of international road maps in close consultation. In a demonstration of initiative, Japan's new Prime Minister had achieved normalization of relations with Peking while the United States contented itself with less than full diplomatic relations.

But the improvement in relations with Peking was not an auto race. It was an endeavor to bridge the chasm between mainland China and the two strongest nations in the Free World. To the people of Taiwan (with whom the Americans declined to break faith) it was a traumatic experience. Yet, it was an inevitable adjustment to the realities of the 1970's. In Japan, the adjustment had unleashed reverberations, but in the end even the loudest critics of Nixon's July 15 announcement had to concede that the long-range effect was distinctly a net gain not only for Japan and the United States, but for a new structure of peace which could not be constructed in the absence of one-fourth of this planet's population.

Chapter 5

Nixon Shock Number Two: Economic Reciprocity

IT WAS MY CUSTOM each morning at breakfast to read Japan's three English language newspapers and listen to the continuous news program transmitted by the United States Armed Forces Radio and Television Service out of Washington. It was the most efficient way to be prepared for the day's heavy schedule at the Embassy.

About 7:30 on Monday morning August 16, 1971 (Sunday evening in Washington), AFRTS reported that President Nixon had been huddling with his economic advisors at Camp David over the weekend and a major Presidential statement would be broadcast three hours later. Still sensitive because of the "Nixon shock" of July 15, it was not surprising that I became suspicious. The suspicions were not allayed when the news reports emphasized that new Presidential economic moves were expected.

Without delay, I asked the Embassy's telephone operator to call Washington. Unfortunately, the top official of the State Department's economic bureau was in Europe, and his deputy's phone produced no answer. After forty-five minutes, contact was made with the Assistant Secretary of State for East Asian Affairs. He had no idea what the announcement might contain, but agreed to undertake an inquiry. My expressed concern was that if the President's statements were to embrace international as well as domestic economic matters, Japan undoubtedly would be affected. The possibility of an import surcharge was specifically noted. I stressed that if the announcement would have an impact on Japan, the Japanese government, which was still smarting from the July 15 trauma, ought to be alerted. Already the hour was late.

About forty-five minutes later, phone calls came simultaneously from the Assistant Secretary and the Under Secretary of State, each reporting that high level messages were being sent immediately to the Prime Minister of Japan and to the Minister of Finance. While those on the other end of the line still were not cognizant of the substance of the President's announcement, they said it was fairly obvious that Japan would be affected.

Twenty-five minutes prior to the President's announcement, another urgent Washington phone call requested that I arrange immediately for Prime Minister Sato to make telephone contact with Secretary of State Rogers. The Secretary would have initiated the call, but since Sato spoke little English, an interpreter would be needed in Tokyo. Regrettably, Teruo Kosugi, the Prime Minister's confidential English-speaking secretary was on holiday. In desperation, an appeal was made to the Vice Foreign Minister, Haruki Mori, to arrange for an interpreter at the Prime Ministry. Getting the interpreter in place took only twenty minutes, but Secretary Rogers's conversation with the

Prime Minister had barely begun when President Nixon informed the world of his "New Economic Policy."

Although performing entirely different functions, Japan's giant "trading companies" are as important to the Japanese economic scene as is Wall Street to the United States. By remarkable coincidence, the heads of the fourteen leading trading companies had been invited to the Embassy residence for "tea" on the afternoon of August 16. It was to be another of a series of mutually beneficial consultations which our Embassy's economic section had arranged with these commercial titans. The purpose on this occasion was intensified discussion of remedies for what had become an alarming trade imbalance between Japan and the United States. Specifically, our hope was to generate from this influential community, which had a vital stake in a healthy relationship with the United States, suggestions for consideration when cabinet members of our two countries convened as "The Japan-United States Committee on Trade and Economic Affairs" (ECONCOM) in Washington September 9-10. ECONCOM, which with few exceptions met annually, had been instituted during the Kennedy administration to help repair what Ambassador Reischauer had rued as "the broken dialogue."

Although the Embassy had received no guidance beyond the President's public pronouncement, and our telephone calls to Washington could produce no further elucidation, it was decided nonetheless to proceed with the scheduled "tea." We were aware, of course, that while the "China shock" had struck at emotions, the Japanese would consider the "economic shock" as affecting very deeply their livelihood.

Promptly at 3:00 P.M., the delegation of trading company presidents arrived at the Embassy residence. Their leader, quite naturally, was Chujiro Fujino, who as President of Mitsubishi Shoji represented the firm doing the largest volume of business. (His trading company's $11 billion volume accounted for about one-third the business annually transacted by the Mitsubishi Group of companies, a sort of conglomerate.) With the self-restraint and politeness for which the Japanese are well known, Fujino opened the discussion by referring to the original purpose of the meeting and the desire of the trading companies to cooperate in achieving mutually satisfactory answers to our serious trade problems. However, the picture had been drastically altered, he said, by the President's announcement.

Fujino went on to point out that Japanese exports to the United States were currently averaging $600 million per month. Of that total, the fourteen companies represented in the room were handling over 50%. For them, therefore, the President's imposition of a 10% surcharge on dutiable imports was a financial blow amounting to $30 million each month. "This," Fujino-san concluded, "is quite a shock." The other trading company chiefs voiced similar unhappiness. President Hiro Hiyama, whose Marubeni corporation was importing more from the United States than it was exporting to the United States, feared that, with America having set a precedent for the unilateral imposition of surcharges, other countries would be likely to follow suit and Japan would be the major victim. In addition to their anxieties about the 10% surcharge, these managers of some $60 billion in domestic and international commerce annually were also concerned about the President's suspension of dollar convertibility into gold.

In response, I urged that the President's measures be considered in broad perspective. For many months, Japanese business leaders had been expressing grave concern about the state of the American economy and had been suggesting strong Washington action. Americans in Tokyo had time and again been reminded by their Japanese friends, "If America sneezes, Japan catches pneumonia." It was pointed out that the President's action did not single out Japan as the target but was in fact a comprehensive program, including courageous measures on both the American domestic and the worldwide economic fronts. The Embassy still lacked details, but it was apparent that with respect to international trade and international monetary exigencies, the President's purpose was to achieve fundamental solutions, within a multilateral framework, and the measures which he had announced were to be temporary in character.

With regard to the surcharge, the Embassy's Economic Minister Lester Edmond pointed out the President's action was not without precedent; it was a procedure previously employed by European nations. We noted that, in fairness, our Japanese friends must recognize that there were many other trade barriers, including in Japan. They were long-entrenched and had disadvantaged the United States to an extent no longer tolerable. Already in the first half of 1971, the American trade deficit with Japan was greater than that of any entire year previously. Worldwide, trade and monetary problems were reaching crisis proportions.

The main thrust of our discussion with the trading companies' leaders was to secure their understanding that the President's action was a necessity, not just for the United States but for the world trading structure of which Japan was a prime beneficiary. Therefore, instead of lending their voices to public outcries about another "shock," these men could play a powerful role in facilitating understanding and a sympathetic reaction in Japan. They indicated appreciation of the fundamental issues, but, because of the direct economic impact on their companies, the news from Washington could not be expected to cause elation. They feared that, coming so soon after the "China shock," the President's dramatic economic moves would have highly adverse repercussions on Japanese public opinion, despite what they might do to place the decision in better perspective. They sincerely hoped the President's measures would truly be temporary. They were also anxious for details, which were then not yet available, of how the New Economic Policy would be implemented.

Although August 15, 1971, would always be remembered in Japan as the day of the "second Nixon shock," it was interesting to note that with regard to the "China shock" the resentment had centered on the surprise and the style more than the substance, but with regard to the "economic shock" Japanese displeasure centered on the substance more than on the absence of prior consultations regarding the President's specific proposals. There had in fact been extensive discussions, almost ad nauseam, in which Japanese and Americans both agreed on the gravity of our economic problems and the need for remedial action, particularly with respect to trade and investment liberalization. However, economic problems tend to become political problems, and the measures which the Japanese were prepared to take were consistently too little, too late, and often not forthcoming. Beyond this basic consideration, any Japanese businessman could appreciate that advance indications of specifics, such as surcharges or dollar non-convertibility, would have caused frenzy in stock markets and national economies throughout the world.

In an address, entitled "The Agony of Success," former Assistant Secretary of State Harlan Cleveland once made the point that on our spinning planet there are no panaceas to produce Utopia. In fact, policies which prove successful can and do breed new sets of problems. He noted that a swain who succeeds in courtship acquires a family of new responsibilities. Similarly, a businessman who achieves millionaire status faces a collection of new challenges to his ingenuity.

Cleveland's thesis is normally overlooked by Americans, nettled by daily newspaper headlines and impatient for tidy answers to every situation. Over the past quarter of a century, our country enjoyed successes in the field of foreign affairs, not always fully appreciated, e.g. George Marshall's European Recovery Program, the Truman Doctrine, George Kennan's "containment" concept, Dean Acheson's creative role vis-à-vis the North Atlantic Treaty, General MacArthur's handiwork in Japan and the Pacific, the Acheson-Dulles architecture of the Japanese Peace Treaty, the Eisenhower Doctrine, Dulles's dike building against the supposed inevitability of the Communist world revolution, Kennedy's courage during the Cuban crisis, and even the oft-maligned upholding of the flag of freedom and decency in Vietnam by President Johnson and Secretary of State Dean Rusk. None of these personalities nor their policies were perfect, but they operated consistent with American character and, what was more important, not without positive results.

Thanks to such past endeavors, new opportunities with their concomitant problems were open to the Nixon Administration. The Cold War was receding. Other nations, great and small, were, with exceptions, ready for a less belligerent world, where citizens could concentrate on improved well-being for themselves and peace with their neighbors. Political polemics were giving way to a desire for more productive economic relationships to enhance mankind's welfare. During the postwar period, with its political preoccupations, the assumptions, ground rules, and norms which had undergirded the world's economic resurgence had remained relatively unchanged. They had to a considerable extent become anachronistic, and with the dawn of the 1970's renovation was overdue.

As the preeminent economic power in the postwar world, the United States had shouldered primary responsibility for much of the non-Communist world. In addition to heavy defense and security expenditures, substantial resources were invested in the recovery of Europe and Japan, and in technical and economic assistance to the developing nations.

With America playing a leading role, institutions were created to improve world economic conditions. At Bretton Woods, New Hampshire, a United Nations conference in 1944 established not only the International Bank for Reconstruction and Development (IBRD) but also the International Monetary Fund (IMF), designed to assure a stable world monetary system. Subsequently, in 1947, the General Agreement on Tariffs and Trade (GATT) came into being to promote the orderly conduct of international trade, and under its sponsorship "Kennedy round" negotiations for tariff reductions were completed in 1967. All these endeavors contributed to the reinvigoration of individual nations and to a vigorous expansion of international trade. Inevitably, however, these successes produced new problems: persistent United States balance-of-payments deficits, doubt as to the continued convertibility of the dollar, the need for supplementary sources of international liquidity, disequilibria reflected in an inveterate balance-of-payments surplus enjoyed by some countries and chronic deficits experienced by others, pressures to revalue undervalued currencies and devalue those which had become overvalued, the increasing frequency of exchange rate crises, a variety of international trade controversies centering chiefly around protectionist barriers, and problems regarding the flow or non-flow of capital across international borders.

At the outset of the 1970's, among the nations which could not escape "the agony of success" was Japan. As the fastest growing economic power in the world, it found itself confronted with pressing problems of adjustment. At home, its "economic miracle," which had been so intensely growth oriented, would have to become more responsive to the broader aspirations of Japan's 104 million people. Internationally, Japan's trade volume had in two decades expanded 22 times globally; its exports to the United States during that period had jumped 32-fold. As an economic superpower, it would be expected to assume commensurate

responsibilities and do business in the international marketplace on the basis of equality and reciprocity.

Since international economic affairs had become unpre-
cedentedly complex and replete with domestic ramifications,
one of the major agonies of the world's foremost economic
power in the 1970's was organizing itself to act with una-
nimity and to speak with one voice. In Washington, where
authority tends to gravitate to those who use their elbows,
the State Department, which should have been the President's focal agency, often found itself shouldered aside by
senior officials in the White House, the Commerce Department, Treasury, Agriculture, the Council of Economic
Advisors, the Special Trade Representative, Ambassadors-
at-Large (literally), and business moguls who had more
frequent access to Presidential corridors than did some
cabinet secretaries.

In an attempt to reduce the confusion, the President in
February of 1971 established the Council on International
Economic Policy (CIEP) with himself as chairman, the
Secretary of State as vice-chairman, and a new Assistant
to the President for International Economic Affairs, Peter
Peterson, as Executive Director. As with most reorganiza-
tions designed to streamline the bureaucracy, an actual
expansion took place. Another senior official was added with
a shop and staff of his own. But the President's objective
was unchallengeable: "a clear single focus for the full range
of international economic issues."

As a first major assignment, Peterson was asked by the
President to prepare a comprehensive review and analysis
of "the changing world economy." It was to serve as background for American policy formulation. Incubated on a
highly confidential basis, the report, complete with vivid
graphics, was presented to the President and other CIEP
principals in April. The impact was such that the President
directed a similar briefing be provided a select group of

Administration officials, Members of Congress, and non-governmental elite. One Tokyo visitor, who confided that he had been among the privileged, hinted that the charts were devastating, particularly with respect to Japan. In December, after the mid-August "shock," an edited version of the CIEP presentation was made public.

Peterson's story was essentially one of "the agony of success." Our postwar recovery, reconstruction, and assistance programs had illustriously accomplished their objectives. Other nations had made remarkable gains in strength. Our crusade since the 1930's, reinforced after the war, for expanded international trade had witnessed a $62 to $310 billion jump in worldwide annual exports from 1950 to 1970. However, our domination of the world economic scene was no longer overwhelming, and other nations were disinclined to assume responsibilities commensurate with their new status. As in other areas of international relations, the challenge was, therefore, to achieve worldwide adjustments to the realities of the 1970's. Peterson was convinced that the American economy was basically strong, but our international competitive position had steadily been weakening and could be in jeopardy, unless appropriate measures were expeditiously adopted at home and by our friends abroad.

The CIEP picture was painted in pastels. The bright American economic indicators were shaded by relative ratings. The United States Gross National Product had risen from $285 billion in 1950 to nearly a trillion ($977 billion) in 1970, thus widening the absolute gap with all our competitors. But CIEP pointed out that America's share of the worldwide GNP had dropped from 40% to 30%. With regard to exports, the United States during the 1950–1970 period registered in absolute terms an increase from $10 billion to $43 billion, but CIEP noted our worldwide share had dropped from 16% to 14%. During the same two decades, farm workers declined from 12.2% to 4.4% of the labor force, but agricultural production increased 20%, the value of production per worker jumping from $2,700 to $6,600. From 1960 to 1970, total American investments abroad had nearly doubled, from $86 billion to $167 billion. Taking liabilities into account, our net worth abroad increased during the decade from $45 to $69 billion, the $24 billion difference exceeding the GNP's of the majority of the world's nations.

But the CIEP graphs disclosed many ominous trends. For the first time since 1893, the United States was headed for a foreign trade deficit, probably over $2 billion. Our basic balance-of-payments deficit, which in the 1960's usually hovered between $1.5 and $3 billion, was plummeting in 1971 to nearly $9 billion. America's reserves, which in 1950 had stood at $24 billion, had by 1970 fallen to $15 billion, a decline from 50% to 16% of total world reserves. America was plowing back only 18% of its total GNP, a rate of investment less than most European countries and half that of Japan. Profits in manufacturing had in 1970 reached their lowest levels in three decades. Our import rate was growing faster than our export rate. In twenty years, our trade in non-technology intensive products (textiles, shoes, et cetera) had shifted from $1.8 billion in our favor to a $9.1 billion deficit (in absolute terms, our exports of these items had risen from $3.7 to $6.8 billion). The overall trade shift from +$6.8 to −$2 billion during the 1964–1971 period was estimated to have cost from 600,000 to 750,000 American jobs. American automobile production dropped from 76% of world output in 1950 to 31% in 1970; steel dropped from 46% to 20%. In 1971, Americans were importing 100% of their 35mm cameras, 96% of their tape recorders, 75% of their calculators, 70% of their radio receivers, and 52% of their black and white television sets. The scramble for raw materials was just beginning, with estimates that the United States would be importing from 30% to 50% of its mineral requirements by the end of the century. Meanwhile, the share of America's labor force engaged in service occupations had gradually risen to 60%, raising questions regarding the maintenance of a manufacturing capability essential to our national interest.

By mid-1971, the unhappy trends to which the CIEP had called attention had taken a decisive turn for the worse. Due primarily to a sharply augmented deterioration in our trade balance and to heavy outflows of short-term capital, the United States balance-of-payments deficit had swollen, during the second quarter of 1971, to a record annual rate of $12 billion. American reserves were being seriously depleted, falling during the first half of 1971 from $14.5 billion to $12.1 billion, or from 16% of total international reserves to 10.6%. Dollars were flowing abroad in record amounts. In Japan alone, the payments surplus was mounting a half billion dollars monthly. Intense speculation was shaking the foundations of the international monetary system.

An immediate objective of the "New Economic Policy," dramatically announced by the President on August 15, was to arrest the deterioration of the American international position. Toward this end, the convertibility of the dollar into gold and other reserve assets was suspended, and a 10% surcharge on dutiable imports was imposed. Being temporary in nature, these measures could also serve as bargaining counters for achieving progress toward the longer range objectives: a realignment to more realistic exchange rates, a sustained "turnaround" in our balance-of-payments position, a reformed international monetary order, a more equitable international trading system, and a broader sharing of international responsibilities. The President realized, however, that no less important was getting the American house in order. Thus, the wage/price freeze and other controls were instituted to combat inflation, while tax incentives were proposed to stimulate domestic growth and productivity, to reduce unemployment, and to encourage new investments which would increase American competitiveness.

In taking action on August 15, the Nixon administration had also to be concerned that unless effective international cooperation were forthcoming, the American people, wearied by their postwar exertions and soured by the Vietnam experience, would be lured by the sirens of protectionism and isolationism. In their view, if the international economic community was to stay in business, all stockholders, including particularly those with mounting surpluses, must assume liabilities as well as assets. But the prevailing attitude was one of procrastination. Thus, the rather brutal action of August 15 was designed by Washington to actuate the negotiations and the reorganization deemed necessary to keep the Free World solvent.

For Americans fortunate enough to have grown up in the first half of the twentieth century, it was a golden era. Our country had come through two world wars with flying colors, and even a terrible economic depression had proved to be a successful test of our mettle. We were convinced there was no way of life superior to ours, and the secret of our success story was devotion and hard work.

By the 1970's, however, American invincibility, invulnerability, and infallibility were no longer axiomatic. In Korea, despite General MacArthur's heroics, we had settled for a draw. In Vietnam, we sought escape. Our European allies were thriving, increasingly allergic to anything smacking of American tutelage. Japan, the only advanced nation in Asia, whose first entry on the world stage had culminated in military disaster, was making one of the most phenomenal recoveries in history. Inhabiting a land area the size of California, with only the most meager of natural resources, the people of Japan were giving new meaning to the concepts of devotion and hard work. It was a more sophisticated nation from that of the 1930's, whose products were

sometimes characterized as "shoddy" and whose all-important silk industry had been vanquished by DuPont's invention of nylon. On the economic ladder, Japan had by
1968 overtaken the Western European countries and was
perched on rung number three, with only the United States
and the Soviet Union above.

It was not surprising that Peter Peterson's survey, "The
United States in the Changing World Economy," would
include a "special review" of "The Japanese Economic Miracle." Although one cabinet member was quoted by *Time*
magazine as contending that Japan was trying to achieve
with the yen what it had failed to achieve by the sword,
Peterson's purpose was a valid one, namely, to draw attention to the Japanese challenge and to stimulate constructive
adjustments to keep America competitive. James Abegglen
and his astute Japan-watchers in the Boston Consulting
Group were stressing that what was transpiring in Japan
might lack "the dramatic impact of the Soviet and Chinese
revolutions" but it could have "equally far-reaching consequences for altering the shape of the world."

In 1945, Japan was a prostrate nation, morally and economically. Thoroughly defeated and shorn of its empire, no
one really expected it to recuperate to the point of once
again becoming a world power. Its viability was still in
doubt ten years later when Frank Gibney wrote his incisive
work, *Five Gentlemen of Japan.* But the viability of Japan was as much in American interest as it was in that of
Japan. Thus, during the occupation, some $2 billion was
invested for relief and rehabilitation purposes and special
dispensations were instituted to nurture Japan's economic
recovery. Then and subsequently, America liberally provided technology and credits, plus by far the largest market
for Japanese products. Ironically, the Korean war was a
boon for Japan. Restraints on the Japanese industrial establishment, which had accompanied the occupation's civil
reform program, were relaxed, while the demand for Japa-

nese goods and services in support of the American military effort on the Korean peninsula gave an immense boost to Japan's economy. Later, the Vietnam conflict would have a somewhat similar effect. Hundreds of millions of dollars of Japanese exports went to Indo-China; our Ambassador, Ellsworth Bunker, sometimes referred to Saigon as "Honda-ville."

For most Japanese, the American contribution to Japan's postwar recovery was by the 1970's ancient history. *Asahi's* 1971 series of articles on "the pervasive American influence on Japan" seemed to go out of its way to dredge up real and imagined grievances, somewhat grudgingly acknowledging that the occupation "showed far more of benevolence than of the harsh vindictiveness that the Japanese had expected." However, according to *Asahi*, this good fortune was "conceived with an eye to the securing of American power or the furthering of long-range American interests in Asia." It was admitted that the American endeavors had been "immediately beneficial to the rebuilding of Japan," but whether they should be "praised as the source of Japan's present stability, influence and power" or "blamed for Japan's difficulties in establishing for herself an autonomous identity" would have to be a question with which historians and scholars would have to grapple. Fortunately, this rather cynical evaluation did not accurately reflect responsible opinion in Japan. The view of governmental and civilian leaders, often voiced both privately and publicly, and endorsed repeatedly by the Japanese electorate, was that which was registered on September 26, 1971, when, during his brief stopover at Anchorage, Emperor Hirohito had said, "Together with the Japanese people, I constantly raise to heart that all the Presidents of the United States, and her government and people, have given us unstinted assistance, materially and morally, after the end of the war, in the restoration and building up of our country. I take this opportunity to express my sincere gratitude for it. I have no doubt whatever that the friendly relations between our two countries, cultivated during the past quarter of a century, will be increasingly sanctioned by close contact and cooperation between our governments and peoples."

While America did make important contributions, it was the Japanese themselves who wrought the "miracle." From occupation days onward, they had assiduously accelerated their economic momentum, and it may well have been the 1960 security-treaty crisis that signaled the take-off. Although it was an act of political hara-kiri, Prime Minister Kishi in effect preserved the postwar success formula. Having made their decision, and having had enough of political turmoil, the Japanese welcomed new Prime Minister Hayato Ikeda's diversion of the nation's attention to the goal of doubling Japanese incomes in ten years. Ikeda knew the resourcefulness of his people, but due to incurable illness he was able to witness only four years of their record-shattering responsiveness.

In point of fact, Japan's Gross National Product of $45 billion in 1960 soared more than four times to $197 billion in 1970, and in 1971 went up to $225 billion. In real terms, Japan's growth rate in the 1960's was an annual 11%, more than double that of the United States, West Germany or any other developed country. Japan's share of the world's GNP was doubling every ten years, from 1.5% in 1950 to 3% in 1960, to 6.2% in 1970. Per capita income, which in 1950 was at a low $130, had rocketed to $2,500 in 1972. In the 1960's, instead of doubling in accordance with Ikeda's goal, the average income, in real terms, tripled. During the 1960's, the consumer price index in Japan was moving upward, but wholesale and export prices remained relatively stable until a minor upswing began in 1968. While output per man-hour in the United States was increasing at a 2.5% rate, the rate in Japan was rising at a merry pace, 9% from 1950 to 1965 and 13.4% from 1965 to 1969. Until 1968, Japanese productivity was surpassing wage increases, even though the latter were rising at a 12% clip or more annually. Industrially, Japan had moved into the major league, competing vigorously with the United States and other world leaders in the production of steel, motor vehicles, shipbuilding, electronics equipment, petrochemicals, et cetera. The pace of Japanese economic progress was symbolized by the world-famous Tokaido "bullet trains" which were shuttling between Tokyo and Osaka via Nagoya and Kyoto at speeds in the neighborhood of 120 miles per hour.

In steel output, Japan had moved up from 2 million tons in 1950 to 93 million tons in 1970, threatening to overtake the Soviet Union and the United States (our 1970 production was 131 million tons). Japan's share of the world market had increased from 6% to 16% during the 1960's. With the merger of the Yawata and Fuji steel companies, the new Nippon Steel Corporation became the world's largest, producing 30.4 million tons in 1971 as compared with the United States Steel Corporation's 24.6 million. Located in Japan were eight of the world's ten largest blast furnaces, as well as the world's largest single steel complex, Nihon Kokan's ultramodern plant at Fukuyama, with a 16-million-ton capacity. While steel production in the United States, West Germany, and Great Britain remained relatively stagnant during the 1960's, Japanese production trebled. It would probably have increased even more had embarrassed Japanese steelmakers not been amenable to agreements for the "voluntary restraint" of exports.

Automobile production was another Japanese industrial triumph. Output increased 25% or more per year throughout the 1960's, representing an increase from 2% to 17% of total world production. Some 5,800,000 Toyotas, Datsuns, and other Japanese passenger vehicles and trucks came off the assembly lines in 1971, more than half the American production (and in a country with less than half America's population). At Hiroshima, the aggressive Toyo Kogyo company perfected the rotary (Wankel) engine and placed its Mazdas on the Japanese and American markets four years before General Motors planned to produce the first American automobile with this revolutionary power unit. (The President of the pace-setting Hiroshima company was Kohei Matsuda, whose family name was conveniently trans-literated to the more familiar word Mazda for international marketing purposes.) Fortunately for Detroit, Japanese in-roads into the American market were largely at the ex-pense of European manufacturers. Total foreign imports to the United States in the early 1970's were holding rela-tively steady at 16% of the American market.

While runner-up as producer of an extensive and grow-ing list of items, Japan had long since established itself as the world's leading shipbuilder. Its 10.6 million gross tons in 1970 represented six times the 1960 Japanese output and one-half the total 1970 ship production in the world. Its mammoth tankers were in such demand that most Jap-anese shipbuilders in 1971 had a backlog of orders which would take many months to fill. A visit to a Japanese super-shipyard was always an impressive experience. At Naga-saki, for example, the Mitsubishi plant, confined to its limited prewar area which was relatively undamaged when the A-bomb missed its precise target, was a model of pro-duction coordination. Under the direction of Soichiro Suenaga, a human dynamo with lifelong experience in his field, huge cranes with split-second timing and pinpoint precision would swing carefully prefabricated sections into place for final welding. Despite the cramped space, ships with deadweight tonnage of 200,000 and more were slipping off the ways every two months. A new dry dock had just been completed at a nearby site, capable of producing a 1,000,000-ton ship, if required, but which in the meantime would serve as cradle for the simultaneous construction of two leviathans, each of less than half-million tonnage.

An integral component, of course, of Japan's "miracle" was its export performance. Outclassing all other nations,

Japanese exports multiplied 22 times from 1950 to 1970, increasing at an average annual rate of 19%. During the 1960's, while American exports were rising 118%, those of Japan quadrupled, mounting three times as fast as total world exports. During the same decade, Japan's share of world exports doubled, from 3% to 6%. In 1971, Japanese exports totaled $23.6 billion (just under half the figure for the United States), and its trade surplus in that single year vaulted from $4 billion to $8 billion. It was a nation of hustlers with quality products at reasonable prices.

Despite a world impression that Japan's economy was export led, the fact was that only 10% of Japan's GNP was being exported. That was, of course, more than the 4% figure for the United States, but considerably less than Belgium's 44% and the 20% ratios for West Germany and Canada. In relation to goods actually produced, Japanese exports amounted to 30%, compared to 13% for the United States, 37% for West Germany, and 63% for Canada. Moreover, the Japanese export thrust was in the sophisticated production areas of major interest to American exporters. Export growth for items such as vehicles, electronic equipment, and chemicals was extraordinary, e.g., 64% for automobiles in 1971. From 1966 to 1970, the foreign market for Japanese electronic desk calculators trebled or quadrupled annually. In short, even though they represented only one-tenth of Japan's GNP, Japanese products were formidable competition in the international marketplace.

To understand Japan's "economic miracle" requires delving deeply into Japan's national character. Growth of such record-breaking proportions was not an accident. It was the result of several forces, the strongest of which was what *The New York Times* reporter Tak Oka had so aptly described as "Japanism." Permeated and complemented by "Japanism," the other forces included: a unique business-economic system, the efficient use of a dedicated labor force, extraordinary collaboration between government and business, and an unusually favorable international setting.

  a. JAPANISM'S "BURNING DESIRE TO CATCH UP." The dominant factor in Japan's success was motivation. As a homogeneous and insular people, not intimate members of the Asian family, and fearful of colonialist Westerners, a feeling of Japan-against-the-world had over the years become deeply ingrained. When their industrial inferiority was underscored by Commodore Perry's "Black Ships," Japanese leaders over a century ago made the wrenching decision to open Japan's doors to foreign technology. Seventy years of remarkable economic progress ensued, culminating in a disastrous military adventure, a major economic setback, and a second implantation from foreign civilization. But there was no surrender of Japanism and its capacity for purposeful communal action. Referring to these historical developments, an article published in 1973 by Japan's Ministry of International Trade and Industry (MITI), entitled "Basic Philosophy of Japanese Industrial Policy," explained that Japanese "feelings of isolation and alienation, anxiety and impatience, have become a burning desire to catch up and a source of national vitality." It was a consensual desire shared by all strata of Japanese— political leaders, commercial officials, bureaucrats, journalists, academics, and workers in offices, factories, vehicles, shops, and rice paddies.

  Consonant with Japanese hierarchical proclivities, the yardstick for measuring progress in "catching up" was the international ladder. During a visit to the sprawling Yawata steel complex in Kitakyushu in October 1969, a large banner was observed near the final rolling mill which read, "We are going to be Number One!" Already Japan's largest producer, Yawata would soon become, via merger with Fuji, larger than the United States Steel Corporation. At

Nagoya, the manager of the Komaki plant where Mitsubishi Heavy Industries (MHI) produced its aircraft was
Teruo Tojo, son of Japan's wartime Prime Minister and, as
a young university graduate, a member of the engineering
team which had designed the Japanese Zero fighter planes
in the mid-1930's. At a briefing, MHI officials described their
programs for manufacturing YS-11 propellor-driven medium-sized transport aircraft, MU-2 executive planes (over
100 assembled and sold in Texas), Hawk and Nike missiles,
and F-4 Phantoms by agreement with McDonnell-Douglas.
Most fascinating, however, was discussion of the chart
which showed that Japan was sixth in world production of
transport air frames. Tojo, who manifested affability and
a warm friendliness toward the United States, left no doubt
that No. 6 ranking was embarrassing and must be remedied. What was disconcerting, of course, was that Boeing
747's and other airliners represented a major category of
manufactured American exports to Japan, which to the
extent that it was lost would make our trade deficit with
Japan that much worse.

Just as successes can breed agonies, so fire can produce
steel. The traumatic adversities which the Japanese suffered at the close of World War II had the effect of rekin-
dling a deep-seated commitment of service to the nation.
From the depths of Japanese culture emerged such
strengths as forbearance, self-denial, sense of obligation,
single-minded determination, hard work, group loyalty,
pride, and the urge to prove Japan's prowess to the outside
world. Directing these strengths successfully into intensive
economic growth, the conservative establishment handily
held the reins of political power throughout the postwar
period, and by maintaining stability permitted the flower-
ing of Japan's new prosperity. The whole saga was one of
Japanism in action.

In our private conversations, Prime Minister Sato al-
luded frequently to foreign characterizations of the Jap-

anese as "economic animals." His references were usually in a light vein, but unmistakably the epithet was resented. Some criticism of this nature was probably unavoidable for, being highly allergic to a resurgence of Japanese militarism, Sato and his compatriots saw no other way to assuage Japan's "burning desire to catch up" than in the economic arena. They no doubt assumed that, with its meager natural resources and relying primarily on the energies of its people, Japan could not pose a threat to its erstwhile conqueror and now valued ally, the legendary American economic behemoth. As it turned out, this was not a safe assumption.

b. UNIQUE BUSINESS-ECONOMIC SYSTEM. As an Asian nation with a cultural background far different from that of the West, it was not surprising that, in becoming Asia's first and only modern industrial society, Japan developed a business-economic system somewhat baffling to Westerners. Concentrating on rapid economic growth, this system was so successful that its main features were well worth noting:

(1) High-Level Savings. Somewhat reminiscent of the Protestant ethic, "A penny saved is a penny earned," the Japanese people traditionally were a nation of savers. Their 1970 personal savings rate, 20% of disposable income, was highest in the world, nearly three times the 7% American rate and well in excess of the rates from 6% to 13% in other major countries.

(2) High Investment Rate. Heavily preoccupied with economic growth, Japan also led the world in percentage of Gross National Product plowed back as investment. During the 1968–1970 period, the rate for Japan was 39% of GNP, double the 18% American rate. More pointedly, Japan was investing 20% of GNP in industrial machinery and equipment as compared with a 10% rate for the United States.

(3) Consumer Demand. Despite its unparalleled

savings rate, Japan had become a consumption society. The popular goal, as previously mentioned, was acquisition of the three C's: cooler (air conditioner), car, and color TV. By 1970, more than 90% of Japanese households possessed at least one TV set, washing machine, and refrigerator. Of the 5,800,000 motor vehicles produced in 1971, 4,000,000 remained in Japan.

(4) Key Role of Banks. A MITI article observed that "as if countless rivulets eventually joined together to become one large river," so "in Japan small amounts of capital were gathered to be channeled in concentration into growth industries." The dams regulating the flow were the commercial banks. The channeling was done with skill and virtually no resources were allowed to stagnate in the dams' reservoirs. The master regulator was the Bank of Japan, which normally stood ready to provide credit facilities to the commercial banks.

(5) High Debt/Equity Ratios. Probably the most striking feature of the Japanese business-economic system was its corporate financing. Massive amounts of debt were employed. For Japan's steel industry, the debt/equity ratio was 5:1, and for Japan's leading domestically owned oil company it was 11:1. During a visit to Nagoya, it was learned that Toyota was doing a $2 billion business, with both equity capital and profits at a $110 million level. Also with a business volume of $2 billion, MHI was operating with equity capital of $275 million and profits of $50 million. Such organizations would be considered in the throes of bankruptcy in the United States where the average debt/equity ratio for *Fortune* magazine's 500 leading United States corporations was less than 0.5:1. James Abegglen and his Boston Consulting Group, who had for years been professional scrutineers of the Japanese economic scene, contended that the Japanese method of growth financing, rather than being dangerous and unthinkable, was a source of great strength, because: (a) growth need not be financed

from retained earnings; (b) provided interest could be paid, there was little constraint on growth; and (c) only small profit margins were necessary while creating substantial growth rates in stockholder equity. In short, Japanese firms could expand faster. The game plan was to grow now, establish market shares, and profit later.

(6) Unstigmatized Big Business. Unlike America, where big business was often berated as rich and reprehensible, "bigness" was not an evil in Japan. The prewar "zaibatsu," which tended to be family-centered holding company operations, were broken up by General MacArthur, but because of loyalties felt by the senior management, as well as for business advantages, it was quite natural for member companies of the old "zaibatsu" to develop special cooperation in the postwar period. Unlike the old pyramided "zaibatsu," which they were often inaccurately labeled, these increasingly powerful postwar industrial groupings were not centrally controlled. In diversification, they were like American conglomerates, but member companies were independent corporations and their collaboration was on an informal and voluntary basis. With the aid of their own commercial banks and trading companies, and often as both supplier and user, these groups spread the risks as well as the benefits of their various enterprises. The result was greater strength and efficiency, and significant market advantages both at home and abroad. The three major industrial groups, Mitsubishi, Mitsui and Sumitomo, accounted for more than a quarter of Japan's Gross National Product. When crises arose, such groups might work out remedial arrangements among themselves, including an equitable division and allocation of resources and markets. These were not cartels, but self-enlightened cooperation among competitive groups having a common love of country.

(7) Survival of the Fittest. In Japan, to him that hath was given. Financial institutions and the government

provided solid backing for the growth enterprises but ruthlessly disdained firms which were marginal and less efficient. In practice, this meant that the smaller and medium-sized companies, some of them serving as buffer subcontractors for the big industrial combines, had a difficult struggle, with several thousand falling by the wayside each year. The result was, however, that the use of human and material resources was constantly being upgraded, and production was increasingly concentrated in the larger and more efficient corporate entities.

(8) More Productive Production. "The secret of a successful strategy is the concentration of fighting power on the main battlegrounds." Japan's MITI cited this Napoleonic and Clausewitz theory to explain basic Japanese industrial strategy in shifting emphasis from labor-intensive sectors, such as cotton textiles, to those which would require the intensive employment of capital and technology, such as steel, oil refining, petrochemicals, automobiles, industrial machinery, aircraft, and electronics, including computers. The rationale: with its 104,000,000 population, Japan would not otherwise have been able to "break away from the Asian pattern of stagnation and poverty" to catch up with Europe and America. Accordingly, Japan's consensus society had shifted relentlessly from what a London *Economist* assessment termed "throw-away industries" toward the most sophisticated stages of industrialization. The result: higher productivity, faster growth, and international esteem.

(9) Optimal Industrial Sites. Most of Japan's coastline, particularly that facing the Pacific, was a veritable palisade of industrial enterprises, all of them capitalizing on the relative inexpensiveness of maritime transportation. Unforgettable among visits to many of these seaside work complexes was a tour of Nihon Kokan's steel-making ''dream plant" at Fukuyama, some 400 miles southwest of Tokyo. It was Japan's newest, and its 16,000,000-ton ca-

pacity was unmatched anywhere in the world. Designed
by a lifelong steelman whose imagination was given free
rein, the Fukuyama complex was located on a man-made
rectangular peninsula. At docks on one side, ships brought
in the coal (via Virginia's port of Norfolk alone, Japan was
importing 19,000,000 tons) and the iron ore (much of it
from Australia). Next to these docks were coking ovens
and sintering facilities. Adjacently placed were the four
blast furnaces, the largest having a 15,000-ton-per-day capacity, with a still larger fifth furnace planned. Next came
the basic oxygen furnaces. Finally, on the other side of the
peninsula were the various rolling mills, from which the
products moved to one of two dock areas, one for domestic
shipments and the other for foreign consignments. In the
center of this well-groomed complex was the master control
room, employing the latest techniques, including compu-
terization and television monitoring. With such an efficient
flow of seaborne raw materials to seaborne finished products, it was little wonder that Japan steel makers could
reportedly lay down a ton of quality steel in Pittsburgh $10
cheaper than the local product.

   (10) Invaluable Trading Companies. With well over
1,000 offices strategically placed around the world, in addition to nearly 10,000 in the home country, Japan's "trading
companies" handled three-fourths of Japan's exports, most
of its imports (predominantly raw materials), and 88% of
its total international trade, in addition to their even larger
volume of domestic business. There were some 4,000 of
these unique institutions, dominated by a dozen or so
giants. By handling hundreds of products, each company
provided capabilities well beyond those of an individual
producer and opened opportunities otherwise unavailable,
particularly for small and medium-sized manufacturers.
The trading companies offered superb worldwide market
intelligence, raw material procurement, distribution outlets, minimal freightage and handling costs, expeditious

trade financing, possible investment funds, and other benefits of Japan's intermeshed business establishment. Noting
that the top five trading companies, because of their huge
sales volumes, could operate on a 0.15% return on sales,
Peterson's CIEP report characterized the Japanese trading
company as probably "the world's most efficient international marketing channel."

c. EFFICIENT AND DEDICATED LABOR. Duly awed by
labor practices which he had observed during a visit to
Japan, one American rendered the indictment, "The Japanese are unfair; they like to work!" It was a succinct tribute to the role of human resources in Japan's economic
miracle.

(1) Full Employment. What was traditionally for
Japan a chronic problem of surplus population had in
economic terms been overcome well before 1970. Partly
responsible was the postwar lowering of the rate of population increase to about 1% (with the help of government-
established abortion clinics), but the main factor, of course,
was the absorption of manpower by Japan's fast-growing
economy. Notwithstanding the steady influx of young people from the rural areas to the urban centers, there was,
in fact, a labor shortage, particularly of workers possessing
technical skills. The classic quotation, attributed to Calvin
Coolidge, "When many people are out of work, unemployment results" did not apply in Japan.

(2) Well-Educated Personnel. Japan's educational
level was among the world's highest. According to the
CIEP report, 91% of Japan's secondary-school-age population was attending secondary schools, as against 78% in
the United States. Japan's universities were also grad-
uating more engineers. Heavy emphasis was placed on vo-
cational training programs, the demand being almost
insatiable for technically minded personnel at all levels.

(3) Wages Up, So Also Productivity. Hourly wage

rates in Japan were in 1971 about one-third those in the United States, only a little less than in Europe, and three times the wage scales in Korea and Taiwan. Semi-annual bonuses plus other fringe benefits nearly doubled the bare salary labor cost. In the mid-1960's, Japanese wages were rising 12% or more annually, but productivity was increasing at a slightly higher rate. The trend changed in 1968 when Japanese wages went up 15.6% and began to outstrip productivity. Unit labor costs in the United States rose more sharply than those of Japan during the 1965–1970 period. While enjoying a distinct advantage vis-à-vis the United States, Japanese labor was not "cheap labor" and it was getting less so. Incidentally, the salaries of the chairmen and presidents of Japan's large corporations were reportedly in the $20,000 per annum range, only a fraction of the remuneration of their American counterparts, but they received substantial subsidies such as housing, chauffered vehicles, and generous expense accounts.

(4) *Cheer, Cheer for Old Matsushita.* One of life's greatest decisions for a Japanese university graduate was the choice of the company with which he would cast his lot. This was because of Japan's unique lifetime employment system. Having virtually made an unbreakable contract with the company, the newcomer would start at the bottom and move upward with his "class" (true also in government) in accordance with an ordained schedule. The salary scale, based on seniority, was skewed to provide the higher increases in the later years. Jam-ups at the top of the escalator were avoided through mandatory retirement at age fifty-five. Those of proven top management caliber faced no age limit. At a get-acquainted luncheon with key Embassy officers, two of the leaders of Japan's fast-growing petrochemical industry were proudly in their mid-eighties, while each of the remaining five was over seventy. The lifetime employment system had its advantages, and they included: the employee need not worry

about his future; the company was paternalistic, usually providing its family members with a variety of fringe benefits such as housing, food and transportation subsidies, daily recreational programs, and vacationing facilities; there was a great amount of job flexibility, allowing an employee to be retrained for another position with equivalent status within the company, if factors such as automation should suggest alterations in the company's operations; and a fast-growing company would gain cost and other advantages by staffing its expansion with recruits directly from the schools. Greatest benefit of all was that the employee identified his own welfare inextricably with that of the company (the very thesis that "Engine Charley" Wilson failed to sell to Americans: "What helps General Motors, helps you"). Typical of an esprit de corps unique in the world, Japanese workers such as those in the employ of that doyen of the electronics industry, Konosuke Matsushita, would begin their day by singing the company song, calling for greater production in the interest of the company, Japan, and customers around the world.

(5) Few Work Stoppages. General MacArthur's endeavors to transplant the glories of American trade unionism to Japan were only partially successful. Aside from undue leftist influences, they ran afoul of deep-seated Japanism. The labor movement, particularly the largest federation Sohyo with some 4,000,000 members, seemed less interested in the welfare of workers than in manifesting political capabilities, such as providing the primary manpower for the "anti-treaty" demonstrations in 1960 and 1970. In 1970, the unions apparently got the message that Japan's increasingly affluent society was disinterested in political turmoil. The fact was that the American concept of cross-company trade unions tended to lack appeal in a country where employees who were being reasonably well treated wanted their particular company to succeed and, rather than create difficulties for it, were personally com-

mitted to assist to the best of their abilities in its success. All of this explained why there were few serious work stoppages in Japan. Occasionally, for an hour or so, a token strike would occur. Often workers would wear red armbands, indicating they were theoretically on strike, but would continue to toil with undiminished vigor. Each year, there would occur the "spring struggle" during which a single union would negotiate the annual wage increase, and when settlement was reached, other Japanese unions would fall in step. There were few complaints, for wages had soared from annual 8% increases in the 1955–1961 period to nearly 18% increases in 1969 and 1970. Under the circumstances, Japanese laborers and their company unions saw no reason to emulate the economic paralyses which frequently plagued the United States. One Labor Minister, Kenzaburo Hara, who may have become slightly infected during student days in Oregon, once gingerly suggested that in some future year consideration might be given to reducing Japan's six-day work week (44 or more hours) to five. The suggestion at that time was not enthusiastically applauded.

  d. BUSINESS-GOVERNMENT COLLABORATION. The Japanese were wont to stress that their economic system was not a textbook model. It was, in their view, a living organism, pursuing the principles of freedom as an ideal but pragmatically responsive via governmental resources to the special problems and goals of Japan. By no means was it a state economy such as in Communist countries. It differed also from the American system, primarily in the greater amount of trust, collaboration, and common purpose which existed between the business community and the government. Attempts to describe this system included: "mixed economy," "consent economy," "concerted economy," and "guided economy," but the expression most frequently heard was, "Japan, Incorporated." To many Japanese this appellation was unsavory, and if the implication was one of unilateral directives from corporate headquarters, it was inaccurate. However, it did usefully convey the thought that Japan's economy was deeply rooted in the national character.

(1) *"Japan, Incorporated."* The dominant roles in "Japan, Incorporated" were played by Japan's political leadership, the administrative bureaucracy, and the business-industrial community. In generating economic decisions, this tripartite establishment could be assisted, as appropriate, by other elements such as academics, research institutes, and labor. The method employed was the tried and true Japanese institution of consensus. Confrontations and sharp disagreements were avoided, but by continual verbal massagings, via committees and informal contacts, decisions would emerge, acceptable to and respected by all interested parties. In an excellent booklet on Japan's government-business relationships, the United States Department of Commerce perceptively labeled this process "participatory partnership."

(2) *Bureaucracy's Powerful Role.* With the inspiration and approval of the political leadership, and in daily consultation with the business community, the powerful Japanese bureaucracy relentlessly moved the economy toward agreed goals. The Economic Planning Agency undertook intensive research and, in full consultation with industry, would produce five- and ten-year projections, along with future priorities. These were general directions to help guide industry toward future growth areas, but they were not detailed production programs. To encourage movement in the desired directions, the Ministry of Finance would manipulate fiscal policies, tax advantages, and, along with the Bank of Japan, commercial credits. The all-important task of "persuasion" and "guidance" of industry to comply with the "vision" was entrusted to MITI (Ministry of International Trade and Industry) with its

manifold resources of carrots and sticks. Other ministries such as Agriculture, Transportation, and Construction might also be involved. On the non-governmental side, "Japan, Incorporated" included, of course, the leadership of the companies, plus an array of business, industry, trade and labor associations, the most influential of which was probably Keidanren (Federation of Economic Organizations), headed by the venerable Kogoro Uemura, often termed "Economic Prime Minister of Japan." The Diet was usually preoccupied with political maneuvering, but it too was melded into "Japan, Incorporated" by means of a continuing dialogue, by committees and individual members, with political and business leaders and the bureaucracy.

(3) Goal No. 1: Healthy Japan Economy. As defined by MITI, Japan's challenge, acutely sensed after World War II, was a threefold one of coping with a surplus population; a scarcity of natural resources, capital and technology; and Japan's "historical peculiarities"—the "seclusive spirit" versus "openness." The need to overcome these problems explained Japan's almost exclusive concentration on rapid economic growth. It also explained the postwar resort to emergency measures, particularly import and investment controls, designed to conserve foreign exchange and ward off balance-of-payment disasters. The policies were eminently successful and the triumph over what MITI termed Japan's three historic enemies was brilliantly achieved. The difficulty was, as once explained to me by MITI Minister Kiichi Miyazawa, that, having grown up during an era when every yen spent abroad was like "giving up a drop of blood," the governing generation of 1971 retained its protectionist instincts and almost reflexively failed to recognize fully the progress made toward the primary goal of a prosperous domestic economy.

(4) Goal No. 2: Export or Perish. Even though Japan's domestic economy was flourishing, with only 10% of the GNP being exported, from the MITI standpoint the

real "nightmare" was that Japan must "export or perish" and it was a "race against the clock" to strengthen its international competitiveness, particularly in the high-productivity sectors. Thus motivated, the government of Japan collaborated with Japanese producers in a vigorous export-promotion program. It featured practices such as subsidies and tax incentives, some of which invited criticism, particularly from those foreign competitors whose operations were governed by a freer play of market forces. But the results were impressive. The teamwork manifested by "Japan, Incorporated" produced an annual 19% export growth.

e. FAVORABLE INTERNATIONAL SETTING. The Japanese economic miracle was significantly facilitated by external factors, not excluding the "Mouse that Roared" principle whereby war-devastated countries are accorded special international sympathy and economic support in their recovery endeavors.

(1) American Assistance. In enlightened self-interest, the United States energetically supported Japan's postwar recovery and its acceptance into the world community. Japan benefited from various forms of American assistance during the occupation, profitable commerce springing from American expenditures in the Korean and Vietnam wars, the American security umbrella in East Asia, and ready access to the enormous American market. Meanwhile, at international fora, such as GATT, the United States pushed Japan's entry, while some other nations were resisting or attaching conditions.

(2) Minimal Burdens. Japan's economic upsurgence was achieved without incurring the encumbrances normal for advanced nations. Its defense expenditures, for example, were only .8% of GNP compared with an 8% figure for the United States. Such circumstances made possible the concentration of Japanese resources on eco-

nomic growth, relatively low taxation (20% of GNP in Japan versus 29% in the United States), the payment of virtually all war reparations by 1971, and for all intents and purposes the nonexistence of a national debt.

(3) Free Trade Environment. With the United States in the forefront of the crusade at GATT and elsewhere, the nations of the postwar world were encouraged to maintain a liberal attitude toward the exchanging of goods and services. During a twenty-year period, the volume of international trade multiplied five times. No nation benefited more handsomely than did Japan.

(4) Technology at Bargain Prices. Its own research and development capabilities interrupted by the war, Japan was able to recover much lost ground by importing technology from abroad, chiefly the United States, at a fraction of its original cost. American businessmen, anxious for participation in Japan's expanding market but frustrated in attempts to invest directly or via joint ventures, often settled for licensing arrangements. In 1970, Japanese royalty and management payments externally totaled $650 million. This was an amount six times the income that foreigners garnered from direct investment in Japan. It was a situation unique in the world.

(5) Available Raw Materials. More powerful than the urge to "export or perish," but not unrelated, was the absolute necessity for Japan to "import or perish." Seventy percent of Japan's imports were raw materials, including 72% of its coal requirements, 85% of its ores, and 99% of its oil. It was said that on the long sea route from the Persian Gulf there was a Japan-bound tanker every 70 miles. With its ability to anticipate the needs of the future, "Japan, Incorporated" was by the early 1970's busily engaged in concluding contracts, usually of a private-barter type, to assure the supply of raw materials for years to come. It may be added that the economics of raw material acquisition had improved markedly with the expansion of Japan's fleet of super-sized commercial ships.

(6) Indulgence of Protectionism. Eager for Japan's postwar recovery, and sensitive to its problems such as the shortage of natural resources, other nations, notably the United States, had after the war accepted as necessary a variety of Japanese protectionist measures designed to conserve foreign exchange and facilitate industrial reconstruction. However, it meant that trade with Japan was not a two-way street. As Japan's prosperity increased, so did foreign irritation at Japanese reluctance to throw away the crutches.

(7) Undervalued Yen. In the contentiousness over Japan's continuing restrictionism, few Americans or Japanese had focused on the anachronistic exchange rate, 360 yen per $1, which had been set in 1949 and which had assured Japanese exports a continuing competitive advantage. One exception was William Blackie, Chairman of the Caterpillar Tractor Company of Peoria, Illinois. At a luncheon hosted by Chase Manhattan's David Rockefeller during Prime Minister Sato's 1970 attendance at the twenty-fifth anniversary of the United Nations, a lively discussion centered on what could be done to remedy Japanese-American commercial frictions, which were obviously reaching alarming proportions. With an instinct for the jugular, Blackie waved aside the bickerings about restrictionism as though the proposed remedies were aspirin tablets, and emphasized that the malady could only grow worse unless major surgery were performed on the unrealistic exchange rate. Such surgery was a major aim of the President's dramatic move on August 15 of the following year.

Although flattered by comments such as those of Herman Kahn that the twenty-first century might well be "the Japanese century," most Japanese were less euphoric. There was pride in their economic miracle, but concern about its imperfections. The driving force of Japanism seemed indestructible, but there were indications that its value system might not be altogether immutable. There was also uneasiness that Japan's glittering postwar economic structure was not without vulnerabilities.

On a number of occasions, Prime Minister Sato referred to Kahn's observations about "the emerging Japanese superstate" and pointed out that, in marveling about Japan's Gross National Product, too many observers were overlooking the existence of large areas of weakness in the Japanese economy. Sato would note that, although Japan was third in the world in GNP, the per capita level of income for this nation of 104,000,000 people ranked only fifteenth.

In the distribution of income, what was often described as a "dual economy" still existed, with substantial disparities between high-wage and low-wage industry sectors. The glamorous, larger, modernized companies were capturing world attention, but twice their number of employees was engaged in the less productive areas of agriculture, services, and the more traditional industries. Even in the more modernized industrial sector, there were inequalities between the treatment received by the regular working force of the major corporations and that accorded the "temporary" and other employees of most of the smaller firms, many of which served as subcontractors for the larger industries and took the brunt of the impact when recessions occurred. A survey in 1965 showed that 52.7% of the households of Japan represented only 25% of the nation's income, while 3.9% represented 16.5% of the total income. The extremes of poverty and wealth were less pronounced than in the United States, but the gap in the "dual economy," which had been narrowed by the war and the occupation, had widened with the rapid economic growth.

Among a good many inefficient economic activities was the Japanese commercial distribution system. In 1968, wholesale sales in Japan were five times greater than retail sales, an important factor being the large number of inter-wholesaler sales. Of Japan's 1.4 million retail outlets, 70% had only one or two employees and only 10% had more than four. The Boston Consulting Group estimated that food and beverage shops, which constituted half the 1.4 million retail outlets, averaged an annual gross income of $2,300 which had to cover all the store owner's expenses, taxes, and the support of his family. By contrast, the take-home pay of a machinist working for a large manufacturing firm could be twice the shopkeeper's net income. Japanese farmers, per household, were relatively affluent, thanks to modern agricultural techniques, government price supports, youngsters moving to the cities, and the fact that most farmers engaged in seasonal supplementary work in factories or construction. The personal welfare of the farmers notwithstanding, the traditional tiny-scale pattern of rice growing was inconsistent with the high productivity goals of the Japanese economy.

Despite its heralded success, Japan's economy had in fact encountered four cyclical economic recessions during the postwar period, one of which was in mid-cycle on August 15, 1971. Featuring a slackening of demand, rising inventories, overcapacity, profit drops, and reduced investment, these recessions were relatively mild and short-lived. Nevertheless, there existed a continuing deep-seated consciousness of a precarious and fragile quality to the Japanese economic structure. Increasingly poignant deficiencies of land, labor, and resources, it was feared, were sure to serve as a brake on Japan's economic development.

The Tokyo Ambassador of an important Asian country was one day bewailing the prospect that because of Japan's economic power, Japanese "hegemony" over most of Asia would be unstoppable. When asked whether he saw no hope for other alternatives, he suggested, wistfully but astutely, that as members of the human race the Japanese conceivably might react to affluence as other mortals normally did, namely, by softening their intensity of purpose. The Ambassador's thesis reflected more than wishful thinking or anthropological considerations. It had economic underpinnings.

In achieving dynamic growth, government and business in Japan had, in MITI's words, performed like two wheels on a cart. It would have been more apt to compare the rate of growth to a motorcycle, inasmuch as rapid forward movement was indispensable to "Japan, Incorporated's" miracle. Once again, success, and particularly the pace of it, stimulated new agonies. Not the least of them was a shortage of labor.

By the early 1970's, the competition in Japan's labor market had become intense. The most immediate effect was the upswing in the wage spiral, with which productivity could not keep abreast. With the demand for their talents and available opportunities increasing, some workers, particularly the young, showed faint signs of restiveness with regard to the conventional work ethic. Was the escalator system sacred? Need loyalty to one's company be unquestioning? Was there not more to life than hard work? Why not higher living standards? It was not surprising that more serious work stoppages began to occur, with the trade unions showing greater interest in social welfare than political issues.

Economists, too, were asking themselves questions: Was continued growth at an 11% clip, or better, realistic? Could an annual 30% return on investment continue? What purpose was served by what MITI described as "blowing more and more air into a balloon, ad infinitum"? With affluence, would Japanese consumption increase, to the detriment of savings and reinvestment rates, thus encouraging "stagflation"? Was the Japanese consensus managerial system capable of quick and bold decisions in times of crisis? Was Japanism flexible enough to adjust to less rapid economic growth?

What was abundantly clear was that the great majority of Japanese, instead of racing along on a motorcycle, wished to ride in a more comfortable four-wheel vehicle. As an affluent society, they felt entitled to the amenities of modern life which they had hitherto denied themselves. Such amenities would include contemporary housing, which because of stratospheric land prices was unavailable to most workers, modern sewage facilities (available to less than 15% of Japanese homes), better schools, utilities, transportation, and highways. Using a Japanese electronic desk calculator, my arithmetic revealed that if the 4,000,000 motor vehicles, produced and remaining in Japan in 1971, were lined up bumper to bumper it would require a road 10,606 miles long. Even allowing 50% for attrition, all four lanes of the 129 miles of expressways, completed in 1970, would be filled bumper to bumper in only 36 days of production. It was no wonder that traffic jams became exasperating, pollution among the world's worst, and urban voters disaffected with the government

By mid-1971, while economic growth was continuing, it no longer monopolized Japanese attention and resources. By popular demand, which politicians would ignore at their peril, attention was directed to the expansion of public works and other programs for improving living conditions. This "social infrastructure" was not without price. Road construction, for example, was extremely costly because exorbitant land costs devoured from 80% to 90% of the government's investment. A new balance in Japanese resource allocations was necessary. All of this was, in effect, a reflection on the Japanese domestic scene of the international phenomenon that the postwar era had come to a close. With top priority economic recovery accomplished, the Japanese citizenry wanted to ease up on the economic accelerator to permit at least some of the enjoyments of travel—comfort, fresh air, new vistas, and a sense of destination.

Inevitably, the continuation of the Japanese miracle was highly vulnerable to international developments. In my initial calls on Prime Minister Sato and his cabinet, questions were anxiously asked about the continued availability of Middle East oil. That area was supplying 85% of Japan's petroleum needs, and energy reqirements were expected to double in five years. If ready access to foreign sources of oil and other raw materials on which Japan was vitally dependent were to be disrupted, the Japanese miracle could overnight turn into calamity. The 1930's provided a chilling reminder of the desperate straits to which the Japanese were once driven.

To a lesser extent, Japan had been dependent on foreign technology via licensing arrangements. It was doubtful that such technology inputs would be as enriching as previously, partly because the cream had already been skimmed off (and often improved by Japanese ingenuity) and partly because of increasing resistance on the part of the suppliers who worried about the boomerang effect on their own companies' interests. In the absence of allowing foreign participation in their ventures, Japanese industries would have to anticipate much larger investments in research and technology. It was estimated that this claim on Japanese resources would increase from $3 billion in 1970 to $13 billion in 1980.

Of greatest consequence, of course, was the absorptive capacity for Japan's products, both at home and abroad. It was difficult to envisage, for example, that Japanese automobile production could continue its meteoric growth of the 1960's. The Japanese market was unlikely to absorb annually many more than the 4,000,000 newly manufactured vehicles which remained in Japan in 1970, and again in 1971. There was also serious doubt that Japan's automobile exports worldwide could for long continue to surge upward at the 1971 rate of 64%. With regard to the total international market, Japan's inroads from a 1% share in 1950 to 6% in

1970 could not be considered limitless. The Europeans, who already had barriers against Japanese goods, were becoming even more resistant. Non-Communist Asia was already taking one-third of Japanese exports. The Communist countries offered unspectacular prospects, whether because of lack of buying power or governmental restrictions. The United States market was Japan's best, and probably would continue to be so, but severe tensions were developing which could seriously impair America's open door policy vis-à-vis Japanese exports.

When the American cabinet delegation, on the occasion of its July 1969 conference (ECONCOM) with its Japanese counterparts, made a ceremonial call on the Emperor, Japan was still entranced by "the small step for man but giant leap for mankind" which had occurred one week earlier. Intrigued by the prospect that Neil Armstrong and his capsule-mates would be bringing back samples from the lunar surface, Emperor Hirohito, encouraged by Japanese officialdom, registered with our cabinet secretaries an appeal that one of the priceless moon rocks be made available the following year for exhibit at Expo 70 in Osaka. Secretary Rogers, spokesman for the delegation, grinned and to the Emperor's amusement observed that at the rate at which our bilateral trade imbalance was growing it might become necessary for the United States to sell the invaluable moon rocks to Japan.

Of all the agonies precipitated by the Japanese economic miracle, none proved more troublesome than the direct impact on Japanese-American trade relationships. In the period from 1950 to 1971, American exports to Japan rose ten-fold, $418 million to $4.1 billion, but Japanese exports to the United States multiplied 41 times, $179 million to $7.3 billion. Until 1965, the trade balance had been favorable to the United States. As late as 1967, the deficit in favor of Japan was moderate. However, in 1968 it jumped to $1.1 billion; in 1969 to $1.4 billion; in 1970 narrowed to $1.2 billion, but in 1971 skyrocketed to $3.2 billion. The $3.2 billion imbalance was in magnitude equivalent to America's global trade deficit in 1971, the first year since 1893 that any trade deficit had been recorded. It was the magnification of the imbalance, at a rate twice that of any previous year, which had triggered the President's international economic measures of August 15, 1971.

Aside from the sheer magnitude of the deficit which American trade with Japan was experiencing, the quality of the imbalance was causing even more alarm in American business and governmental circles. Of the $7.3 billion in Japanese goods exported to the United States in 1971, virtually all of it was directly competitive with American manufactured products, such as steel, electronics, textiles, and automobiles. On the other hand, 67% of America's $4.1 billion exports to Japan was in raw material or agricultural products, including coal, iron ore and scrap, lumber, soybeans, wheat, corn, and cotton. The remaining 33% was primarily capital equipment not manufactured in Japan. Only 3% of Japan's worldwide imports was in consumer goods.

Despite the fact that ninety percent of Japan's GNP was absorbed by the domestic market, economic growth was so rapid and export ingenuity so effective that remarkable export records were being set, particularly with respect to the American market. In 1967, 69,000 Japanese automobiles had entered the American market. By 1970, the number had reached 354,000, and by 1971, 943,000, a staggering 168% increase in one year. Meanwhile, less than 5,000 American motor vehicles were being imported to Japan annually. Japanese steel exports to the United States jumped from $72 million in 1960 to $975 million in 1971. Over $1.6 billion in Japanese electronic equipment went to the United States in 1971, while Japan received about $300 million, primarily advanced computers not manufactured in Japan. Japan's TV exports to the United States jumped from $62 million in 1965 to $327 million in 1971. In brief, the United States was the customer for: three-fourths of Japan's total exports of television receivers, plywood, nails, bolts, nuts, and woven wool products; more than one-half of Japan's exports of footwear, pottery, sound recorders, radios, toys, sporting goods, clothing, and steel items; and only a little less than half its exports of automobiles, sewing machines, cutlery, ball and roller bearings, and motorcycles.

The response to the rising tide of Japanese products in the American market was a crescendo of American displeasure. Loudest outcries, quite understandably, came from those industries most endangered by the rigorous Japanese competition. No less concerned was the United States Government, which was in effect fighting a two-front war domestically: high unemployment, unused productive capacity, and inflation on the one hand; and compulsions toward protectionism and isolationism on the other. Reflecting the upsurge of anxiety was a *Time* magazine cover story in the spring of 1971, entitled "The Japanese Invasion." Japanese readers were stunned by acerbic comments in the article, including some by American businessmen who were well known in Japan, whose companies were doing a quite profitable business in that country, and whose language when in Japan lacked such overtones of hostility. Not a few memories sensed some of the anti-Japanese emotionalism of the Pearl Harbor era.

The essence of the American displeasure was the contention that the competition was unfair. The list of complaints against the Japanese was long: cheap labor, government-business collusion, the protection of so-called "infant industries" which had long since become major world competitors, no antitrust problems, no work stoppage handicaps, no anti-pollution expenses, export subsidies, tax incentives, preferential discounts, dumping, discriminatory freight rates, an array of import quotas, restrictive import deposit system, import duty exemptions for some industries, "Buy Japanese" governmental procurement, discriminatory commodity taxes, other tariff and non-tariff barriers, exploitation of cheap labor via investments in neighboring countries, and, in general, governmental "administrative guidance" based on xenophobic philosophy dating back to the slogans of Meiji days, "Honor the Emperor; expel the barbarians."

To back up the complaints, various trade statistics were cited. It was pointed out, for example, that for a California customer the cost of a Toyota or a Pinto was about the same, about $2,000, but in Japan the retail price of a Pinto was about $5,500, more than double that of a Toyota, due to such factors as assessing customs on the CIF price, slightly higher duties, discriminatory commodity tax schedule, westbound freight rates higher than eastbound, et cetera. America's largest motor vehicle exporter, General Motors, could secure only an infinitesimal .1% of the Japanese automobile market. An $8,000 Cadillac had a $30,000 price tag in Japan. It was said that in 1970 only ten Pintos were imported to Japan, one for each of the motor companies to scrutinize.

Although always congenial, Chairman Joseph Wright of the Zenith Corporation was among the most vocal in his criticisms. In exchanges with the Embassy and in discussions with the Japanese, he stressed the plight confronting the American radio-TV manufacturing industries, noting that 90% of radio receivers (excepting automobile sets) sold in the United States were being produced in foreign countries, as were nearly half the black and white TV sets and a growing proportion of color television receivers. When Assistant Secretary of State for Economic Affairs Philip Trezise delivered an address defending the liberal trade point of view, Wright telegraphed a request for permission to reprint four thousand copies. He explained that he was being forced to discharge four thousand employees from his Chicago factory, and, in sending them termination notices, he wanted to include the reason why!

As American Ambassador in Tokyo, I often felt as though I were on a torture rack. Thousands of Americans were clamoring against the flood of Japanese imports, particularly those affecting their own livelihoods, but at the same time most of those same Americans were merrily purchasing the high-quality Japanese tape recorders, transistor radios, TV sets, cameras, automobiles, et cetera. A vice president of one of America's major motor companies one day observed to me that there was nothing so discouraging as to look out from his office window into the company parking lot and note how many employees were driving foreign-built automobiles.

As the American trade deficit increased, so did tensions with Japan. Bitterness, enkindled by Japanese barriers to trade and investment, imperiled the broad political cooperation which the two countries had so fruitfully cultivated since the war. It tended also to distort the economic panorama, but there were a number of factors which needed to be kept in perspective:

a. RECORD-BREAKING TRANSOCEANIC TRADE. Although overshadowed by the upsurge of Japanese products coming to the United States, American exports to Japan were increasing at a rate considerably higher than our worldwide export growth. Meanwhile, from 1960 to 1971, the Japanese-American bilateral trade volume burgeoned 4½ times, from $2.6 billion to $11.4 billion. Each year new records were being set for transoceanic trade. The United States absorbed 31% of Japan's exports and supplied Japan with nearly the same percentage of its imports. Only Canada was for us a better customer; Japan had none better than the United States. The then MITI Minister, and twice Foreign Minister, Masayoshi Ohira, pointed out at a Japan-America Society luncheon that Japan was transacting more business with California alone than with the Common Market countries combined. Ohira added his gratification for our federal union, for otherwise, he quipped, he would have to cope with fifty American Ambassadors and Secretaries of Commerce.

At a symposium of Japanese and American business leaders sponsored by *Fortune* magazine in September 1971, I referred to the fact that our bilateral trade with Japan was each year reaching unprecedented heights and compared it to driving an automobile: "If the car goes faster down the road, the ride is apt to be more bumpy. But if it's more bumpy, it doesn't mean that we dismantle the automobile or go back to a horse and buggy. It means that we must give our attention to the rough spots in the road, to the necessity for repairing or oiling the machinery."

Particularly to be noted was the importance of Japan to American farmers. By far their best customer for soybeans, wheat, corn, and other products, Japan in 1970 became America's first $1 billion agricultural market (actually $1.2 billion). Shipments to Japan represented one-sixth of our agricultural exports, which in turn represented one-sixth of America's total exports. Having had the good fortune of growing up in Lincoln, Illinois (the only town named for Lincoln before he became President), it was for me a source of pride to encourage Japanese receptivity to the harvests from "the broad green plains that nourish our land." In my youth the prime crop from the rich black soil of central Illinois was corn, but more recently its primacy had been challenged by soybeans. Equally as important as the miracles wrought by America's tillers of the soil was the indispensability of lucrative markets, among which externally Japan was the foremost. The value of Japan's 1971 imports of American soybeans and corn exceeded $500 million. Although these prairies had furnished solid electoral support for the administration, it was not always clear that their interests were adequately taken into account in White House formulation of economic policies vis-à-vis Japan.

b. HAPPY CONSUMERS AND IMPORTERS. American consumers, too, were unmistakably benefiting from Japanese-American trade, but in a different manner. They were able to purchase high-quality products at reasonable prices. Theoretically, foreign imports should impel American industries to be more competitive and efficient, but for many of them the magnitude of the influx was considered to be disruptive. Meanwhile, large corporations such as General Electric and RCA were pragmatically having most of their radio receivers manufactured in Japan and elsewhere abroad, but selling the units in the United States under their own labels. Similarly, the great retailing organizations, such as Montgomery Ward and Sears Roebuck, were stocking their stores with tens of millions of dollars' worth of Japanese goods, most of which bore their own retail nomenclature. A few American firms had advantageously taken root in Japan during occupation days and were faring well. One of the cola companies, for example, was netting $45 million yearly from its Japanese operations. In Tokyo, the Embassy would meet once each month with the Board of Directors of the American Chamber of Commerce in Japan (ACCJ). The purpose was to exchange views with this fine group of compatriots about common problems, particularly the nettlesome one of trade and investment. On more than one occasion, a participant would confide to me afterward that, while he shared the prevalent unhappiness about Japanese restrictionism, his own company was doing very well and it was his hope that the Embassy would not rock the boat.

c. MULTILATERAL CONSIDERATIONS. In assessing Japanese-American trade problems, the picture was not so bleak when viewed in a multilateral, rather than merely a bilateral, context. For example, Japan was 75% dependent on oil as an energy source; 85% of its oil came from the Middle East; and 50% of that was handled by American companies. According to conservative estimates, the United States balance of payments was benefiting by at least one-half billion dollars annually, via profits to the American importing companies and via highly favorable American trade balances with the Middle East nations, which were receiving substantial royalties traceable to Japan. There were also numerous triple plays; for example, Australian raw materials to Japan, Japanese products to the United States, and American products to Australia. American firms usually participated in such trilateral ventures. Also helpful were the Japanese trading companies with their "third country" activities. It was estimated that they were marketing $500 million in American goods to non-Japanese areas. All these various transactions could not, of course, close the $3.2 billion trade gap, but their existence and potentialities were not to be ignored.

d. PROBLEM TRANSCENDED TRADE BARRIERS. The general impression in the United States, particularly in the business community, was that Japanese restrictive practices against American imports were the root cause of our trade deficits with Japan. Restrictions did exist, and some were continuing, despite considerable progress in securing their reduction. The fact was that even if all the items still remaining under import quotas (between forty and fifty in mid-1971) were to be freed, the net effect, according to responsible economists, would be an improvement of not more than $300 to $500 million in the 1971 $3.2 billion imbalance. There were obviously other important contributing factors, not the least of which was the challenge to American competitiveness. As for the Japanese, their restrictive trade practices, as the Embassy repeatedly pointed out, were causing far more irritation than they were worth.

e. DIFFERENT GROUND RULES. Determining what were "fair" and "unfair" Japanese practices was difficult. This was pointed out in the July 1971 report of the President's Commission on International Trade and Investment Policy headed by Albert Williams of the International Business Machines Corporation. "At the heart of the matter," said the Williams report, was "the fact that Japanese economic activity takes place within a political and social system so distinct from our own and from other industrial countries that it is difficult enough to understand Japanese business practices in detail, let alone render valid judgments as to their 'fairness.' " The Japanese admired the American system but felt under no obligation to copy, for example, American work stoppages or the application of American antitrust laws. On the other hand, the international community had sought via GATT and elsewhere to establish a code for international commercial conduct. Insofar as Japan's import quotas and other practices were in direct violation, they were indefensible. But among the complaints lodged by American businessmen were many gray areas. It was in areas such as these where the Americans cried "foul" and where the Japanese resented what MITI called American "lectures."

f. CONSENSUS TAKES TIME. While the Japanese "consensus" decision-making process possessed striking advantages in securing purposeful communal action, it also had its drawbacks, notably in deferring action sometimes to the point of near-paralysis. The Japanese-American trade imbalance had not become serious until 1967. On an issue with such widespread impact, it was not surprising that it would take "Japan, Incorporated" two or three years to generate an awareness of the problem, and a similar time span to undertake decisive action. After the President's August 15, 1971, announcement, Japan absorbed heavy financial losses for several months before effective remedial measures were actually taken. As late as March 1972, Finance Minister Mikio Mizuta was writing publicly of the need for a "national consensus" that would allow the Japanese "nation which has become the largest holder of foreign exchange reserves" to comport itself, with respect to international monetary reforms, as "a country that has matured and grown in stature."

g. INCREMENTAL PROGRESS: "MILLIMETERS PER DECADE." It was almost axiomatic that, pursuant to the consensual system, governmental progress in Japan, whether in the trade field or elsewhere, would normally occur in bits and pieces rather than in bold sweeps. The name of the game was to educate the people, avoid provoking serious controversy, and deprive the opposition of ammunition. What this meant was that innumerable judicious steps were in fact taken, as in the trade liberalization field, but without securing the desired impact or appreciation in public opinion outside Japan. In grappling daily with our economic problems, a new unit of measurement occurred to me: "millimeters per decade." Cumulative progress was indeed being made in removing trade barriers, in fact at a geometric rate, but the units seemed only to be millimeters per decade. To gain true appreciation of the achievement, it was necessary to compare the state of affairs of one, two, or five years earlier. What was important was that movement was taking place, and at a constantly accelerating pace.

h. EXHORTATIONS OF LIMITED VALUE. Unfortunately, the gap between Tokyo's trade and investment liberalization and Washington's impatience grew wider. A virtual parade of American VIPs, official and self-appointed, arrived in Japan to plead, appeal, cajole, exhort, and threaten. Their Japanese listeners, with traditional politeness, would readily acknowledge the problems, express a desire to effect remedies, but, when it came to action, the "millimeters per decade" prevailed. The Japanese press, with its nationalistic tendencies, seldom allowed the American side of the story to be told, but would report American exhortations in terms of "pressure" and "high-handed demands," with overtones of an American "occupation mentality." Under the circumstances, the progress actually achieved was quite remarkable.

Needless to say, the Embassy, with or without instructions, lost no opportunity to seek Japanese understanding and cooperation. Carefully chosen public rostra included the Japan-America Society shortly after my arrival, the prestigious Research Institute of Japan with the Prime Minister and most of the cabinet present, the World Trade Center, the Japanese Press Club on the subject "The Mills Bill in Perspective," International House, et cetera. The common theme was the importance of reciprocity if the trade relationships between our two countries were to continue to flourish and if the international trading system, so advantageous to Japan, were to remain viable. These public expositions were made with sincerity and frankness. In urging more of a "two-way street," I stated in my September 1969 Research Institute speech, "The United States cannot tolerate unendingly a trade deficit with Japan soaring into the billions of dollars." Such straightforward remarks caused some concern among the State Department's politically-minded Japan hands, and, at the same time, invited comments such as those of *Asahi* that Japan's "tendency to depend on a certain 'softness' and 'special consideration' in the American attitude" had been a "characteristic feature of Japanese-American relations since the war," but Ambassador U. Alexis Johnson and I had "set the new tone of frank, straight talking with Japan" and shifted the emphasis from "explaining Japan to Washington to explaining the United States to Tokyo." Indications from White House and Department of Commerce sources, however, sought to give the impression that our economic woes with Japan were, at least in part, the Embassy's fault for not thumping tables hard enough. Thus our endeavors were caught in somewhat of a crossfire, but we pressed on, operating on the basic premise that while selected public discussions were valuable contributions educationally, the resolution of differences was more apt to be achieved by effective diplomacy than by vitriolic verbal outbursts.

With reference to the foregoing, Masaru Ogawa, editor of *The Japan Times* and knowledgeable observer of the Tokyo political scene, took the occasion of my departure and the appointment of a prominent American businessman as my successor to comment, "There is some feeling of trepidation in Japanese circles that the United States may take an even stronger stand on economic matters than before. Contrary to rumors purportedly emanating from Washington, they had found Ambassador Meyer to be exceedingly 'tough,' emphasizing at every opportunity the imbalance of trade between the two nations and arming himself with charts to prove his point. How much 'tougher' can the new Ambassador be?"

i. AMERICA'S LACK OF STONE-CASTING CREDENTIALS. In championing idealistic international economic doctrines, our American practices did not always live up to our preaching. At a meeting in Geneva in October 1969, when American experts tabled a catalogue of seventeen irritating Japanese non-tariff trade barriers, the Japanese responded with a list of twenty-one alleged American economic mal-practices—"Buy American" procurement, overzealous im-plementation of anti-dumping and countervailing duty laws, and a variety of import specifications designed to keep out foreign agricultural and industrial products. It was true that the United States itself was engaging in export subsidies, as on farm products, and invoking import controls, as on beef and dairy products. Furthermore, from personal experience, I knew how the Shah of Iran and other Middle Eastern producers were irked by our tight controls on petroleum imports (a policy which was to take an ironic switch later). While the Japanese from 1963 to 1972 were reducing their number of items under import quotas from one hundred and thirty to thirty-three, the number of items under American import controls rose from seven to sev-enty. Probably even more irksome was our forcing other nations to institute export restraints, euphemistically termed "voluntary controls," on such broad sectors as steel, textiles, apparel, ceramic products, and stainless-steel flatware.

Our European allies, accepting only 6% of Japan's ex-ports, aggravated our problems. By discriminatorily re-stricting seventy-three specific categories of Japanese imports, the member nations of the European Economic Community in effect accentuated Japanese competitive pressures on the United States. Their practices were based on concessions which they had extracted in return for approving Japan's admission to GATT. Under the circum-stances, not particularly welcome or praiseworthy was the vociferous support which our European friends accorded the Japanese in opposing American requests for "voluntary controls" on exports already restricted in Europe, such as synthetic textiles.

j. THE UNWISDOM OF PROTECTIONISM. Understandably resentful that trade with Japan in competitive industrial products was virtually a one-way street, frustrated American businessmen and their Congressional representatives turned in desperation to thoughts of protectionism. That was not their preference, and it had been contrary to United States Government policy since the mid-1930's. Few Congressmen, however, could ignore growing unemployment problems in their districts and allegations by the influential textile lobby and others that foreign imports, notably from Japan, were responsible. After many delays and much reluctance, the Ways and Means Committee of the House of Representatives in mid-1970 reported out legislation which would set quotas for the importation of textiles and shoes. The prospect was that there would be many additions, that the bill would become a "Christmas tree" if and when it would be taken up in full session. "Once you open the gate," the Committee's astute and powerful Chairman Wilbur Mills told me, "they will break the fence down."

Most Americans who in the early 1970's were proposing restrictions on trade, investment, and the flow of technology realized that economic tribalism was the wrong road. Aside from such retaliatory actions as Japanese cutbacks on $1.2 billion in American agricultural imports, a retreat to protectionism would ultimately mean a less competitive and less productive American economy. Apparently, some of the proponents hoped that the mere threat of protectionism would intimidate the Japanese, but the latter had great confidence that America would not legislate against its own best interests. The quota bill died on Capitol Hill, but one could not rule out a battering of the fences if the economic situation became more critical and if

our legislators were put to the test by a vote for the
record.

Telescoping the 1969–1972 period, the cumulative results
of Japan's incremental progress in resolving international
trade issues were quite substantial. The progress was not
always readily apparent or fully appreciated, but the fact
was that the Japanese were moving.

a. YEN REVALUATION. The move of greatest consequence
was the revaluation of the yen. The rate of 360 yen per
dollar, set in 1949, simply was not realistic in the 1970's. By
sustaining Japan's strong competitive advantage in world
markets, it was a key factor in Japan's mounting trade and
payments surpluses, with a 1970 trade balance of $4 billion
rising to $7.8 billion in 1971. In the first nine months of
1971, Japan's balance of payments recorded an overall surplus of $7 billion, and reserves by the end of the year
reached $15.2 billion (exceeding the United States total,
including the value of the gold in Fort Knox). It should be
noted, incidentally, that at no time did the Japanese try to
raid our gold reserves. On the contrary, they had taken a
number of quiet measures designed to keep the dollar
strong.

Nations in chronic surplus have a responsibility no less
than those in chronic deficit to take corrective actions, but
being rich is less uncomfortable. Politically and psychologically, there was an instinctive Japanese resistance
against tampering with the fixed parity system which had
served Japan so well. Like Tokyo, Washington danced
around the yen revaluation issue, taking the position, publicly and privately, that it was a matter for Japanese decision. When during a Tokyo visit Assistant Secretary of
State Philip Trezise vaguely suggested that the yen appeared to be undervalued, he caused a stir in Japan, but
the Washington reaction seemed to be one of embarrass-

ment and irritation. Thus the Japanese were somewhat miffed when it became clear that a major aim of the President's August 15 announcement was currency realignment. They had had no previous official indication of the seriousness of this American desire. A redeeming feature was that the President's objective was worldwide monetary reform, not just the revaluation of the yen.

The December 1971 Smithsonian agreement, described by President Nixon "as the most significant monetary agreement in the history of the world," featured a 16.88% revaluation of the yen along with an 8.57% devaluation of the dollar. Japan's Foreign Minister Takeo Fukuda publicly bemoaned Japan's "greatest economic shock since the war," and Finance Minister Mikio Mizuta would "never forget as long as I live the atmosphere of extreme tension and pathos that prevailed." Nonetheless, Fukuda, Mizuta and Prime Minister Sato were gratified to have "uneasy feelings" eliminated. There was an atmosphere of gloom and doom in Tokyo, but Japan's highly favorable trade balances continued month after month with only minor declines. Raw materials were less expensive, but retail prices in Japan for foreign manfactured goods remained unchanged. Japan's trade surplus continued throughout 1972, and the bilateral imbalance with the United States hit a record $4.1 billion. Everyone agreed that a time lag was inevitable before the yen revaluation would take full effect, but impatience prevailed. A second revaluation was instituted before a turnaround was noted, with the prospect of a $2 billion deficit in 1973. Meanwhile, the Japanese economy was manifesting a resilience more than equal in magnitude to the fearfulness of those who did not realize their own strength.

b. TRADE LIBERALIZATION. At the time of my arrival in Japan in mid-1969, there were, according to OECD definitions, 120 categories of imports under quota restrictions. By mid-1970, the number had been reduced to 90; by

January 1971 to 80; by June to 60; by October, in accordance with plans which Foreign Minister Aichi had affirmed
to us prior to the President's August 15 announcement, the
number was reduced to 40; and by the time of my departure
at the end of March 1972 the number was down to 33, a
figure below that for European nations or even our own. In
chopping away at the Import Quota system, Prime Minister
Sato and his colleagues had to undo two and a half decades
of accepted practice. When Phil Trezise during an October
1969 visit reported how discouraging he had found his talks
with Japanese officials, Aichi insisted Trezise could return
to Washington with a "happy face." Despite press criticism
about "bowing to United States pressure," Sato and Aichi
were at that very moment prevailing on the cabinet to cut
in half the number of Import Quotas before the end of
1971. In point of fact, they did much better—from 120 to
under 40.

One of the hottest issues was "the grapefruit war." On
the one side were the citrus growers of California and
Florida, with our Agricultural Attaché Elmer Hallowell and
the rest of us at the Embassy pressing their cause. On the
other side were Japan's "mikan" (like a tangerine) growers
with the Japanese Ministry of Agriculture as their staunch
ally. The Prime Minister was in the middle, for the mikan
growing center was in his Yamaguchi constituency. After
several delays and much reluctance, the Japanese government removed grapefruit from the quota list but at the
same time legislated a seasonal tariff of 40% for imports
from December through March (America's growing sea-
son). Our citrus growers were undaunted. In the one month
of November 1971, more American grapefruit were sold in
Japan than during the entire preceding year.

Other significant Japanese trade liberalization moves
during the 1969–1972 period included: advancing by nine
months Kennedy round tariff reductions (Japanese tariffs
on dutiable goods averaged 10.7%, not much higher than
the American level of 8.3%); abolition of the restrictive

"import deposit" requirements and "Automatic Import Quota" licensing systems; relaxation of "standard method of payment" procedures; reduction of preferential rates for discounting export accounts; increased supply of yen for import financing; reduction of commodity taxes on automobiles; expanded quotas for the importation of beef, oranges, and other agricultural products; lowered tariffs on a variety of items such as automobiles (from 17.5% to 10%), machine tools, X-ray and color films, turkey meat, and soybeans.

Besides the seasonal grapefruit tariff, there were numerous other instances where items would be removed from the Import Quota list but simultaneously heavy duties would be imposed. One particularly annoying case, of concern to Senator Henry Bellmon and Oklahomans, was the imposition of a $135 per head tax on the importation of feeder calves. Prime Minister Sato, to whose attention I brought these matters, agreed that it made no sense to take items off the quota list only to attach prohibitive tariffs. Instead of such shenanigans, Sato said he favored the initiation of a new round of tariff reduction negotiations which, he hoped, would be called the "Japan Round."

Also on the negative side was the fact that most of the thirty-three categories which still remained under import control as of the end of March 1972 were of avid interest to American suppliers—computers, integrated circuits, and fruit juices. Much of our hope for reducing our trade deficit centered on the increased export of high technology products such as computers. But in response to entreaties by Economic Minister Lester Edmond and myself, MITI Minister Kiichi Miyazawa expressed doubt that computers would ever be decontrolled. The Japanese conviction, he said, was that he who controls the computers controls the country. Nonetheless, there was an insatiable Japanese interest in American computer technology, and reluctant agreement to the importation of peripheral computer equipment, as well as advanced computers not manufactured in Japan. Irritating to Americans was Japanese insistence that computers produced by International Business Machines in Japan be considered as "imports." IBM, whose manufacturing in Japan had been authorized in 1960 in return for licensing its patents to thirteen potential Japanese producers, was doing quite well, but its percentage of total Japanese production was only 30% compared with 70% in the early 1960's. Its exports were by far Japan's largest for computers, and its contributions to Japan's computer technology were inestimable.

The reduction in tariffs and commodity taxes cut by 25% the sales price of American automobiles in Japan. This fact, plus factors such as the "snob appeal" of imported products, improved our export prospects. However, due to other reasons, such as the substantially lower manufacturing costs for Japanese vehicles, the undervalued yen, and freight discrepancies (Toyota, for example, had its own special car-carrying transport ships), the cost of an American compact was still nearly double that of its Japanese equivalent. This underscored the point that United States-Japanese trade problems were more complex than quota restrictions alone.

Tourism was a notable success. Foreign-exchange allowances for Japanese travelers were raised first to $1,000 and then to $3,000. Incredible as it may seem, Japan by the end of 1971 had surpassed Great Britain as the supplier of the most visitors to our shores. Highlighting the Embassy's weekly "Country Team" meetings were the reports by Consul General Ron Gaiduk of new records being set in visas issued, despite staff reductions. Curious and group conscious as they were, the Japanese came, in Shakespeare's words, "not single spies but in battalions." One could, as I did, encounter a contingent of forty Japanese butchers in transit at Denver airport, or a score or more of Japanese metalworkers at Henry Ford's Greenfield Village, the latter group somewhat disappointed that our major automotive companies did not expose all their production procedures to the incessantly clicking Japanese cameras. (The late Ambassador Adlai Stevenson classified Japan as a photocracy!)

c. "VOLUNTARY" RESTRAINTS. The tide of Japanese exports to the United States being what it was, few Americans in 1971 appreciated that 32% of those exports (seventy specific items) were being limited by export quotas enforced by the Japanese themselves. These restraints were pursuant to so-called "voluntary" agreements negotiated by the United States Government under the tacit threat that failure to do so would result in more severe mandatory American import quotas.

An agreement on steel exports, negotiated in 1968, had proved reasonably effective in limiting the growth of Japanese steel imports in the United States to 5% per year. Not surprisingly, some Japanese steel makers shifted their emphasis to the more profitable higher-grade steel products, while still keeping within the tonnage quotas. Similarly, there was a concentration on the more accessible West Coast markets. These weaknesses, which nettled American steel executives, were remedied in a new agreement negotiated in early 1972. Without these "voluntary restraints," there was little doubt that the Japanese, because of their cheaper prices for quality products, could have caused serious disruption to the American steel industry.

Early in the 1960's, at the initiative of the Kennedy administration, the United States, Japan, and other countries had concluded a Long-Term Cotton Textile Agreement (LTA) which protected the United States from a disruptive growth of cotton textile imports. In the mid-sixties, production worldwide shifted heavily away from cottons to synthetic fibers, not covered by the LTA. Our struggle, beginning in 1969, to achieve a "voluntary" agreement with Japan to restrict the export growth of synthetic fabrics and apparel became such a cause cèlébre, so disproportionately affecting the Japan–United States relationship, that the whole affair deserves special attention. The story is recounted in the chapter which follows.

Aside from "voluntary restraints" attained via governmental auspices, some self-enlightened Japanese manufacturers themselves recognized the wisdom of not overloading the American import circuit. Two major automobile firms, for example, suspended temporarily the allocation of new dealerships in the United States. They obviously realized that the more than doubling of Japanese motor vehicle exports to the United States in 1971 was excessive, and wisely decided to be less provocative vis-à-vis an already bruised Detroit. With an assist from the yen revaluation, Japanese auto makers during the first half of 1972 increased their shipments to the United States by only 44%.

Somewhat embarrassed by the ease with which Japan seemed to be out-producing and out-competing industries elsewhere, Japanese government officials were giving serious thought to a unilateral across-the-board voluntary export-restraint program. They called it "orderly marketing." As it was explained by MITI Minister Kiichi Miyazawa to George Shultz, then Director of the Office of Management and Budget, and John Ehrlichman, Director of the White House Domestic Council, during their September 1970 visit, the objective would be to avoid the disruption of foreign markets by imposing automatic restrictions if and when the export of a commodity to a foreign country exceeded a modest growth rate, e.g., 15% to 20%. By mid-1972, the concept was still being discussed, but was overshadowed by the August 15, 1971, aftermath.

As was pointed out in the Williams report, all "voluntary restraint" and "orderly marketing" programs are fundamentally restrictionist, to be employed only as temporary measures. In addition to causing irritations, as they did with Japan, by placing the onus for the protectionism on the wrong party, such measures if prolonged could provide pretexts for countries like Japan to retain import controls and could, in general, cause serious damage to the entire structure of freer trade.

d. INVESTMENT LIBERALIZATION. During my Ambassadorship to Lebanon, oil-rich sheikhs from the Persian Gulf area were lustily buying up hotels, large percentages of business ventures, villas, and other valuable real estate. When my good friend Foreign Minister George Hakim was asked whether he was worried by the prospect that wealthy outsiders might buy up the whole country, he smiled and said, "They can't carry it away."

Endemically, there was no such equanimity in Japan. In explaining Japanese aversion to direct investment by foreigners, MITI's Naohiro Amaya as recently as 1973 stressed that, while he hoped the "defect" would be overcome, xenophobia in Japan "is a fact that exists even today." The United States, he said, was "disregarding such delicate sentiments of the Japanese people" in "demanding the liberalization of capital completely and without delay." Urging that the problem be "understood as an historical process of contact and fusion between two different nations or two different cultures," Amaya observed that "a one-sided, direct, and high-handed approach as the north wind trying to strip a traveler of his mantle will little serve the purpose of improving international relations."

Given the almost congenital instinct to "be on guard against Westerners," which was reinforced by chronic postwar payments deficits, it was no mean feat when in 1967 the Japanese government launched a bold four-stage capital-liberalization program. The time schedule was subsequently accelerated and the final stage completed in August 1971, almost coincidental with the President's announcement. During the four-year period, 228 industries had been opened up for 100% foreign investment, more than 500 for 50%, and only 7 areas were retained on a "negative list."

Among those not qualifying for automatic approval, were nuclear and defense-related industries (including computers), agriculture, mining, real estate, and public utilities.

Despite those welcome statistics, American direct investment in Japan did not increase substantially. The cumulative total remained well under $2 billion and under 2% of total American foreign investment. For most American investors, preoccupied with the vast American market, a special effort was required, one not particularly attractive. It involved coping with Japanese xenophobia, the labyrinth of red tape, seemingly interminable negotiations, consensus decision-making, Japan's unique labor-management practices, and the archaic Japanese distribution system. Moreover, the opening of the doors to 50% and 100% investment applied only to new industrial ventures in Japan. For established enterprises, without special dispensation there could be no more than 25% foreign equity, and no individual shareholder could own more than 10%. Obviously, MITI was worried about the vulnerability of Japan's high debt/equity corporate structure to "takeovers" by foreign capital. Given the uniqueness of the way of doing business in Japan, any American or other foreign investor would, in my judgment, be foolish not to seek a Japanese partner. But it was the apparent coercion to do so that was not welcomed by foreign investors.

Making the required special effort and securing the required special dispensation were the American motor companies, in what turned out to be a dramatic investment breakthrough. For several years, Japan's two major automakers, Toyota and Nissan (Datsun), as well as MITI, opposed Japanese-American joint automotive ventures. Three of the weaker Japanese companies, for their part, resisted being forced into mergers with the Japanese majors. Refusing foreign investment on grounds of protecting an "infant industry" no longer made sense in a country whose total production was second in the world and was doubling every three years, and whose exports to the United States were doubling yearly. By 1971, therefore, MITI reluctantly approved an agreement which the Chrysler Corporation had reached with Mitsubishi Heavy Industries (MHI) for an eventual 35% ownership of MHI's motor vehicle company. Mitsubishi gained needed capital strength plus an American marketing outlet for its "Colt." A short time later, Chairman James Roche secured approval for a similar General Motors tie-up with Isuzu, a company specializing in truck production. Henry Ford II negotiated intensively with Toyo Kogyo, the Mazda producer at Hiroshima, but difficulties developed in the negotiations. While joint ventures of these types were not greeted with enthusiasm by American labor leaders, the American manufacturers argued that it was a choice of either "getting a piece of the action" in Japan's booming market and in East Asia, where the Japanese had marketing advantages, or being left out in the cold.

During visits to Japan in January 1969 and May 1971, Senator Jacob Javits of New York impressed upon Japan's top officials how it was in Japan's interest to step up its liberalization of trade and investment, including outward financial flows both to the developing countries and to the United States. Citing his own credentials as a free-trade advocate, he noted that Congress was in a protectionist mood and ready, if our economic situation got worse, to shake the international trade structure. During one session with MITI Minister Miyazawa, the latter disclosed with some pride that Japan had recently raised the ceiling for direct investment abroad to $300,000. The Senator replied that that sum would not finance six hamburger stands in California. A short time later the Japanese foreign investment limitation went up to $1,000,000, and when in late 1971 Japan's foreign-exchange reserves reached mountainous proportions, the investment outflow ceiling became virtually unlimited. Particularly welcome were enlightened moves such as that by Sony's Akio Morita in establishing a television-manufacturing plant in San Diego. Meanwhile, a task force of Japanese and American businessmen was studying how joint investments from the two countries could be better organized for the benefit of the developing nations.

There were other long-sought developments in the capital-liberalization field which came to fruition in 1971. For the first time, foreign securities were approved for sale in Japan. Various foreign-exchange restrictions were eased, such as sending remittances abroad. Approval was given for the purchase of real estate in foreign countries. The first foreign bond issue was authorized. The limits on the magnitude of loans which could be extended by Japanese branch banks abroad were removed. After considerable tension caused by the prospect that California, complaining of a lack of reciprocity, was taking steps against Japanese banks (which were doing better than other banks in that state), greater hospitality was accorded American banking activities in Japan. Two new United States branch banks were, for example, given authorization to operate in Tokyo. The incremental progress was accelerating at an exponential rate. But every millimeter required patient endeavor, and the progress was by no means complete.

e. EXPANDING JAPANESE FOREIGN AID. Neither Japan, nor its friends or rivals, were eager to see the Japanese economic juggernaut become armor-clad. At the same time, a nation with such power could not escape responsibility for the furtherance of a safer and more prosperous world community. Obviously, its contribution could best be made through assistance to what was formerly called the "underdeveloped" world. It was a challenge which the Japanese government and people accepted for two reasons: short-term benefits in terms of markets and access to raw materials, and a long-term desire for a sound world economy as a requisite for peace. As Foreign Minister Aichi observed in October 1970, "To dream of long-term prosperity for our country while being isolated from other countries is like climbing a tree to find a fish."

At a May 1970 OECD meeting and subsequently at a Ministerial meeting of the Southeast Asia Development Conference, the Japanese publicly committed themselves to a foreign aid target of 1% of GNP by 1975. That goal had been recommended by a special World Bank committee and by OECD. By 1970, Japan had already attained a .93% of GNP figure, which exceeded the American percentage for foreign economic aid (our military outlays, of course, were a heavier drain). The problem with Japan's increasing financial flows to the developing countries was that they tended to be in the form of hard-term private investment and export credits. Since the American GNP was much larger, and two-thirds of American aid was "concessional" as against one-third for Japan, the Japanese in actuality were providing, despite the percentage of GNP figure, only one-seventh as much non-commercial assistance (government grants, technical assistance, and soft-term loans) as was the United States. Nonetheless, Japanese "economic cooperation" was improving. In volume, the outlays had risen from $600 million (.62% of GNP) in 1966 to $1.8 billion (.93% of GNP) in 1970. In quality, "concessional" aid, or what was termed in Japan as "official development assistance," had doubled in two years to reach an $800 million level in 1971. Loans at 3% interest, with seven-year grace and twenty-five-year repayment periods, were being extended to Korea, Indonesia, and other East Asian neighbors. Additionally, recognizing that multilateral aid can have advantages, Japan was gradually increasing its support for international lending institutions such as the Asian Development Bank.

Southeast Asia, which was providing a market for one-fourth of Japan's exports, was the logical area of greatest opportunity for Japanese assistance. Japanese reparations payments had been helpful but they were nearing completion. The United States, with enormous security expenditures and extensive economic aid, had borne too heavy a burden in that area for too long. Prime Minister Sato himself expressed concern about the economic insecurity which was likely to result from the American withdrawal from Indo-China. The Japanese, therefore, intensified their plans for "economic cooperation" with both Saigon and Hanoi among others, and United States officials never ceased to provide encouragement. The subject was included in discussions by the President, Secretary Rogers and other cabinet members, East Asian USAID coordinator Rod O'Connor along with a stream of other Washington officials, and, of course, the Embassy in Tokyo.

The expansion of Japan's foreign-assistance operations in Southeast Asia unquestionably helped the development of the region, but the successes were not without some agonies. Although equity investment was being extended and was increasing, Japanese financial flows, whether governmental or non-governmental, tended more often to be in the form of export credits. For any given project, the host country would agree to purchase from Japanese companies the construction materials, the machinery, the technology, and the spare parts, and to effect repayment as circumstances warranted in products, notably natural resources. Outward "indirect investment" of this kind benefited Japan in several ways. It was a convenient mechanism for assuring the long-term supply of raw materials. The Japanese non-equity role was less visible politically, and disengagement was easier in times of crisis. In projects for the processing of raw materials such as oil and aluminum as well as in low-productivity consumer goods industries, the Japanese could take advantage of cheaper labor, and also, in effect, "export pollution." Multifaceted operations of this type were tailor-made for Japan's giant trading companies. However, as Japan's economy boomed and its "economic cooperation" expanded, the dependence of the Southeast Asian nations on Japan both for exports and imports increased, while Japan's dependence on them became a smaller percentage of Japan's worldwide exports and imports. Indonesia was exporting 80% of its oil to Japan, but that represented less than 10% of Japanese oil imports. While a $3.2 billion trade deficit with Japan was causing America so much difficulty, the weaker nations of Southeast Asia were in 1971 experiencing a $2.2 billion deficit with Japan. What all this meant was that Japan was becoming increasingly vulnerable to allegations of "creeping economic domination" of the region.

In several ways, the Japanese foreign-aid experience paralleled that of the United States. On the home front, there was a lack of enthusiasm and a need to demonstrate the effectiveness of the program in terms of direct Japanese interest. Among the recipient countries, there was the desire for help but resentment against the helpers. Stories were heard to the effect that the Japanese were joining the Yankees as targets for "go home" slogans, particularly because of the heavy commercial accent to Japan's assistance, the presence abroad of Japanese in increasing numbers, and their tendencies toward clannishness. The challenge facing the Japanese in the conduct of their assistance programs was, as declared by Aichi, the development of a spirit of "partnership." During a visit to Taipei, the Acting Foreign Minister of the Republic of China quoted to me the proverb, "To lead, one must learn to follow." His point was that, in exercising their destined role in regional affairs, the Japanese would need to perform what was for them the difficult task of placing themselves in the other fellow's shoes. Only by truly understanding the feelings and aspirations of its poorer neighbors, and adjusting its assistance accordingly, would Japan be able to achieve optimal results from its "economic cooperation."

f. MORE REALISTIC JAPANESE GROWTH. Although the Japanese economy continued to grow in 1970 at an annual rate of 11% (18% in nominal terms), what had begun in the fall of 1970 as an inventory adjustment with limited effects on the economy had by mid-1971 turned into a down-phase of a medium-term investment cycle, mostly in manufacturing. Investment in private plant and equipment, which had been increasing consistently at an annual rate of more than 20%, dropped in 1971 to 3.2%. Many observers believed that the President's August 15 "shock" gave further impetus to this investment slowdown and, in any case, helped to prolong it. Ironically, it was the Japanese recession which contributed to Japan's burgeoning trade surpluses, which in turn had been responsible, at least in part, for the drastic American action. Japanese exports were continuing to increase at their 20%+ pace, but, due to the slowdown, imports had fallen back to only a 5% increase. Although many sectors of the economy continued their strong expansion, the cumulative effect of the slackening of investment in plant and equipment reduced Japan's overall growth rate in 1971 to 6% in real terms (11% nominally).

Expansionary fiscal policies, employed by the government of Japan to deal with the investment turndown, coincided in mid-1971 with what MITI described as a "drastic turn from the slogan of expansion of production capacity and promotion of exports to the slogan of concentration on social capital and social welfare." Shaken by electoral reverses in the metropolitan centers, and under strong international pressures, the LDP government realized that the time had come for a basic realignment of the Japanese economic system. Instead of almost exclusive preoccupation with a high rate of economic growth, the new pattern of investment, with a larger role for the public sector, would include as a primary goal what the powerful Industrial Structure Council defined as ensuring "a humanly rich life for every Japanese." Not surprisingly, the initial emphasis was on stimulating business recovery, particularly for the small and medium-sized industries, which had previously been treated rather cavalierly. But the government's fiscal outlays, in tandem with the resources of the private sector, were by late 1971 broadened to encompass assistance designed to improve the living standards of the whole society —construction of housing units numbering in the millions, regionalization and decentralization of governmental services, organizing optimum land utilization, improving woefully inadequate sanitation facilities, expanding the transportation system and making it more efficient, relieving the vexatious automobile congestion countrywide, increasing the effectiveness of secondary education by quadrupling resources during the coming decade, moving toward a five-day week, and instituting good health care and old-age security programs.

Well up on the list of priorities was the quality of the environment. Sato often referred to GNP as "Gross National Pollution." According to a report in one of the major newspapers, the death rate in Tokyo on days of high pollution was three times that on clearer days. For no city in the world was this a more serious problem. Similarly, the coastal waters were heavily contaminated. Flying from Nagoya out over Ise Bay in a MU-2 with MHI's Chairman Yoichiro Makita, the coastal waters near Yokkaichi were observed to be blood red from the refuse of a chain of petrochemical companies. A week or two later, the press reported most of the fish in those waters were dead. Recognizing pollution to be as major a problem for Japan as it was for us, I spent two highly profitable days in Pittsburgh during my first visit home, with a view to being able to speak with firsthand knowledge of what could be done to clean up an environment. At the Embassy's suggestion, Chairman Russell Train of our Council on Environmental Quality visited Japan, as did Special Assistant to the Secretary of State for environmental matters Christian Herter. Minister Sadanori Yamanaka, who had been chosen by Prime Minister Sato to coordinate Japanese environmental endeavors, visited Washington, and agreements were signed for cooperation between our two countries in meeting the environmental challenge. Japan established its own Environmental Protection Agency, but its work was concentrated primarily on protection of places of scenic beauty and natural resources. The problem for Japan, as with the United States, was that, like Mark Twain's weather, it was easier to talk about the "quality of life" than to secure effective action. Nevertheless, Japan's new economic policy envisaged that at least 7% of all industrial investments during the coming decade would be allocated to environmental protection.

Thus, Japan was undergoing a major reallocation of resources. The "social infrastructure" would not be inexpensive, but it would signify an essential Japanese adjustment away from the postwar fixation on "GNPism" toward the realities of a mature and modern society. Of interest to foreign nations, notably the United States, the realignment should stimulate imports to Japan, offering opportunities to foreign suppliers in such fields as modular housing, interior furnishings for homes, heating and air-conditioning equipment, office machines, sporting and other leisure-time equipment, pollution-control equipment, et cetera. In 1971 alone, the Japanese government increased its fiscal outlays for social capital by at least 40%, including its Fiscal Loan and Investment Program, which funded public works projects. Over a ten-year period, government allocations for these purposes were to be four times what they had been in the 1960's. Pursuant to this rearrangement of priorities, plans called for a more realistic GNP growth, to a rate reduced to about 8% annually.

As a matter of historical record, it should be noted that more than two months before President Nixon's announcement of August 15, 1971, the Japanese government had already made a basic decision to take what it considered to be important steps to ameliorate the fast-evolving international economic crisis. On June 6, the Sato cabinet had approved an "Eight Point Program," the components of which were: 1) accelerated liberalization of imports; 2) trading preferences for imports from the Less Developed Countries (LDCs) ; 3) further tariff reductions; 4) capital liberalization; 5) reduction of non-tariff barriers; 6) expanded foreign aid; 7) consideration of an "orderly marketing" program so that Japanese exports would stop short of disrupting other nations' economies; and 8) "flexible" fiscal and monetary policies, including massive government support for what amounted to a New Deal for Japan's hardworking populace.

Growing anti-Japanese sentiment in the United States had for many months been of deep concern to Tokyo. It had shocked Finance Minister Fukuda two years earlier during his attendance at a World Bank meeting in Washington. As our trade imbalance increased, and particularly when it took an alarming turn in early 1971, the Sato government knew that drastic steps were required. The Emperor himself became concerned, an anxiety which, incidentally, prompted his personally taking the initiative to send a congratulatory message to President Nixon on the occasion of the successful Apollo 14 mission in February. In early May, when *Time* magazine published its blast about "The Japanese Invasion," the occasion was taken to hand to a high Foreign Ministry official an informal summary list of measures which the Japanese government should urgently consider if emotionalism in the United States were to be dampened. My list, which included the key issues long under discussion, not surprisingly resembled the subsequent "Eight Point Program." One exception was my unauthorized suggestion of yen revaluation. In mid-June, the Japanese were to convene a meeting in Washington of all their diplomatic officers in the United States to determine what could be done to improve Japan's "image." Stressing that the problem was much greater than public relations, a more comprehensive list of specific suggestions was handed to my Foreign Ministry colleague on June 2. Hope was expressed that effective measures could be initiated quickly so as to have a salutary impact prior to the joint cabinet meeting scheduled for Washington in September. Four days later, the Japanese "Eight Point Program" took shape.

At the reception following the ceremony on June 17 when the Okinawa reversion documents were signed, Prime Minister Sato was reminded that Washington had scrupulously avoided linking the return of Okinawa with our trade problems, but that, in response to the Okinawa agreement, effective progress in trade matters would be appropriate. Such progress could even be critical in ensuring Senate ratification of the agreement. Having just returned from a special trip to Washington, I gave as my impression that our legislators were well disposed regarding Okinawa, but the bread-and-butter concerns of their constituents could affect their votes. Being truly Japanese, Sato was more motivated by the desire to repay an obligation. The following morning, according to the press, he called a special meeting of the six Ministers involved in economic matters and "instructed all-out efforts for the implementation" of the "Eight Point Program."

Never was Sato's sincerity to be doubted. On June 21, Finance Minister Fukuda, the strong man in the cabinet, came at his initiative to the Embassy residence to explain the government's plans for implementing the "Eight Point Program." It was a two-hour session during which Fukuda divided measures to be taken into those which would be carried out immediately by cabinet action, such as reduction of import quotas, and those which would require Diet action in early autumn. The major portion of the program should be completed, he said, by the end of August, prior to the joint cabinet meeting in early September. Economic Minister Edmond and I welcomed the Japanese determination to take action, but urged that there be no underestimation of the gravity of our economic problems and the profundity of the remedial measures necessary. Fukuda confirmed press reports of a cabinet reshuffle the first week in July, stressing that the new Ministers were being carefully selected so as to reinforce the government's efforts in the economic field. A week later, on June 29, the Japanese cabinet reaffirmed the "Eight Point Program"; liberalized twenty import quota items including grapefruit; raised the rediscount rate .5% ; lifted ceilings on outward investment; pledged to take favorable action at the earliest practicable date with respect to beef quotas, soybean tariffs, commodity taxes, and twenty additional quota items; and authorized sizable increases in governmental outlays for "social infrastructure." Fukuda reportedly insisted to his cabinet colleagues that it was "time for action, rather than words." One unhappy bureaucrat complained about such decisions being made at the cabinet level and described it as being "very un-Japanese." The cabinet action was all the more remarkable because it took place two days after Sato had suffered a stunning defeat in the House of Councillors, where his candidate for the Presidency had fallen victim to a hostile strategy involving some of Sato's own party associates.

Fukuda's prediction about the new cabinet came true on the July 4 weekend. He himself was named Foreign Minister. The new Minister of International Trade and Industry was the redoubtable Kakuei Tanaka, who, during my courtesy call, pointed out that the new cabinet included four strong personalities each of whom had served as Finance Minister at times when Japan was having economic woes and the United States had provided invaluable assistance. Both Tanaka and the new Finance Minister, Mikio Mizuta, expressed their determination to repay the remembered American helpfulness, now that America was experiencing economic difficulties. (In Japan, a sense of obligation was not only a strong motivating force, but actions taken because of it seemed to be more defensible politically.) Mizuta expressed to us his eagerness to redress the trade imbalance, particularly in anticipation of the joint cabinet session in September. He was confident that our bilateral trade gap could be narrowed to the $1 to $1.5 billion range by greatly increased Japanese government expenditures designed to stimulate domestic demand (and imports), and by further Japanese trade liberalization measures. Prime Minister Sato, the fourth ex-Finance Minister in the cabinet, declared publicly that the chief purpose of the new government would be to alleviate the rising economic tensions between Japan and the United States. All of these developments were, of course, fully reported to Washington.

Then came the "Nixon shocks." The July 15 announcement with regard to China plunged Sato into political hot water. The August 15 economic surprise knocked the world's highly touted new economic giant into a daze. The initial reaction of the Japanese, when confronted by the import surcharge and dollar convertibility restrictions, was to scuttle the "Eight Point Program." Calmer heads prevailed, however, and it was decided to cite the "Eight Point Program" at the September joint cabinet meeting as the best road for emerging from our bilateral economic morass. Meanwhile, the Japanese lessened their foot pressure on the liberalization accelerator while trying to ascertain precisely what it was that America's New Economic Policy wanted from Japan.

From the outset, there was no doubt that the Japanese "Eight Point Program" was well intended. It was, however, highly doubtful that it would have been adequate. All too soon, it became clear that important elements of the program, such as liberalization of competitive agricultural products, would be undermined by strong domestic political resistance. Furthermore, even if the program were carried out in its entirety, it lacked the most critical element, monetary realignment. Multilaterally or bilaterally, the revaluation of the yen was a sine qua non if economic disequilibrium was to be corrected. Yet that subject was for the Japanese the most painful, if not unmentionable. The major thrust of the "Eight Point Program" had been to avoid this unavoidable eventuality. In fact, in Japan it was known as "the yen defense" program.

As with the China issue, and more glaringly so, the "Nixon shock" of August 15 was more faulty in style than in substance. Exhibiting a characteristic insensitivity, seemingly directed more toward allies than toward foes, Washington had: a) not once, at least to the knowledge of the American Embassy in Tokyo, communicated officially its desire to see the yen revalued; b) neither opposed, nor acknowledged, nor even shown an awareness of the Japanese "Eight Point Program"; c) concentrated with ferocity on the textile problem, leaving the impression that both "Nixon shocks" were some sort of reprisal for Japanese intransigence on textiles; d) spoken with a cacophony of voices, either via public pronouncements or via a plethora of presumed spokesman who infiltrated Tokyo or were in contact with the Japanese in Washington; and e) unfairly transferred the blame for some of our own shortcomings to the hard-working Japanese. It was no secret, of course, that there was abundant American displeasure with Japan's restrictive trade practices, and that Japanese remedial action had hitherto been inadequate. In dealing with the

Japanese at all levels, Embassy representatives never failed to stress these points. But the Japanese were moving. The shock of August 15 would have been more defensible, therefore, if, before the boom was lowered, there had been opportunity to explain through a single authoritative channel that the "Eight Point Program" was deficient and that monetary realignment was a necessity.

Even though, with respect to Washington, the Embassy often felt itself to be in the dark, our spirits and our effectiveness were always buoyed by the solid cooperation of the American business community. In the American Chamber of Commerce in Japan (ACCJ) were men who knew not only how to conduct profitable trade but also how to respect Japanese cultural sensitivities. Many of them had lived in Japan for years and had learned the subtle combinations for unlocking the opportunities which existed. They also knew, as ACCJ President James Adachi phrased it, that when subjected to pummeling, a Japanese proverbially "resists with the midsection." Others who served in the ACCJ Presidency were no less perceptive, e.g., William Dizer of Dupont, Vincent Coe of Price Waterhouse, George Purdy of Dresser Industries, and Howard Van Zandt of ITT, who distilled the wisdom of his years of Japanese experience into an instructive booklet on how to do business in Japan.

At the monthly ACCJ-American Embassy conclave in July 1971, a report was presented by the ACCJ representatives who had attended the annual plenary meeting of Japanese and American business leaders, sponsored by ongoing special Japanese-American committees and backed by the Chambers of Commerce of both countries. The ACCJ participants believed real progress had been made, not by lecturing the Japanese about their iniquities, but by explaining that the United States economy was in trouble and needed Japan's help. The delegation's report led to extended discussion, and to a specially arranged meeting in which suggestions were sought from our ACCJ friends for rectifying the trade imbalance, which was heading for the $3 billion mark. They doubted the "Eight Point Program" would fill the bill. Almost unanimously, they were against protectionism, and thought the emphasis should be on "fair trade." There was some mention of yen revaluation. In answer to the key question of how to persuade the Japanese to move, most thought that words were inadequate and that some sort of "leverage" was needed, but what that leverage might be was more difficult to say. They considered that the linkage of trade problems with political issues like Okinawa would not be wise. A crucial factor, in their view, was shoring up American competitiveness. These consultations, the second of which took place three days before August 15, produced no startling panaceas, but they were valuable, and the results were reported to Washington.

There were many other manifestations of productive collaboration between the American business community and the Embassy in Tokyo, such as the staging of trade exhibits at least once a month; discussion of individual company problems and intercession with the Japanese when appropriate; capitalizing on the stream of visiting presidents and vice presidents of American firms for promotional activities, commercial and social; special missions by ACCJ members into the prefectures to discuss trade problems in public forums; facilitating joint ventures and other Japanese-American business cooperation; "Know Your Embassy Day" and other occasions for bringing the American community together as at the congenial and lively American Club. No overseas group of Americans ever worked more closely together, a point generously echoed in writing by Far East American Chamber of Commerce Chief Lew Burridge, ACCJ's 1972 President George Purdy, and ACCJ's Executive Secretary Bart Jackson.

Unfortunately, there has long been an assumption in some American business and governmental circles, includ-

ing even among our friends in the Department of Commerce, that the American Foreign Service is insufficiently
attentive to our commercial problems. It is an unfair allega-
tion and was manifestly untrue in Tokyo, where the Embassy had a tireless and dedicated crew of economic officers.
Collaborating fully with the State Department contingent
were Treasury Representatives, the Commerce Department's Trade Exhibits staff, plus top-notch attachés in such
fields as Agriculture (Japan was our best customer), Civil
Aviation (American aircraft and equipment were in demand), Maritime Administration, Fisheries, Customs, Internal Revenue, Atomic Energy (Japan was a major
buyer of enriched uranium), Defense Assistance (military
hardware), Science (space and environmental cooperation),
and the United States Travel Service (tourism was booming). Even sections of the total United States Government
mission remote from economic matters were under orders
to enhance American commercial interests wherever possible. Every dollar of American goods we could sell would
help with our staggering trade imbalance.

Arriving via San Francisco and Williamsburg, Japan's
Foreign Minister Takeo Fukuda, still not fully recovered
from a gall bladder operation, and six of his cabinet col-
leagues met with their American counterparts in the State
Department's conference room September 9 and 10, 1971.
It was the annual meeting of the Japan–United States Committee on Trade and Economic Affairs (ECONCOM). The
Japanese were still recoiling from August 15. The twin
American worldwide objectives, monetary reform and more
equitable trading relationships, were now clear, but the
Japanese remained perplexed as to what specifically was
expected of Japan and, therefore, what positions should be
taken at ECONCOM. The Ministry of Agriculture, for
example, favored holding back on liberalization until the
elimination of the American import surcharge could be

negotiated. The prevailing view, however, was that the "Eight Point Program," even though it had been prompted by the imminence of ECONCOM, had the broad objective of improving Japan's international position. That program should, therefore, go forward and serve as basis for the delegation's talks in Washington. A number of specific liberalization measures, pursuant to the "Eight Point Program," were authorized for disclosure in Washington.

To assist in making ECONCOM as productive as possible, Assistant Secretary of State Philip Trezise had visited Tokyo at the end of August. Describing attitudes in Washington as being on the verge of hostility, Trezise impressed on Foreign Minister Fukuda and other Japanese officials the importance of a forthcoming Japanese attitude at ECONCOM. As to format, it was decided that the opening meeting would be limited to statements by the chairmen of the two delegations. Next on the program would be luncheon discussions between American cabinet members and their Japanese counterparts, and it was in these meetings where the Japanese had planned to get down to specifics. As it happened, the President scheduled at short notice a speech before Congress on the first mid-day, requiring the attendance of the American cabinet members and the postponement of the counterpart meetings for twenty-four hours. Inevitably, without the mellowing effect of the tête-à-têtes, the plenary sessions took on the nature of a public debate, with each side defending stated positions. The posturing was somewhat reminiscent of the famous Japanese theatre known as "kabuki."

In order to foster dialogue, the prepared text of Secretary Rogers's opening remarks was provided to the Japanese delegation in advance, only to have it published in the Japanese newspapers the day before the conference began, along with the gist of the remarks planned by Foreign Minister Fukuda. Nonetheless, both spoke extemporaneously, confining their remarks to the economic problems

between the two countries. The Secretary, contending that
the yen was undervalued and that a basic balance-of-payments disequilibrium existed, urged a major revaluation of
the yen and the removal of Japanese restrictions on imports
and foreign capital. In response, Fukuda referred to the
"painful confusion" caused by the August 15 measures,
cited liberalization progress completed and in train, contended that Japan's trade surpluses were primarily due to
sluggish imports because of the current recession and to
lack of American competitiveness, pointed out that the
parity problem was multilateral in nature, and urged the
early termination of the American import surcharge, noting among other things that if prolonged it could invite
retaliation. Much of the debate the first day and a half
centered on whether or not a "disequilibrium" existed. The
Japanese saw no fundamental imbalance and no bilateral
ailments which could not be corrected by the "Eight Point
Program." At one point, when responding to a challenge to
prove the existence of "disequilibrium," Treasury Secretary
John Connally produced a round of mirth, but not necessarily agreement, by making the elementary observation,
"You are winning, and we are losing."

Although delayed twenty-four hours, the counterpart
meetings broke much ice. The Japanese came forward with
a number of scheduled moves in accordance with the
"Eight Point Program." These included the abolition of the
"Automatic Import Quota" (AIQ) restrictive licensing system, a status report on investment liberalization according
to which 94% of Japanese industry was said now to be open
to foreign capital, and tariff reductions on a number of
items of considerable interest to the United States such as
refrigeration and air-conditiong equipment, cosmetics, and
soybeans. The ambiance that was created by the personal
contacts was such that the conference on the final afternoon
was marked by an abundance of pleasantry, even though it
was short on substance. The high point of the two-day

ECONCOM was a White House dinner in honor of the Japanese delegation. The Japanese returned to Tokyo happier, but not much wiser.

Following ECONCOM, Japanese and American financial representatives met in London in mid-September at a meeting of the "Group of Ten," consisting of the Finance Ministers and Central Bank Governors of the major industrialized nations of the Free World. There were further consultations during the annual IMF meetings late in September. The major stumbling block to progress on the monetary front was the aversion of most countries, including Japan, to allowing their currencies to float. This, at least on a transitional basis, was the essence of the initial American objective. At the end of August, Finance Minister Mizuta had called on his fellow countrymen to "endure the glorious suffering" and announced that the yen would be allowed to float within unspecified limits. But there was unobtrusive intervention by the Bank of Japan, involving only a minor revaluing of the yen, and Japan's trade surpluses continued at their half-billion-dollar-per-month pace. The pressures were on, but no single nation, including Japan, wanted to take steps that might redound to its future disadvantage. It was this reluctance to bite unnecessary bullets which no doubt motivated the Japanese in their continuing efforts to ascertain the specifics of a solution acceptable to the United States.

The kinds of questions for which the Japanese were seeking answers came up during my lengthy conversation with Prime Minister Sato on September 30. He noted that in one of the international conclaves, Treasury Secretary Connally had mentioned that a $13 billion "turnaround" would be required in the American balance-of-payments situation. He noted that his advisors considered this "Texas talk." In their view, a $6 and $7 billion figure was more realistic, and they were awaiting the results of an expected

IMF study on the subject. Another question was whether Japan must unilaterally revalue its currency, or whether it should await a multilateral solution to what was essentially a multilateral exchange-rate problem. For Sato, the most important problem was, of course, the extent of yen revaluation, and he said he could not agree with the 20% figure which had apparently been mentioned to Finance Minister Mizuta in Washington. His own preference was to revalue in stages, announcing a modest increase in the value of the yen and basing further adjustments on ensuing market forces. An additional problem, cited by the Japanese for deferring revaluation, was the replacement of the dollar by the yen in Okinawa upon reversion. Ultimately, this problem was resolved through a Japanese subsidy which permitted Okinawans to convert their dollars at the pre-revaluation 360 to 1 rate.

At this juncture, in early October, President Nixon sent California Governor Ronald Reagan to the Far East to assure our allies that the breakthrough with Peking would not be at their expense. In Tokyo, the Governor was inevitably grilled on economic matters, and specifically asked what Japan would have to do to get the import surcharge eliminated. He gave assurance that the August 15 measures were only temporary. Foreign Minister Fukuda, noting that our two countries represented 60% of the GNP of the Free World, assured Governor Reagan of Japan's determination to see our economic problems resolved.

A month later, there arrived in Tokyo another Presidential emissary, Secretary of the Treasury John Connally. His exploits on the political scene in Washington were well known in Japan, as was his key role in the formulation of the President's New Economic Policy. As usual, in trying to detect the true intentions of American policy, Tokyo had been receiving signals not all on the same wavelength, the particular sounds depending on the particular interests of the source, whether it was White House, Congress, State Department, Treasury, Commerce, or other. Unclear, therefore, as to American requirements, fearful of further American blockbusters, and deeply reluctant to bite bullets which had to be bitten, the Japanese regarded the Treasury Secretary's visit with some trepidation. The common concern, publicly advertised, was that some new Texas-sized power play was imminent. The newspapers published advisories on "Typhoon Connally."

Not enraptured by the epithet, Secretary Connally told newsmen shortly after his arrival of his inability to understand how anyone could consider him a "typhoon" when he was really only a "gentle breeze." In official discussions, he indicated that it was unthinkable that he would have come to twist any arms, mount any pressures, or present a package of proposals. His purpose, he avowed, was merely to explain the problems which the United States was facing to anyone willing to listen and, for his part, to hear what others might wish to discuss. The Secretary's innocence may not have been quite as pure as implied, but, tactically, the Japanese were disarmed. Eager to get to the point, they repeatedly inquired what Japan must do to secure the removal of the import surcharge. The Secretary responded that he had no proposals, but if his Japanese friends had any suggestions he would make himself available, in Washington, Hawaii, or Tokyo, immediately or at any future time convenient to them. While taking this low-key approach, the Secretary did not hesitate in official conversations to defend American positions taken at the Group of Ten meetings or elsewhere. For example, he insisted there would have to be an $11 billion turnaround in the American balance-of-payments situation (down from the earlier $13 billion figure). Similarly, Connally disavowed any official United States position with respect to the extent of yen revaluation, but adroitly dropped the hint that there were some economists who felt that a revaluation to be meaningful ought to be around 24%.

One of the most fascinating exchanges took place during a luncheon at the Embassy residence to which the stalwarts of the Japanese business establishment were invited. Included were the venerable "Economic Prime Minister" from Keidanren, Kogoro Uemura; Shigeo Nagano, who was President of the Japan Chamber of Commerce and Board Chairman of the Nippon Steel Corporation; and Yoshizane Iwasa, Fuji Bank Chairman and indefatigable promoter of Japanese-American business harmony. During the discussion, one of the Japanese leaders ventured the customary contention that the root problem was the inadequacy of mutual understanding. With his well-known charm, Connally registered some reservation. He said he had little trouble in understanding that while a Toyota and a Pinto were selling for about the same price in California, the cost of a Pinto in Japan was double that of a Toyota. Similarly, he had no difficulty in understanding that the deposits in two Japanese banks in California exceeded the grand total for all the foreign banks in Japan. He could also understand that, while the Japanese government had removed feeder calves from quota restriction, it had at the same time levied a $135 import tariff for each calf. There was no pounding on the table. Amicability and good humor prevailed. But the points were driven home.

As summarized in my telegraphic report, Secretary Connally in his mission succeeded in: a) dispelling Japanese illusions that there might be an easy way out, including a sort of *force majeure* of economic proposals from the United States; b) placing the ball in the Japanese court and stimulating more serious Japanese realization that painful adjustments to reality were inevitable; and c) establishing himself as the voice of unmistakable authority, thus nullifying the many previous confusing signals. While the Japanese had to go back to their own drawing boards, they were gratified that dialogue had been established with a true power source in Washington and hopeful that means could be found via further consultations to resolve our bilateral and international trade difficulties. A welcome dividend for the American Ambassador in Japan was that Secretary Connally believed in keeping the Ambassador informed of the intricacies of our policies, and even of the contents of a "back channel" message which he had received from the President for delivery to Prime Minister Sato.

After further international discussions at Rome and elsewhere, the "Smithsonian Agreement" was concluded on December 18. Although a number of major problems remained in the international monetary field, including a reform of the basic structure, the realignment of currencies was a giant step forward. Despite the anguish which they had experienced, the Japanese were relieved that the boil had been lanced. They were also delighted that the American import surcharge was lifted. Meanwhile, progress in developing greater reciprocity in our trading relationships, entrusted by the President to Special Trade Representative William Eberle, was still only at a moderate pace. The fact was that Japan was a formidable competitor, and resolving our bilateral trade problems was apt to be, like diplomacy itself, a continuing process.

Peter Peterson had in early 1972 moved from the Council on International Economic Policy to become Secretary of Commerce. When talking about our economic problems to California bankers a few months later, he referred to the Charlie Chaplin gag, "I met the enemy, and he is us." If there was one message to be brought back from Japan during the 1969–1972 period, it was that the United States could not rest on its past laurels. The realities of the 1970's would also require some painful adjustments by Americans.

Although Washington's predominant interest was securing Japan's compliance with the Golden Rule, the Japanese challenge was not without positive values for Americans. By offering competition which could not be ignored, it provided a stimulus for improved American performance and even afforded some useful lessons. Without a strong domestic economic base, Americans could not expect to continue to play a highly productive role in the world economy, nor for that matter could they expect to maintain superior standards of living for themselves. Determining the adjustments which ought to be made became the subject of intensive study by such groups as the President's Commission of International Trade and Investment Policy (Williams's Commission) and the Council on International Economic Policy. A few of the key areas requiring attention are worth noting.

a. INTERNATIONAL COMPETITIVENESS. With an output of 30,458,000 metric tons from 23 furnaces, the Nippon Steel Corporation in 1971 outproduced the United States Steel Corporation, which was utilizing 69 furnaces to turn out 24,647,000 tons. When asked to explain the greater efficiency, one Japanese steel executive jocularly observed, "You bombed us out during the war and thus our equipment is more modern." Postwar reconstruction, however, was not the whole story. The fact was, as reflected in the ultramodern Nihon Kokan complex at Fukuyama, that, on an industrywide basis, Japan was consistently investing a higher percentage of its GNP in new plant and equipment than any other country in the world, notably 20% versus 10% in the United States.

Thus, if the United States wished to stay competitive in the international marketplace, increased investment in plant modernization was advisable. With the assistance of fairer exchange rates, some lost ground might be recovered in non-technology intensive areas such as shoes and textiles, but, according to most observers, investment emphasis should be in the high-productivity areas, where the United States enjoyed comparative advantage. This would require stepped up research and development to strengthen the chief American asset, technological leadership. It would also require more efficient education and training programs to fit manpower skills to job requirements. While a governmental Economic Planning Agency might not be feasible in the United States, much could be said for taking a leaf from the Japanese book in organizing coordinated and concentrated research to determine the likely areas of high-technology growth in the future, such as automobiles compatible with future energy resources, and encouraging innovative industrial movement in those directions. Critical to the maintenance of high productivity, of course, was the need to control inflation and the domestic wage-price spiral.

The prospects were not without hope. Taking advantage of the spin-off from our space program and cooperation with North American Rockwell, one forward-minded Japanese company got the jump on the market with attractive electronic desk calculators, at a price between $200 and $300. Subsequently, however, American ingenuity devised means for producing calculators which were more compact, boasted added features, and sold at half the price. Similarly, even in the production of TV sets, and aided by yen revaluation, American firms in 1972 were recovering some of the American market which had been yielded to foreign producers.

b. COOPERATION OF LABOR. Having toured three Japanese automobile factories, occasion was taken during a stop in Detroit after my return in 1972 to revisit one of the major American companies. Aside from the contrast between Toyota's spick-and-span, ultramodern Nagoya plant and the war-weary and relatively grimy American facility, more impressive was the difference in the work habits of the employees. For each hard-working, undistractable Toyota-man at a position on the computerized Japanese assembly line, there appeared to be two or three men at each of the positions in the American plant, one resting, and none so engrossed in his work as his Japanese counterpart. The thought occurred that there ought to be some happy medium between the almost slavish diligence of Japanese workers and the carefree, almost careless, attitudes of Americans.

These work attitudes were reflected in statistics. While Japanese productivity was increasing 90% from 1965 to 1970, that of the United States went up only 10%. Wage costs were rising in Japan at record rates, and in 1968 began for the first time to outstrip productivity, but, as Peterson's CIEP report noted, the rate of United States wage increases exceeded our gains in productivity by wider margins than in Japan or other countries. Inevitably, our exports became less competitive.

More damaging in our efforts to compete internationally were our lengthy work stoppages. A West Coast dock strike in 1971 cost us $50 million in agricultural exports to Japan, and, once lost, foreign markets cannot always be regained. Meanwhile, it was not surprising that motor vehicle production costs in Japan, where strikes were minimal or merely red-armband exercises, were less than in Detroit, where in 1971 General Motors, at considerable added expense, had to stockpile a three months' supply of steel in anticipation of a steel strike, which in the end did not materialize. In terms of man-hours, work stoppages were forty times more costly per annum in the United States than in Japan. The hope had to be that means could be devised whereby just solutions could be found for American labor disputes without so seriously crippling our international competitiveness.

c. MORE AGGRESSIVE FOREIGN MARKETING. With trade promotion being a top-priority Embassy objective, no effort was spared to support, via publicity activities, receptions, and opening ceremonies, the projects of the Department of Commerce's Trade Center in Tokyo. By staging a major exhibition at least once a month, we helped American companies, particularly the smaller ones, to sell varieties of products, including fluid power systems, avionics, waste treatment equipment, sporting goods, and computer peripherals. Under Trade Exhibits Manager Ed Simmons's direction, these endeavors in 1971 added $130 million to the total value of American exports to Japan. In the "they said it couldn't be done" category, an American textile and apparel mission, comprised of representatives from twenty-five companies and headed by the Commerce Department's Stanley Nehmer, sold the Japanese $7 million worth of American textiles. Meanwhile, full support was also accorded such projects as a major grapefruit exhibit, introduction of hotelkeepers to American beef, and the gift to Japan of a prize 4-H Club bull. Such initiatives were among many organized by Agricultural Attaché Elmer Hallowell and his five-man Department of Agriculture team, who worked closely with various American commercial cooperatives. When it was noted, during my first briefing at Hallowell's office, that the import of American farm products to Japan was at a level just over $900 million, I made a pledge to obtain special United States Government recognition if and when the $1 billion barrier were broken. It was a happy moment a little over a year later to redeem that pledge with special citations to our Agriculture colleagues directly from their highly appreciative Secretary, Clifford Hardin.

The fact was that, across-the-board, Japan was America's fastest growing market, as well as our best transoceanic customer. Moreover, Japanese consumer demand was increasing from 10% to 15% annually. However, the United States economy was only 4% dependent on foreign exports, and the problem was to stimulate American producers, so preoccupied with their vast American trade, to take the trouble to study market possibilities in Japan, to brave the admittedly resistant Japanese system, and to tailor their products to increase their attractiveness for Japanese customers. Japanese producers were more export-minded. For example, Japanese automobile companies were designing emission-controlled engines to be produced to meet proposed American government standards well before Detroit considered the goal attainable. Our Embassy, through every channel available, sought to apprise American businessmen of the Japanese market potential and to provide pertinent information. High technology products offered the greatest promise for American exporters, but opportunities were also opening up for merchandising consumer goods.

Encouragement was given by the Embassy to the giant Japanese trading companies to step up their purchase of American products, either for delivery in Japan or to "third countries" where their endeavors were already benefiting the American balance of payments by at least $500 million. But the primary responsibility had to be American and, as both Williams and Peterson emphasized, export expansion was a field requiring intensive cultivation by both the American government and industry. Tilling that soil might include: plowing up weeds such as unfair tax restraints, discriminatory freight rates, and excessive application of antitrust laws to our export trade; providing fertilizer through further liberalization of Export-Import Bank financing already initiated by Chairman Henry Kearns; and getting the harvests, industrial as well as agricultural, to foreign markets, perhaps through the development of export associations for small producers or of American trading companies like those in Japan.

d. REDUCING NON-PRODUCTIVE OUTFLOWS. The American economy at the outset of the 1970's was suffering two special handicaps. Internationally, financial outflows to support what the United States deemed necessary for peace and security constituted a $7 billion drain on the balance of payments. This included foreign economic assistance and military expenditures in Vietnam and elsewhere. Domestically, outlays for defense, foreign aid, foreign investment, and the space program reduced resources for investment in economic growth. Thus Japan, which had only modest military and space disbursements, was able to allocate twice the percentage of its GNP for industrial performance. As pointed out by MITI's Maohiro Amaya, this accounted for "the wide gap in increase rates of wholesale prices and export prices of the two countries," which in turn led to the acute trade imbalance.

It behooved the United States, therefore, to reduce wherever possible its non-productive outflows. Other nations would be expected to assume primary responsibility for their own welfare and would share in the international security burdens. Thus, in Japan in 1971, it was possible through realignment of American military facilities and force reductions to effect savings totaling $50 million. Further belt-tightening was being planned, while the return of Okinawa to Japanese political administration envisaged financial savings several times that figure. Such developments were good for all parties concerned and of direct benefit to the American economy.

e. FIRMNESS AGAINST UNFAIRNESS. As the Williams report had indicated, one difficulty was ascertaining whether certain Japanese practices were fair or unfair. Unfortunately, the international code negotiated at GATT could be quite murky. Nonetheless, if the United States had grievances, there should normally be no hesitation to seek remedies via the pertinent articles of the General Agreement. Even though the GATT forum was time-consuming, relatively ineffectual, and sorely in need of strengthening, its enforcement capabilities would not be enhanced by being ignored or bypassed, nor would the American cause, if justifiable, be as well supported in the court of world opinion.

Meanwhile, for malpractices such as "dumping," the United States had laws of its own which could and should be invoked. They authorized the levying of additional assessments on imports which were found by the Treasury Department to be selling "at less than fair value" and determined by the Tariff Commission to constitute "injury" to domestic producers. Under Assistant Secretary of the Treasury Eugene Rossides, the time span for conducting these anti-dumping procedures was reduced from more than two years to a few months. A dozen or more cases involving Japanese exports were investigated by our Customs attachés in Tokyo. In most cases the complaints were not upheld, mostly because the archaic distribution system in Japan had tended to give the false impression that factory prices for exported products were lower than those for domestic consumption. Interestingly enough, when an American complaint was registered against Japan's television manufacturers, unexpected allies appeared in the form of a group of Japanese housewives who organized a boycott; they saw no reason why they should be paying more than Americans for a TV set produced in Japan. Many Japanese, however, suspected that these anti-dumping actions were being prosecuted by Washington more rigorously than warranted because of frustrations over other economic matters. This suspicion was not entirely without substance.

f. CONSULTATIVE APPROACH. While punitive leverage could on occasion be effective (and in the case of yen revaluation it was probably inevitable), the consultative process was by far the most desirable approach. As the Free World's top two economic powers, neither Japan nor the United States could ignore their interdependence and their need to pull together to preserve the type of world that had

brought prosperity to both nations. Beyond the reconciliation of present differences, there was constant need to discuss the economic world of the future. For example, our
views should be harmonized on the broad subject of trans-
national investment, including such areas as: Japanese
funds in the United States, and vice versa; cooperative joint
ventures in the developing countries; investment risk insurance; multinational corporations with their potential
for improving the use of the world's resources—if they could
overcome charges in the developed countries of being "job
exporters" and in the developing countries of infringing on
sovereignty; and greater roles for multilateral organizations such as the Asian Development Bank (ADB), the
Overseas Private Investment Corporation (OPIC), and the
private European-American-Japanese joint venture known
as the Private Investment Corporation for Asia (PICA).

Another challenge requiring extensive consultation was
"the international division of labor" which MITI described
as "progressively giving away industries by way of sophis-
ticating the industrial structure of one's own country, much
as big brother gives away his now too small suit to his kid
brother." Related was the subject of adjustment assistance
for industries which would be phasing down in such industrial upgrading. Then there was the whole realm of bal-
ancing ever-higher industrial production with a livable
environment. Other fruitful subjects for consultation included the need to tighten GATT's rules and its enforcement capabilities, "orderly marketing" safeguards, further
cooperation in OECD, the relationship between trading
communities such as the Common Market and the rest
of the world, Japanese-European-American collaboration,
and the creation of an international monetary structure
with sufficient flexibility to be responsive to the world of
tomorrow.

In the halcyon postwar days, when the United States
became guardian of the Free World and the dollar was

almighty, the American concept of consultation with foreigners understandably tended to become one of preaching the gospel of salvation according to Uncle Sam. When, in 1971, economic conditions took a decided turn for the worse, the Washington administration, heavily business-oriented, urged "more assertive" methods of diplomacy. While firmness of purpose in the nation's interest could not be questioned, there was a danger, as cautioned by Japan's MITI, of a "protectionist reaction" to "one-sided lectures" and having American idealism "prejudicially forced" on other nations. Earlier, Americans had learned that the American political system was not one which could be tidily transplanted all over the world, regardless of such factors as literacy, natural resources, and cultural heritage. Americans had now to learn that economic concepts, which seemed so sacrosanct to us, might also require some adjustments, if they were to be compatible with the realities of the 1970's in the international community. American economic idealism, as MITI observed, contained a large measure of "universality," but permanent converts were more likely to be retained through persuasion than by browbeating.

Although there may have been room for improvement in preparing for the moment of truth, there was no way that the demise of what economist Paul Samuelson described as "a dream world" could have been made painless for the Japanese. Inevitably, there was a linkage between Japan's soaring trade surpluses, specifically vis-à-vis the United States, and the deteriorating American trade and payments situation, which by mid-August 1971 left the President with little choice but to take action designed to bring about more equitable international trade and monetary systems and to shore up via such measures as wage and price controls the performance of the American domestic economy. With a firm belief that the economic health of

Japan and that of the United States were interdependent, and that both were prerequisites for international stability, we at the Embassy in Tokyo did not hesitate to defend the "New Economic Policy," as in the meeting with the Trading Company executives.

Even though they could understand the importance to Japan of the vitality of the nation that was in effect the centerpiece of the international economy, and with which they were doing a booming business increasing some $2 to $3 billion annually, most Japanese reacted to the President's moves with strong displeasure. Primarily, it reflected fear of the unknown. The range of consequences was difficult to predict, but there was a general foreboding that Japan's rate of economic growth would be cut at least in half. Serious economic dislocations were anticipated. For those so motivated, there would be opportunity to blame August 15 for a variety of Japanese ills, no matter how unrelated. For serious and thoughtful Japanese, however, there was a realization that adjustment to the realities of the 1970's was necessary, probably to an extent that would have been politically unfeasible if left to Japanese initiatives.

Once again, the Japanese underestimated their own strength. Their economy was so robust the 16.88% yen revaluation pursuant to the Smithsonian agreement was taken in stride. Japanese producers and exporters were able, by absorbing some of the cost, to hold down the increase in dollar prices. During the first half of 1972, Japan's worldwide trade continued merrily in surplus at a $700 million monthly rate. Exports to the United States continued to increase 20% above the previous year's volume, while due to the prolonged recession in Japan imports remained sluggish. The year 1972 would show a record $4.1 billion American bilateral trade deficit with Japan. Faced with seemingly irrepressible surpluses, as well as American impatience, the Japanese in February 1973 undertook a flotation of the yen, the net effect of which, since the pre-

Smithsonian period, was a 35% revaluation of the yen vis-à-vis the dollar. A short time later, a turnaround in Japan's surplus accumulation was detected; the problem, for the Japanese, then became one of not having the pendulum swing too far in the other direction.

In the trade field, Special Trade Representative William Eberle conferred vigorously with the Japanese on several occasions in 1972, but the results were mostly of short-term cosmetic value (it was election year in the United States). To help ease the American balance-of-payments problem, Japan agreed to more than $1 billion in "emergency purchases"—agricultural products, aircraft, and other imports. It was a gimmick, in effect borrowing on what Japan would in any case be purchasing in the future. The problem was, as Assistant Secretary of the Treasury John Petty observed earlier, that our two countries had over the past half-dozen years just about run out of gimmicks. In addition, there was the danger that Japan would increase its vulnerability to the return swing of the pendulum. With respect to import quotas, the number had been reduced via normal diplomatic processes from 130 to 33 during the three years preceding April 1, 1972, leaving Eberle with less than sensational opportunities for progress, particularly since the remaining 33 items were relatively "hard core." Japanese restrictionism in its various guises was, nonetheless, still a legitimate object of American concern. Of more critical significance, however, were the yen-dollar adjustment and the continuing challenge to American competitiveness.

Japanese and American newsmen often asked me about progress being made with regard to our economic problems. Almost reflexively the response was, "The measures being taken by the Japanese government are indeed welcome and encouraging. But more needs to be done." It was a comment inherited from my predecessor and one which could be bequeathed to my successor. Yet, the reciprocity gap had been narrowed significantly and, stunned by August 15, Japan had, nevertheless, manfully met the challenge of participating in international councils in a manner befitting what was for it still the unbelievable status as No. 2 economic power in the Free World.

Nothing during my sojourn in Japan was more inspiring than witnessing how tragedy had been converted into triumph at Hiroshima. It was thrilling to meet people who, more than any other, had the right to be obsessed with the horror of the past, but who instead devoted their thoughts and their energies to the present and the future. I visited Hiroshima on two occasions, and my impression was that those who had experienced the deepest human suffering were the most capable of forgiveness, compassion, and friendliness.

There was, to be sure, the unforgettable museum with its grim reminders of the most lethal day in the annals of conflict between nations. There were the reverent thousands who assembled every August 6 to pay silent homage to those who perished at the clock-stopping moment of 8:15 in the morning. There was the simple and dignified cenotaph at which they gathered, with its inscription avowing that such an event should never happen again. There was the scientific research by Dr. George Darling and his Japanese and American associates in the Atomic Bomb Casualty Commission. But with the sense of honor so precious to the Japanese, there was for Hiroshimites an absence of self-pity, and a revulsion against unseemly exploitation of the 1945 holocaust.

A stricken Hiroshima had devoted all its energies to rehabilitation. The reconstruction in recent years had come into full flower under the leadership of Governor Itsuo Nagano. New structures were springing up throughout the Hiroshima delta, and also new industries. Toyo Kogyo, the Matsuda automobile enterprise, was to be first in the world to mass produce the advanced rotary engine. The prefectural newspaper, the *Chugoku Shimbun*, more influential than the great dailies emanating from Tokyo, had constructed a most modern edifice for its talented organization. Such were the monuments which Hiroshima was building.

Although Hiroshima and, in like manner, Nagasaki were by far the most dramatic testimony, these history-chosen cities were reflective of the prevailing spirit in postwar Japan. For the Japanese, the answer to adversity was hard work. Just as the disaster of August 1945 had been overcome, so also the "shock" of August 1971 would be surmounted, even though its being the handiwork of a valued friend would leave a special scar. There would surely be more trials and tribulations in the future. Even those prophets outside Japan who so confidently predicted the unretarded upward growth of the Japanese economy occasionally recognized that counteracting contingencies were not inconceivable. In their calculations, it was to be noted, the possibility of a realistic revaluation of the yen had been almost overlooked, or was not expected to occur for a number of years. Similarly, highly optimistic assumptions were made regarding Japan's long-term access at reasonable prices to energy and other natural resources on which it was so vitally dependent. While not concurring with the prophets of an ever-upward straight-line growth for the Japanese economy, my own judgment was that the indomitability of the Japanese spirit would assure Japan's continued status as a leading economic power. However, Japanese growth in the future was apt to occur at the more normal levels experienced by other advanced nations.

What was true for the Japanese economy applied also to the Japanese-American relationship. There were bound to be differences and frictions, with neither side faultless and both sides convinced of the righteousness of their respective positions. The United States considered it essential to take its unilateral action of August 15, but the Japanese believed such action was contrary to mutual trust between the two countries and inconsistent with the Nixon Doctrine's emphasis on "negotiation rather than confrontation." Later, the Japanese would take unilateral action in the protection of what they considered their national interest in assuring oil supplies from the Middle East, but Americans believed that action undermined their efforts to foster peace in that area, as well as global energy cooperation. Each country had to recognize and respect the fact that the policies of the other would not always be identical with its own. Under the circumstances, full and intimate consultations would be required to guard against the emergence of an "adversary" spirit, which once before in history had taken on a catastrophic manifestation. Any such parting of the ways, as MITI's Naohiro Amaya so well phrased it, would be "blasphemy" against the millions of lives lost by both nations due to an earlier "barren" relationship.

Neither Japanese nor Americans could allow economic difficulties, serious or petty, to blind them to the larger picture. No two nations had enjoyed closer and more fruitful ties during the postwar era. Both countries were producers and traders. Both believed in international trade, the freer the better. Both had troubles typical of advanced societies, such as cyclical recessions, inflation, and the need for higher productivity. Both nations were pragmatic. America had welcomed Japan's resurgence, and Japan counted on America's vitality. Both knew how much they meant to each other, not just in the economic domain but in their common dedication to peace in the world. For both, the challenge was that which had been mastered by "the spirit of Hiroshima," the conversion of troubles into opportunities, adversities into hard work, and tragedies into triumphs.

Chapter 6

Textiles: Taxing Tokyo's
Tensile Strength

IN 1971, WHICH THE PRESIDENT was to describe in his subsequent annual report to Congress as "the watershed year"
in American foreign policy, the Japanese were shaken on
July 15 by the China announcement and on August 15 by
the President's dramatic economic moves. All Tokyo waited
to see what would happen on September 15. That date
passed uneventfully, but October 15 became another red-
letter day in United States-Japan history. After an ultimatum threatening severe imposed quotas, the Japanese on
that date agreed to a "voluntary restraint" program limiting the growth of Japanese synthetic textile exports to the
United States.

The textile saga was a long and sad one. No issue during
my three-year sojourn in Japan was more vexatious. It

poisoned the atmosphere, far out of proportion to the issue's intrinsic worth. A review of my personal files testifies to the fact that more telegrams by far were written on the subject of textiles than on any other. Hundreds of hours were invested in seeking a resolution of this problem. It was an irrepressible topic in discussions with the Embassy staff, with officials of the Japanese Ministries, in public addresses, and in the background sessions which I held biweekly at the Embassy residence with newspaper editors, university professors, and other influential citizens. All this, despite the fact that the Embassy was never involved in the actual negotiations. They were conducted either in Washington and/or by special negotiators designated by the White House.

The common charge by critics was that the Nixon administration's concentration on the textile issue was motivated by nothing more than paying off election debts. Senator Strom Thurmond and some of the South Carolina textile leaders were said to have been the architects of Mr. Nixon's so-called "southern strategy," of which the welfare of the textile industry was an integral part. The Republican Presidential nominee in 1968 was known to be an advocate of liberal trade, but according to insiders, a decision was made in the heat of the campaign, and with indications that his opponent was about to come out in public support of the textile industry, that Mr. Nixon himself would make a public commitment to slow down the importation of synthetic textiles from foreign countries.

It would be a mistake to believe that responsiveness to textile interests was limited to one candidate and one campaign. In the early 1960's, consistent with campaign promises, President Kennedy's administration was successful in achieving an International Cotton Long Term Agreement (LTA) for limiting the importation of cotton textiles. In the mid-60's manufacturing shifted heavily to synthetic textile products not covered by the LTA. Thus, by 1968, the clamor was for an LTA-type arrangement for man-made fiber fabrics and apparel. After 1968, the Nixon administration, as pointed out by Senator Thurmond and others, had to be concerned that in the next political campaign the opposing party would accuse the Republicans of empty promises whereas Democratic administrations delivered the goods (or limitation thereof).

The ubiquity of American political interest in the problems of the textile industry was brought home to me on October 24, 1969, during a visit to Tokyo by the unsuccessful 1968 Presidential candidate, Hubert Humphrey. Invited to attend one of my regular background sessions at the Embassy residence, he obligingly came and was immediately asked by one of the twenty editors present whether American insistence on a "voluntary agreement" restricting textile exports was not due merely to a Republican political commitment. Without hesitation, the former Vice President gave an eloquent ten-minute dissertation based on his familiarity with the problem, the main point of which was that the textile question was indeed a political-economic matter in the United States. He noted that in addition to the social aspects (percentage of minority workers employed), there were areas in the South where textile manufacturers were in trouble due to the flood of foreign imports from Japan and other places. Senators and Congressmen from those areas, he pointed out, were only too ready to legislate quotas against foreign imports. As an advocate of freer trade, Humphrey was distressed by the prospect that if quotas were to be legislated against textiles, similar measures would soon be invoked with regard to shoes, electronics, steel, and other imports. This, he said, would be a calamity for Japan even more than the United States. He concluded that as a matter of urgency the Japanese should agree to voluntary textile controls. Given the fact that these top Japanese editors were hoping for some wedge-driving, Humphrey's comments, which had a clearly authentic ring, were highly effective.

The hard political facts regarding textiles included: a) it was an industry more fragmented than most with at least one factory in most Congressional districts in the United States; b) half the spindles of the American textile industry were concentrated in the Carolinas and northern Georgia (in South Carolina alone, two-thirds of the industrial workers were in textile-related industries); and c) a total of 2,500,000 American workers were dependent on the textile industry, namely one out of every eight factory workers. There was little wonder that the industry packed political clout.

Because of the highly advertised political ramifications, many observers in Japan and even in the United States had serious doubts that there was economic justification for the textile restraint program demanded of the Japanese by the American administration. They cited the fact that foreign imports represented only 3% of American consumption. More broadly, and more correctly, they expressed the view that it would be preferable to concentrate American efforts on securing "fair trade" over the whole spectrum of trade relationships, and it was a shame to evoke so much bitterness over the single issue of textiles. Strongly holding such views were Don Shannon of *The Los Angeles Times*, Bernard Krisher of *Newsweek*, and other members of the American press corps in Tokyo.

Given this controversy, I took occasion on my first return to the United States (when Prime Minister Sato came to discuss Okinawa with the President) to visit the Carolinas in early December 1969. I found that it was true that our major textile plants gave the appearance of prosperity. There were many modern plants, and salaries were four times those of textile workers in Japan. It was also true that the volume of production was high and going higher.

Where the primary trouble lay, I learned, was in the impact of foreign imports on the price structure. Our textile industrialists viewed their markets as exceedingly precarious; foreign exporters with their lower prices were already making massive inroads in a huge market.

Thus, despite constantly rising production costs, wholesale prices for American textiles had scarcely risen. The result was a sharp decrease in profit margins. The per-share quarterly earnings of Springs Mills, for example, had tumbled from $2.48 to 22¢ over a four-year period. Per-share earnings at Dan River Mills had plummeted to 5¢ during the latest quarter (six Dan River factories in Spartanburg County had closed in the preceding two years at a cost of 1200 jobs). Meanwhile, smaller companies were going out of business. The demise of the Arista Mills of Winston-Salem during the week of my visit was accompanied by newspaper headlines to the effect that 400 people had been deprived of their livelihood due to Washington's inaction over the restriction of foreign textile imports.

Globally, the United States in 1958 had had a virtual balance in textile exports and imports. Eleven years later, America's textile trade deficit had grown to a staggering $1.3 billion. In what had become a typical year, American textile industry total sales had in 1969 dropped by 2% while foreign imports went up 16%. Dow Jones averages in 1969 were down 15% but textile stocks had taken a 39% nose dive. Meanwhile, in contrast to the countries of Europe and elsewhere, America virtually alone was keeping its doors open to textile imports.

In 1969, Japan had sold over $500 million worth of textiles to the United States, while purchasing only $10 million worth in return. In addition to direct exports, the Japanese were also profiting via fiber sales to lower-labor-cost areas like Hong Kong and Korea from which apparel products were moving to the United States, also at an excessive rate of growth. Beyond that, Japanese investors were constructing textile factories as far away as Central America with the American market in view.

Upon returning to Japan, I tried to make these facts clear. I think I made headway in securing Prime Minister Sato's understanding, though less so with his Minister of International Trade and Industry. In general, there were few willing to listen.

In an attempt to gain public understanding, I delivered a major address, "Of Looms and Linch-Pins," at Osaka on February 20, 1970. Although all of Japan was aware that the textile problem had reached critical proportions, the substance of my remarks was largely ignored by the vernacular press. *The Japan Times* provided excellent coverage, but that English-language newspaper was primarily read by and published for the foreign community in Japan. The Embassy, of course, sent copies of my speech to influential leaders throughout Japan and this helped to get our story across. Subsequently, there were a number of items in the vernacular press which were obvious attempts by Japanese textile leaders to controvert points which I had made at Osaka.

That my Osaka remarks had had effect was also reflected in a crescendo of criticism in the press and even in the Diet to the effect that the Japanese Embassy in Washington was not as energetic as the American Embassy in Tokyo in telling its version of the textile story. This was grossly unfair to Ambassador Takeso Shimoda, who was one of the best emissaries Japan had sent to America. His sin apparently was that he could evaluate the vexatiousness of the textile problem and wished to see a compromise resolution before the frictions between Japan and the United States would become more emotional. A year later he was replaced by a successor who was able to maintain his credentials on the home front by frequent speeches, reported more extensively in the Japanese press than the American, emphasizing American shortcomings while glorifying Japanese behavior. Particularly irksome to the American press corps in Tokyo were the new Japanese Ambassador's frequent speeches describing his country's trade doors as being wide open if only reticent American businessmen would walk in.

The fact was that the textile problem was as formidable in Japanese politics as it was in American. In Japan, the industry was also fragmented, although there were concentrations in Osaka and in Fukui prefecture. Those areas were thriving on the textile bonanza with annual export increases to the United States of 50% and higher. More disturbing, there seemed to be an illusion that such meteoric growth would continue. This was evidenced by sizable new investments in textile plant capacity. Thus, there was strong resistance to any thought of curbing the growth. As in the United States, the industry—management and workers—used its political clout. In the Diet elections at the end of 1969, one hundred victorious candidates of Prime Minister Sato's own party had, in return for the textile industry's electoral support, made public commitments of unrelenting opposition to any textile restraints.

There was never any doubt in my mind that Prime Minister Sato wished to get the textile issue settled at the earliest possible moment. Without specific commitment, he twice promised President Nixon that he would do so (during the November 1969 and the October 1970 visits to Washington). Given the hopelessness of securing the inevitable Japanese political "consensus," he failed to deliver. Despite the usual assertions about "Japan, Incorporated," this was one of the few times in postwar history that a Japanese industry balked despite considerable government pressure.

In its own way, the textile tension was reflective of the new nationalism emerging rapidly in Japan in the late 1960's. In the Japanese press, the American position was invariably portrayed as "demands" of utmost "inflexibility" requiring Japanese "surrender." This reporting was part of of a well-mobilized campaign by the textile leaders, particularly Toyosaburo Taniguchi and Kagayaki Miyazaki, who headed the Japanese Textile Federation and who had as their allies the bureaucrats in Japan's powerful Ministry of International Trade and Industry. Thus the textile leaders would quickly learn from MITI the most minute details of American negotiating tactics (regarding which we at the Embassy were not even aware) and leak them to the press in a distorted and inflammatory manner. Time and again, we would beseech Japanese government officials to desist from foreclosing negotiating options by such misguidance of the press. But MITI's unfortunate disclosures persisted, and we had little success in persuading the government that a solution might be more easily found if the Japanese people could be led to a better understanding of the American side of the case.

For our part at the Embassy, we tried to understand the difficulties on both sides of the textile controversy. Personally, I found Japan's textile leaders tough but not malicious. They were sincere people, as were our textile leaders in the Carolinas. The same could be said of the bureaucrats on both sides. But when it came to the textile issue, concerned parties on both sides, particularly the bureaucrats in MITI, viewed the future as a matter of survival.

To postpone coming to grips with realities, the textilists in both countries were in effect engaged in a battle of overproduction: the Japanese on the assumption that their textile industry, like their whole economy, would be in jeopardy unless high rates of growth could be continued; the Americans with a view to maintaining company solvency through increased output despite decreased earnings. Backed in each country by powerful political forces, this was a collision course. Heading off the collision required two and a half years and eventually a daredevil confrontation.

During the two and a half years, the textile drama passed through various stages. None of them were pleasant.

Shortly after the Nixon administration took office, Secretary of Commerce Maurice Stans tackled our increasingly difficult international trade problems. In May of 1969 he visited Japan, the news having preceded him that his mission was to secure Japanese agreement to restrain the growth of textile exports. Japanese reaction was strong. By the time of his arrival, the Diet had passed by unanimous vote a resolution opposing any restrictive measures for textile exports.

In talking with Secretary Stans before taking up my assignment in June, he had impressed me with his distress at the way the Japanese had misconstrued our government's request. The Japanese press in particular, but even some Japanese officials, portrayed the Secretary as heavy-handedly demanding the virtual cessation of textile exports to the United States. The Secretary made clear to me, and hoped I could do so in Japan, that the United States was asking neither a cessation of textile exports, nor a diminution, nor even a leveling off. Our request, which to me sounded reasonable, was that instead of increasing textile exports by percentages of from 50% to 100% annually, the Japanese agree voluntarily to more modest growth, something more in consonance with American market expansion.

In my first call on Prime Minister Sato, the subjects of trade and textiles inevitably arose. We spoke enthusiastically of our record-breaking volume of bilateral commerce, and the inevitability of such success producing new ranges of problems. The Prime Minister attributed Japan's "economic miracle" to the excellent United States-Japan postwar relationship. With respect to textiles, he thought a recent visit to the United States by Japanese textilists might at least pave the way for progress. I, of course, stressed that Secretary Stans had not asked the impossible, such as the closing down of factories or loss of jobs in Japan, but merely cooperation in "orderly growth" of

United States imports. The Prime Minister was confident that moderation of exports would be the course of wisdom for Japan. He specifically looked forward to the forthcoming joint cabinet meeting (ECONCOM) in Tokyo and was hopeful that Secretary Stans, who would be attending, would be able to return to the United States with assurances of appropriate cooperation.

It has long been my belief that success in diplomatic negotiations is inversely proportional to the number of people attending the negotiating sessions. Thus, while the United States-Japan joint ministerial meeting had once had much value, probably more at the time of its institution in 1961 than in later years, it now resulted only in an improvement in climate. The meeting held in Tokyo July 29–30, 1969, struck me as particularly unproductive. Our Secretaries of some six Departments and their Japanese Ministerial counterparts each in turn delivered a prepared statement, with several hundred deputies and spear-carriers in the conference hall. Subsequently, at a post-mortem at the Embassy, our Secretaries agreed that at future conferences prepared statements should be submitted in advance and the conference time used more advantageously for informal give and take. More useful, of course, were the bilateral counterpart meetings where subject matter and attendance could be limited. Even in that forum, however, the Tokyo ECONCOM in 1969 showed negligible progress as far as the textile problem was concerned.

The hard political fact was that Sato was nearing the end of his third two-year term as Prime Minister. Depending on progress with regard to Okinawa, he hoped to preside over a successful transition to leadership of a type which had characterized the Liberal Democratic Party since the days of the outstanding postwar leader Shigeru Yoshida. The press, opposition parties, and even rivals for the Premiership within the LDP were watching carefully

for an opportunity to attack Sato on the grounds that he
had achieved his goal of Okinawa reversion only by a shady
deal on economic matters, specifically textiles. Thus, the
textile issue languished through the summer and fall of
1969, as Sato prepared for his meeting with President
Nixon in November.

In the Sato-Nixon communiqué of November 21, 1969,
the leaders of Japan and the United States by mutual
agreement made no reference to the textile problem. The
primary subject was, of course, the future reversion of Okinawa. Of the communiqué's fifteen paragraphs only two
touched on economic matters: one describing our desires
for greater and freer trade; the other setting forth
our common interest in economic assistance to emerging
nations.

Although the President's meetings with the Prime Minister were tête-à-tête, there was good reason to believe that
some informal discussion of the textile problem did take
place. Inevitably, the Japanese press charged that Sato had
made a "deal." My own impression was that the Prime
Minister did express his desire to get the textile problem
solved, but not as a quid pro quo for Okinawa. Certainly
neither he nor the President were in a position to discuss
specific details of a solution.

In January 1970, following the impressive Diet election
victory in December of Prime Minister Sato's Liberal
Democratic Party, efforts were resumed to resolve the
nettlesome textile issue. The negotiating was done in Wash-
ington by two professional diplomats, Ambassador Takeso
Shimoda of Japan and Under Secretary of State U. Alexis
Johnson. But the real locus for possible progress was in
Tokyo.

In Prime Minister Sato's reshuffled cabinet, the new
Minister of International Trade and Industry was Kiichi
Miyazawa. He was a veteran economist and government
official, with much international experience. There was no

question he shared Sato's desire to resolve United States-Japan economic tensions, for he was fully aware of the consequences to Japan of a blowup. But as far as textiles were concerned he took a rigid position that the Government of Japan was powerless and its only instrument was to persuade the textile industry to cooperate. The only hope he saw for such persuasion was unequivocal proof that the American textile industry was being injured. Furthermore, progress would be possible only if GATT procedures were followed.

Weeks passed in deadlock. Various American proposals were rejected out-of-hand, with Japanese reaffirmation both officially and in the public media that "injury" must first be proved. The array of facts which I had brought back from my visit to the Carolinas was shrugged off by Minister Miyazawa, who argued that the textile industry in Japan was also suffering and that it was on the decline in all advanced industrial countries. Prime Minister Sato was more impressed by our "injury" data when I saw him shortly after seeing Miyazawa, but the MITI view prevailed that Japan's industry must be persuaded that injury was being sustained. Our figures, including a lengthy compendium especially supplied by Washington, were described by MITI and the textilists as unconvincing.

During a visit to Japan at the end of January, Senator Jacob Javits weighed in heavily with the Japanese authorities. With well-established credentials as a free trader, and personally disliking the textile issue, the Senator made clear that that issue could be "the flash point" for a flood of protectionist legislation highly detrimental to United States-Japan relations and to the whole international trade structure. In response to the claim that the Japanese government was helpless without the voluntary cooperation of the textile industry, New York's senior Senator maintained, as had Illinois Senator Charles Percy during a talk with Foreign Minister Aichi the preceding September, that the purpose of government is to head off disasters. Officially and publicly, Senator Javits was eloquent, but there was little budging on the Japanese side.

While the head of the Japanese Textile Federation Toyosaburo Taniguchi was adamant, his deputy (and probable rival for the Federation's presidency) Kagayaki Miyazaki seemed frenetic. Through third parties I invited Miyazaki for a talk. Word came back that he could not come to the Embassy but would be willing to talk "on neutral ground." He suggested the Okura hotel, where with our advisors we spent a whole evening with no meeting of minds. For every bit of data we would put forward, Miyazaki, armed with encyclopedias of reference material, would retort with countering statistics, frequently quoting United States Government sources out of context. At their request, we held a similar session at the Embassy residence in late February, with Taniguchi, Miyazaki, and nine other textile leaders attending. Japan's textile leaders stuck to their guns; we had failed to convince them of injury to the United States textile industry. The only point of agreement was that United States–Japan ties should not be disrupted.

Increasingly, it was clear that "proof of injury" and "recourse to GATT" were tactically dead-end streets. Instead of looking at the forest, our Japanese textile friends were asking that we measure each tree, and their measuring rods differed from ours. What they were asking, I once suggested, was not proof of injury but of death. The GATT issue was only secondary, and as Senator Javits pointed out, it could perhaps somehow be employed "as a tent," once basic bilateral agreement had been achieved. In a private two-and-one-half-hour chat with Taniguchi in Osaka, I detected a slight shift in emphasis away from "injury" to some binding commitment that any restraint program would be "temporary." He cited the international LTA as having started out as a "temporary" mechanism but as having since acquired permanence. I responded that if peace was achieved on the trade front and if the industries in both countries continued solvent, as proved true for the LTA and the steel voluntary-restraint programs, we should be thankful.

Despite the best persuasive exertions of those Japanese and Americans constructively concerned, the Japanese textile industry had dug in its heels. The press was its solid ally in mobilizing public opinion against America's "unreasonable demands," and in the Diet the industry was collecting on its election debts. Hajima Fukuda, chairman of the Diet committee handling textiles, called at the Embassy residence on several occasions. He too was well intentioned, but it was clear that while most Diet members put a high premium on United States-Japanese relations, none of them would wish to antagonize Japan's textilists.

Quite a galaxy of distinguished Americans appeared in Japan for the opening of Expo 70 on March 14, 1970. Among them was Donald Kendall, whose credentials for the Japanese included the Presidency of Pepsi-Cola (which does flourishing business in Japan), the Chairmanship of the Emergency Committee for American Trade, long-time friendship for Japan, and close friendship with President Nixon. Interested in broader issues, particularly ECAT's endeavors for expanded fair trade, Kendall sought diligently to avoid entanglement in the textile issue, but Japanese leaders sought his help. One idea which emerged was a one-year moratorium on textile export increases during which a Presidential task force would study the situation and produce a viable proposal for the future. The Japanese were at first reluctant but subsequently showed a favorable interest. Meanwhile, however, and despite earlier seemingly favorable soundings in Washington, Kendall discovered that the moratorium concept was by no means acceptable to the American government.

A factor, no doubt, in Washington's strong negative

reaction to the "Kendall Plan" was that by that time a protectionist head of steam was building up in Congress. What was to become known as the Mills Bill was designed to impose stern restrictions on the importation of textiles and shoes. With Congressional prospects thus brightening, it was clear that American textilists would not settle for a mild and vague moratorium proposal. What was interesting, however, was that the Japanese side had shown movement away from flat opposition to any restraints, and even away from the insistence that injury must be demonstrated to their seemingly unrequitable satisfaction. The consensus process was at work, albeit too slowly.

With White House and Congressional impatience increasing, with our Washington negotiators urging a "ball park" Japanese proposal, and with the Kendall Plan having proved to be a non-starter, Prime Minister Sato in late April 1970 renewed endeavors for an intergovernmental solution. Privately with Foreign Minister Aichi, he contemplated a proposal for Ambassador Shimoda to introduce in Washington, but then in late May told me that the subject was so "highly technical" he would have to await Trade Minister Miyazawa's return from a European trip. He was confident, however, of a "final solution" within a few days. He noted that Miyazawa had balked at going to Washington from Europe but would go later. Upon Miyazawa's return to Tokyo, I sensed some backsliding as the newspapers reported his renewal of consultations with the textilists, moratoriums and other suggestions already having proven fruitless. Nonetheless, and while the content of its new proposal was still greatly in doubt, the Japanese government announced that Miyazawa would proceed to Washington on June 24, to be accompanied by Foreign Minister Aichi. This was a dramatic move, the common assumption being that a final settlement was at hand. What was at that time not known to any of us at the Embassy was that the

MITI Minister had been involved in some secret negotiations with a secret emissary from the Department of Commerce.

A pre-departure conversation with Minister Miyazawa disturbed me by its fatalistic tone. He said he would try to avoid an unfortunate outcome but his hands were tied, presumably by the textile industry. At the same time, he said, he was feeling rather pleased, for the mission would "put a period" to this pestiferous issue. He might succeed or he might fail. Either way he would probably lose his job. My impression was that while he might make a gallant try, Minister Miyazawa would not produce a proposal adequate to Washington's needs, that he would accept the inevitable breakdown in negotiations and in effect welcome the enactment of Congressional legislation. The latter route would at least get the Japanese government off the political hook, particularly at a time when a decision regarding Sato's succession was only a few weeks away. I wagered these instincts of mine against the views of my Embassy staff of Japan-experts who contended that failure of such a dramatic mission was unthinkable.

In Washington, at first there seemed to be hope. But when the negotiations came down to the core issues, it was evident that considerable misunderstanding had developed in those earlier talks between Minister Miyazawa and the Commerce Department's secret emissary. There was also a feeling that the Japanese negotiators backed away the second day from forthcoming positions taken the first day. It was yet another example of how easy it is to have confused communications between cultures. In the end, Secretary Stans and Minister Miyazawa agreed to disagree and a communiqué was put out to that effect.

In Tokyo, Prime Minister Sato the following noon was hosting a delegation of American governors. He, Finance Minister Fukuda, and other cabinet Ministers had been up much of the night in last-ditch efforts to avert the collapse of the Washington talks. They were in great distress, but grateful that the tone of the communiqué was more in sorrow than in anger. Sato and I and the others stressed to each other the importance of confining the damage and not letting it spill over to other aspects of the vital United States-Japan relationship. According to the Prime Minister, domestic political repercussions would be limited—no cabinet resignations. The Japanese textile industry, he asserted, was responsible and should bear the consequences. Above all, we agreed that, with the Mills Bill now imminent, Japanese spokesmen should eschew talk of "retaliation." Meanwhile, Sato, Fukuda, et al., resolved to rededicate themselves to the broader trade issues, such as reducing Japan's trade barriers. During a Tokyo visit a month later, Secretary Rogers assured worried Japanese that as far as the American administration was concerned the collapse of the textile negotiations would not adversely affect plans for the reversion of Okinawa.

The failure of the Aichi-Miyazawa mission was the first such open rupture of negotiations in United States-Japan postwar relations. Ironically, it coincided almost exactly with the day, June 23, when the United States-Japan Treaty of Mutual Cooperation and Security celebrated its tenth anniversary and was extended automatically.

Through the summer and fall of 1970, the textile issue lay fallow, but emotions did not. In Japan, there was gratification, particularly in the press, that the government had not knuckled under as had been anticipated. Meanwhile, the export of synthetic textiles to the United States continued merrily, at a pace more than 50% higher than the previous year. In Washington on July 15, the Mills Bill was voted out of the House Ways and Means Committee. Japan's top businessmen were deeply concerned by the possibilities of a trade war. At the same time, there were those in Japan, including the textile leaders with their own monitoring system in Washington, who had serious doubts that the

United States Congress would in the end approve the Mills Bill. They considered it more a threatening gesture than a potential reality. It was, incidentally, worth noting that as a result of his Horatio-at-the-bridge endeavors, and due to new worries arising from his Samsonian handiwork, textile leader Miyazaki had so exhausted himself that he was hospitalized in late July and never resumed his previous active role.

In late October 1970, Prime Minister Sato attended the 25th anniversary of the founding of the United Nations and stopped for discussions with the President in Washington. Despite our best efforts in Tokyo, Japanese officials expected no progress during the talks regarding the textile issue. Nonetheless, the issue still existed, and at the conclusion of the White House meeting the press was informed that negotiations regarding textiles would be resumed. Before disclosing this publicly, however, there was a memorable scene in Dr. Henry Kissinger's office when it was explained to the Prime Minister that the announcement should not be made unless there were assurance that a mutually satisfactory solution was imminent and that there would be no second breakdown in the intergovernmental negotiations. The Prime Minister was determined to settle the question, and confident he would do so shortly after his return to Tokyo.

Intensive negotiations then got under way between Japanese Ambassador Nobuhiko Ushiba and the Assistant to the President, Peter Flanigan. There may have been some general consultation between the Japanese government and the Japanese textile industry, but by this time it seemed clear that the Japanese government must take a courageous initiative, with a view to securing later acquiescence by the industry. A number of textile leaders told me privately they wanted the government to do just that. Obviously, this was buck-passing.

Again there was no doubt of Sato's earnestness. However, the Tokyo press and textile circles loudly accused the government of "starting the train without the passengers." There was also the usual unhelpful leakage from MITI sources, reflecting in press stories describing an alleged "American plan" as "not even worth studying."

At the Embassy, we tried to help the cause by building an awareness that Japan's textile exports were causing America serious problems. "No nation," I stressed in a speech before the Japanese press club on December 9, "can be expected to be complacent when an industry which accounts for one out of every eight factory workers is seriously threatened with intolerable disruption by sharply rising foreign imports." I cited the fact that 113,000 American textile workers had lost their jobs in the first eleven months of 1970 and that during the immediately preceding two-year period 400 United States textile factories had been compelled to shut down.

Weeks passed as the Washington negotiators debated how many items in how many categories would be subjected to specific restrictions. Considerable progress was made and the gap narrowed. Meanwhile, the pressures were building up as the end of the Congressional session neared. At first, there seemed every likelihood that the Senate would approve some version of the House-passed Mills Bill. But it soon became clear that many aspects of that bill were controversial. When Congress adjourned without enacting such legislation, the negotiations inevitably slowed down.

New proposals by Flanigan in January were described by Japanese officials as "in the wrong direction." In mid-February the Japanese were considering new proposals of their own, but on condition that Flanigan's January proposals be considered "non-existent." In short, without the Congressional Damocletian sword, progress proved to be backward. Flanigan and Ushiba had in late December come within a hairbreadth of reaching agreement. The new divergence was a pity, but the negotiators continued negotiating.

While locked in negotiations with Flanigan, Ambassador Ushiba in mid-February 1971 reported to Tokyo that during a call on Chairman Wilbur Mills the latter indicated he would be satisfied with a Japanese program restraining the growth of textile exports in their aggregate to 5%. This, of course, would be a much softer deal for the Japanese than that being negotiated with Flanigan, which involved items and categories. Reporting this news to Washington, I quoted a high Foreign Ministry official as observing that Chairman Mills's proposal would inevitably undermine the Ushiba-Flanigan negotiations.

Meanwhile, the Tokyo newspapers were reporting that the Japanese textile industry might itself volunteer a "unilateral restraint" program. Also reported was a mysterious visit to Tokyo by a brilliant young lawyer, who was serving as a lobbyist for the Japanese textile industry in Washington, and who reportedly had been in contact with Chairman Mills. (There also appeared for a private talk with Sato one of the staff members from Peter Peterson's Council on International Economic Policy, but the Embassy was assured that his visit was unrelated to textiles.)

On March 8, 1971, Foreign Minister Aichi tipped me off that later that day the Japanese Textile Federation would announce a voluntary program unilaterally restraining its exports of textiles to the United States to an overall growth factor of 5%. According to the Minister, Ambassador Ushiba was so notifying Washington officialdom. Later the same day, Prime Minister Sato's Chief Cabinet Secretary issued a public statement endorsing the "unilateral restraint" program and adding that it obviated the need for further intergovernmental negotiations.

White House reaction was not long in coming. Foreign Ministry officials, in no little distress, phoned me to inquire about wireservice reports indicating the American administration's extreme annoyance. Concerned by reports that a public statement was to be issued, Foreign Minister Aichi and then Sato himself called me in to urge that we not quarrel in public. They insisted that the new program was privately engineered without Japanese government participation and they explained that the statement breaking off intergovernmental negotiations, which obviously had angered Washington, had been intended as conditional. At the same time, they stressed that the Japanese government was in no position to reverse the "unilateral restraint" action. In Washington, it was decided that, the Japanese explanations notwithstanding, there was no choice but to make clear via public announcement that the Japanese actions were unwarranted and unacceptable. In a personal message to Sato, the President explained his lack of alternatives.

The strength of Washington's reaction stunned Tokyo. Ambassador Ushiba claimed that during the month that a "unilateral restraint" program was being cooked up, he had detected no displeasure as grave as that precipitated. There were many in Tokyo, not excluding some of us in the Embassy, who had suspected there might have been some sort of tacit understanding between the White House and the Ways and Means Chairman. In any case, there had been no indications either to the Japanese or to our Embassy to forestall the "unilateral restraint" movement. The only comment heard by the Embassy in response to an earlier telephone inquiry was from a State Department official who had suggested that Washington would probably wait to see what the Japanese would produce.

Despite a desire to make amends, particularly for the unquestionably rude manner in which the intergovernmental negotiations were broken off, the Japanese authorities insisted they had no choice but to let the "unilateral restraint" program go forward. They pledged themselves to try to assure that in its execution it would be as effective as the program which Ambassador Ushiba and Flanigan had been negotiating. They would also, if Washington concurred, seek cooperation from the other major East Asian textile exporting entities, notably Korea, Taiwan, and Hong Kong.

The Ushiba-Flanigan negotiations did not resume. After a brief period of apparent uncertainties, it became clear that even if the Japanese were to execute the unilateral restraints as effectively as envisaged in the Ushiba-Flanigan negotiations, and their ability to do so was open to considerable doubt, it still would not be acceptable in Washington (perhaps because Chairman Mills and not the administration would get the credit). Only an intergovernmental agreement would suffice.

On April 23, former Secretary of the Treasury David Kennedy arrived in Tokyo during the course of an East Asian tour. His stated purpose was to discuss broad financial and trade problems in the region, but the Japanese had little doubt that he would tackle the textile problem. Their assumption was correct. For the next six months Secretary Kennedy, accompanied by special assistant Anthony Jurich, other aides, and security officials, carried out a series of visits to Tokyo. While there were occasional side issues to be dealt with in the East Asian area, the focal point for these highly secretive visits was the securing of agreements with Japan, Korea, Taiwan, and Hong Kong for the restriction of synthetic textile exports to the United States.

As former President of the Continental Illinois Bank of Chicago, which had financial interests in Japan, Secretary Kennedy was well acquainted with the country and many of its leaders. His diplomatic technique was to deal only with the key leaders, to the extent that the secret nature of the meetings allowed. He disliked any sort of publicity. His diplomacy was essentially Theodore Rooseveltian:

"speak softly but carry a big stick." Often he would simply hibernate in his hotel room, relying on his mere presence to exercise pressure. Meanwhile, as occasion warranted, his key aide would be in communication with the Japanese.

Obviously, this type of negotiating was highly unorthodox for old diplomatic hands. My Embassy colleagues, particularly in the economic section, were less than happy, particularly since such details as they did learn were gleaned from Japanese sources. Secretary Kennedy did, however, from time to time give me a general overview of progress made.

Secretary Kennedy's efforts, not surprisingly, had ups and downs similar to those which had characterized the preceding two years of wrangling over the textile issue. Just about the time when hopes would rise, some hitch would dash them. Eventually, and as a last resort, it was decided by top Washington authorities that only strong action would achieve success. Accordingly, in mid-September, Secretary Kennedy served notice that October 15 was the deadline. If a voluntary agreement were not negotiated by that time, the United States would impose a settlement, the terms of which would be much more severe. There was some difficulty in ascertaining under what authority our government could execute such a settlement, but where there is a will there is a way. One possibility, for example, was a legislative provision which would permit the United States Government to impose on a third country an agreement worked out with, say, Korea or Taiwan. A more likely course was invocation of provisions from the "Trading with the Enemy" Act.

No one likes ultimatums, neither the recipient nor the deliverer; but, as in this case, they can produce results. On October 15, Kakuei Tanaka, whom Sato had chosen as Minister of International Trade and Industry in a July cabinet reshuffle, signed an intergovernmental agreement with Secretary Kennedy. There was little joy in MITI, but Tanaka, with the energy that characterized his behavior, bore up as cheerfully as one could expect. Saddled with an onerous task, he had lived up to his reputation as a man of courage and decision.

At long last, the textile problem was off the agenda. Bitterness and resentment there were, and there would be scars. But there was an overwhelming sense of relief. Textiles disappeared from the front pages of the newspapers. Japan-American diplomacy returned to normalcy, to preoccupation with broader trade issues.

Throughout the two-and-a-half-year period, the pre-ultimatum negotiations seemed unproductive. However, looked at in perspective, much progress was made. From their initial absolute intransigence, the Japanese, as I reported to Washington, had over the months: a) given up their insistence on proof of injury; b) concurred in a bilateral agreement rather than requiring referral to GATT or other multilateral forums; c) as to duration, agreed to a one-year moratorium and then to a two-and-a-half-year time period for an agreement; d) compromised to some extent on the base year (one possible reason for the sharp rise in export growth in 1969, 1970, and 1971 was to build up a high volume to serve as the base period); and e) recognized that instead of higher disruptive levels, growth of exports should be held to under 10%.

Throughout the negotiations, including the final ultimatum stage, the nature of the coverage was invariably the chief stumbling block. Essentially, the American textile industry insisted on coverage which would be "comprehensive," placing specific restrictions on the various product items in the textile spectrum. The Japanese resisted strongly, but reluctantly agreed in principle to an overall, or "aggregate," growth figure. In the Flanigan negotiations, the Japanese went further, agreeing to restrictions on seventeen selected items in six categories. This was a position not too far removed from our earlier insistence on twenty-eight items. There were problems, however, as to how much shifting would be allowed within and between categories. Also unresolved was how "residuals," items not under specific restriction, would be handled. The general idea was that if increased exports for any of the residuals became disruptive, the American side could call for "consultations." The question was whether quotas would be applied, regardless of the results of those consultations.

With regard to the coverage question, both the American and the Japanese sides had good cases. The American side believed that unless specific items were restricted, Japanese exporters would shift their production into the most attractive categories, thereby capturing the most profitable sectors of the textile market and placing the American industry at an intolerable disadvantage. As illustration, the Americans could point to the "voluntary agreement" on steel. A 5% growth factor had been applied, but only on an overall tonnage basis. During the original three-year time frame, Japanese steel exporters shifted to the higher grade steels (and concentrated geographically on our West Coast), to the chagrin of the American steel industry. (In the renewal of the steel agreement in 1972 these weaknesses were remedied.)

On the other hand, the Japanese position with regard to coverage was also readily understandable. Their contention was that textiles are far different from steel. Fashions change and change rapidly. Therefore, if Japanese exporters were locked into narrow categories or specific-item quotas, it would be impossible to shift production as fashions shifted.

Thus, the coverage issue was a most complicated one.

It involved woolens as well as synthetic material. It involved fabrics and yarns as well as apparel. It also required agreement on whether to use yardage of fabrics, numbers of items of apparel, or the value of either.

The consensus decision-making process in Japan seemed inherently incompatible with strong individual leadership. Two of Japan's most aggressive postwar leaders, Yoshida and Kishi, had fallen from power as a result of confrontations with Japan's group-conscious mentality.

With such precedents, it was fully understandable that Sato wished, if at all possible, to achieve resolution of the textile issue through consensus, especially within his own Liberal Democratic Party. There was strong resistance not only from the Ministry of International Trade and Industry, but from a large number of LDP politicians. More than any other party, the LDP represented the establishment of which the textile community was a part. Thus, in contradistinction to other political problems, such as the security treaty, this was the first occasion when Japan's postwar leadership was experiencing a serious revolt from within the establishment itself.

The Prime Minister's predicament was not made easier by the fact that his own days at the helm were numbered. His chief aim was to effect a transition of power to leadership which would continue the policies responsible for Japan's postwar success story. Because of rivalries within the LDP and his inability to secure party consensus as to his successor, Sato in October 1970 decided to stay in office for a fourth two-year term. This postponed the problem, but perhaps increased Sato's difficulties. Most politicians assumed there would be no fifth term and this tended to identify him as a lame-duck Prime Minister. The opposition parties exploited these circumstances, as did, of course, the LDP pretenders for the Premiership. Whether it was the succession issue, ratification of the Okinawa agreement, the military budget, rapprochement with China, or the textile issue, securing consensus became for the Prime Minister more difficult than ever.

There was a buck-passing element in the consensus concept. No individual wished to get stung. Therefore, with a distasteful issue like textiles, the federation leaders wanted the support of their industry; the government and the industry each wished the other would take the responsibility; and Diet members were all for a solution provided it was acceptable to the industry. In the LDP the Maeo faction, of which Miyazawa was a member, wished the onus to go elsewhere, as did other LDP factions. The MITI bureaucrats could not be expected to take courageous action even if they could overcome their protectionist myopia. With the superb craftiness which he had developed over the years, Sato sought to bring all these elements aboard. It was an impossible task.

In July 1971, Sato had selected a cabinet which included strong men like Fukuda and Tanaka, capable of energetic assumption of responsibility. Since these two, however, were themselves Prime Ministerial hopefuls, their enthusiasm for having the buck stop at their desks was not unbounded. Nevertheless, as head of MITI, Kakuei Tanaka on October 15, 1971, signed the agreement hammered out with Secretary Kennedy. At the time, he said it would probably cost him politically but, exuding the resilience for which he was famous, he predicted his fortunes would rebound after six months. The fact of the matter was that the textile issue was by that time such a nauseating topic for all Japanese that both Sato and Tanaka gained in respect for having shown the courage to liquidate the problem. All Japanese, particularly the buck passers, breathed a sigh of relief.

Despite the to-ing and fro-ing on the textile issue, and the increasing impatience and irritations in Washington, Sato through it all remained a solid friend of the United

States and of the principles which our two great countries share. This dedication motivated his endless endeavors with the textile issue. Beyond this was a deep sense of personal debt on his part, a quality which is not always readily discerned in Japanese. He wanted to reduce United States-Japan economic tensions because, as he often told me, it was America's generous understanding and cooperation which had made Japan's postwar "miracle" possible. Similarly, he considered President Nixon a good friend of long standing.

The return of Okinawa was in effect the goal of Sato's political life. In his mind, the historic nature of this event would be sullied by linking it with textiles; his motivation for resolving the textile problem was, therefore, more personal. In Japan, honor tends to require returning a favor with a favor. Thus, Sato believed that a satisfactory resolution of the textile issue was the least he and Japan could do for a President and a nation which had treated Japan so well.

When as a result of the Japanese "unilateral restraint" end-run the Ushiba-Flanigan negotiations blew up in March 1971, I wrote a personal letter to Secretary Rogers trying to explain some of the misunderstandings which contributed to the sorry state of affairs. Among other things, I noted that with numerous emissaries shuttling between Washington and Tokyo, it was confusing to the Japanese. A year earlier, in conversation with the then Treasury Secretary Kennedy, Prime Minister Sato had urged that the textile issue be handled through "a single window" and he suggested specifically that it be via the Embassy-State Department route. On another occasion, the Prime Minister asked me if it was not awkward for me as Ambassador not to be a direct participant in the negotiations. I replied by saying that it was for the President to decide how a special problem of this type was to be handled.

My reply contained a certain amount of clairvoyance, for in reply to my letter to the Secretary I was informed that the textile problem was a special matter to be handled in a special way.

Ironically, the Prime Minister's concerns were prompted by the fact that there were many well-intentioned individuals who wished to be helpful. Some of them were officials; some were private citizens. Some were Japanese going to Washington; some were Americans coming to Tokyo. Some operated in the open; others furtively. Some had official blessing; some did not. Some claimed contact with various officials in the White House; others had been in touch with Congress, the Department of Commerce, the Department of State, the Department of the Treasury, the textile industry, or other centers of presumed influence. Minister Miyazawa, for example, told George Shultz and John Ehrlichman when they visited Japan how he had tried unsuccessfully to track down the author of an outline of a draft settlement scribbled in Japanese on yellow tablet paper and supposedly emanating from the White House. I am confident that neither the President, nor the Secretary, nor those designated by them to handle the textile negotiations were ever fully aware how many uninvited, albeit well-meaning, chefs there were in the kitchen.

Although suggesting the normal diplomatic channel, Sato in urging "a single window" for handling textiles seemed primarily interested in identifying emissaries who spoke with the voice of authority. With better coordination, it would have been possible to avoid side-tracks which resulted in increased bitterness. Kendall himself would not have proceeded with discussion of the moratorium proposal had he been able to get a clear reading that it was a non-starter. In preparing for their mission to Washington in June 1970, Ministers Miyazawa and Aichi might have forestalled the collapse of negotiations had there been better coordination of American expectations. With respect to "unilateral restraints," it would have been an easy matter for us at the Embassy to have stopped this maneuver while it was in that one-month rumor stage. We had killed other false moves, such as Japanese government suggestions to American spokesmen to leave the resolution of the textile problem to the textile industries of our two countries.

Part of the difficulty lay, of course, in the fact that with regard to international economic matters various American departments and agencies inevitably were involved. After the announcement of "unilateral restraints," the State Department's top authorities were taking the line with Japanese officials that the only hope lay in making the unilateral restraints meaningful, in effect assuring that the category-item restrictions envisaged in the Ushiba-Flanigan negotiations would be carried out. Later, it became clear that the White House ruled out any consideration whatsoever of the unilateral-restraint program, and insisted on an intergovernmental agreement. Cued by the State Department conversations, the Embassy in Tokyo unfortunately, for a fortnight or so, was off on a tangent, pushing the idea of making the unilateral restraint program meaningful. Compounding the confusion, this tangential line was even reflected in the President's explanatory letter to Sato.

Regardless of negotiating lapses, the textile issue with Japan was bound to be supremely difficult. While the American request for non-disruptive exports sounded reasonable, the fact was that any "voluntary restraint" program was a misnomer. There was nothing voluntary about it. It was the imposition of an American barrier that called upon the Japanese to shoulder the political responsibility. Given the rising tide of nationalism in Japan, there was marked aversion to letting America put the monkey on the Japanese back. The Japanese government, despite a desire to find an amicable solution, found itself between two tremendous pressures. The domestic pressure placed limits on the Sato government's maneuverability.

Under the circumstances, it was not surprising that at times there was sentiment within Japanese officialdom privately welcoming what amounted to American *force majeure*. Despite the broader repercussions it was likely to produce, some Japanese officials hoped the Congress would pass the Mills Bill; it would take Tokyo off the political hook. Similarly, the eventual American ultimatum made it possible for the Japanese government to say that it had no choice but to accept the lesser of two evils.

Given the complicated forces involved, and the unhappy history of the textile problem, it could be argued that an effective agreement, such as that of October 15, 1971, might never have been reached without *force majeure* tactics. What concerned us in Tokyo was that the "get tough" enthusiasts in the White House might prescribe such brutal tactics as standard operating procedure in dealing with the Japanese, who, incidentally, were still recoiling from the July 15 and August 15 gauntlets. In our view, confrontation diplomacy should be employed only as a last resort. If in this instance it was successful, it was because an impasse had been reached, created by unnecessary mistakes by both sides in the earlier stages. The powerful textile industries in both countries had shown an allergy to compromise, and inducing their cooperation was difficult for both governments. On the American side, it was not clear at the outset precisely what was wanted, and the unavailability of what Sato called a "single window" added to the confusion. Both sides tended to view the textile problem in isolation. Neither related its solution to the resolution of broader trade problems such as yen revaluation. Nor was adequate weight given to the debilitating effects on the overall Japanese-American relationship. Many feelings were bruised and there would be scars of resentment, but, fortunately, the long-range damage was not as severe as it might have been.

It is an ill wind that blows nobody good. The textile episode was so unpleasant that neither Japanese nor Americans would wish its repetition. Hopefully, lessons were learned from the mistakes of both sides, so that in the future clashing interests of a similar nature could be better handled.

In an irony of fate, within two years of the 1971 Ides of October, Japan and the United States found themselves on the same side in discussions at Geneva, both countries pressing for the extension and the widening of the original long-term textile agreement (LTA). During the interim, Japan itself had become a major importer of textiles and the Japanese industry had come to view the international textile trade much the same as did the American industry. Thus, after all the sound and fury, and genuine unpleasantness, Japanese and American international textile interests had come together.

Chapter 7

The Changing Art
of the Possible

OFTEN, IN PASSING THROUGH the outer office of the Ambassadorial suite in the Tokyo chancery and viewing the gallery of photographs of my distinguished predecessors, I would think of that golden era when diplomatic life was less hectic. In those bygone days, before the balkanization of the world and the revolutions in communications and transportation, our diplomatic establishments were relatively small families, consisting almost exclusively of personnel assigned by the Department of State and observing niceties dating back to the Congress of Vienna. Most posts were Legations, with only a few at the major capitals having Embassy status. (With postwar inflation, Legations, headed by Ministers, became virtually an extinct institutional species.) The Staff in Ambassador Grew's prewar Tokyo

Embassy totaled only thirty. The bulk of diplomatic correspondence was exchanged by seaborne pouch, although as problems magnified and communications facilities improved, so did the telegraphic "traffic." Travelers came by ship, perhaps once or twice per month through the ports of Yokohama or Kobe.

Diplomacy had changed considerably by the 1970's. The Embassy in Tokyo had a complement of more than 300 Americans, only one-third of whom were on the State Department payroll, while the rest represented a score of other Departments and agencies. (In addition, the Ambassador had responsibilities vis-à-vis some 40,000 American military.) More than 100 telegrams were sent every day, and a similar number received. Nearly 1,000 American visitors, including business executives and government officials, were deplaning daily at Tokyo's Haneda International Airport. Tokyo was a lively and fascinating post, even though on occasion a three-platoon system sounded tempting: one Ambassador to work the day shift with its flow of vital paperwork, plus a full schedule of appointments, including discussions with Japanese officials and opinion leaders; a second Ambassador to work the night shift of three or four social functions per evening, where opportunities were afforded for informal consultations and problem solving; and a third Ambassador to act as a sort of Grover Whelan taking care of the flood of important visitors. Even such a setup would not allow much time for reflection, or for the "graveyard shift" which was my valued solitude lasting well beyond midnight and devoted to "cleaning out the inbox." Years earlier, Ambassador George Wadsworth, one of the unique personalities in the Foreign Service before it became more homogenized, had taught me never to go to bed without dealing with the last scrap of paper in the inbox. Sufficient unto the day would be the next day's evil.

Prior to the war, American diplomacy abroad was conducted by an elite corps of Foreign Service professionals.

Their basic functions were reporting, representation, and negotiation. In accordance with time-honored diplomatic custom, their dispatches were addressed to the Secretary of State with the words, "I have the honor to report . . ." Their ranks included giants such as Ambassador Grew in Tokyo and my first "Chief of Mission" Loy W. Henderson, both of whom were to leave an invaluable imprint on our postwar diplomacy. As in any organization, there were also some officers less outstanding. Unduly influenced by Talleyrand's hallowed advice, *"Surtout pas trop de zèle,"* there were those who took the caution against overzealousness too literally, reporting meticulously developments within the country of their assignment but taking few initiatives unless specifically instructed, and then serving more or less as a mailman for a verbatim message. Quite naturally, our prewar diplomacy tended to reflect the detachment with which an isolationist-minded America viewed the outside world.

After the war, with recognition that a more active American role was inescapable, there was a veritable revolution in American diplomatic endeavor. The American Foreign Service was expanded from a few hundred officers to several thousand. Practices which had served well in the past were replaced. For example, Deputy Under Secretary of State for Administration John Peurifoy with his coterie of iconoclasts discarded the "I have the honor, sir . . ." dispatch format in favor of less formal "airgrams." In earlier days, our international problems had been predominantly bilateral in nature and treated as political phenomena. Now there would be an explosion of international interests. In both Washington and the field, major attention was accorded and manpower devoted to such issues as collective security, technical assistance, economic development, trade expansion, scientific cooperation, and informational and cultural affairs. Our problems became more multilateral in nature, requiring broad international discussion and the extensive travel of special emissaries. Thus, instead of presiding, as previously, over what amounted to a special State Department preserve, our Ambassadors abroad were required to supervise the activities of a disparate group of United States Government representatives, the great majority of whom had their own home offices in Washington. To assure the necessary teamwork and optimal effectiveness, President Kennedy and his successors issued strong directives stipulating the authority of the Ambassador over what was to be considered a fully coordinated United States mission.

In extending after the war over $140 billion in assistance to nations whose people were trying to improve their lot in life, as well as preserve their freedom, American motives were of the best. Much good was accomplished, although history books are unlikely to accord full credit. Frictions were inevitable, primarily because with the help came the helpers. For the recipients, there was the instinctive aversion to being considered, in effect, inferior. For the assistors, there was the tendency to develop a "Father knows best" mentality. As Senate Foreign Relations Committee Chairman J. William Fulbright suggested, it was easy to confuse power with virtue. When those to whom our advice and protection were extended showed less responsiveness and appreciation than many Americans desired, questions increased as to whether our assistance programs were worthwhile. Was the recipient of American largess adequately anti-Communist? Was it taking the steps we considered necessary to achieve the magic goal, so graphically described by Walt Rostow as "economic take-off"? Was the recipient at least potentially a democracy or was its leadership too authoritarian? In short, was it shaping up in our own image?

Such questions were asked by a Congress dutifully concerned as to whether the large outlay of taxpayers' dollars was justifiable. They also provided criteria for newsmen to gauge the state of affairs, or any new turn of events in aid-recipient countries. Unfortunately, the American people were not always given a fair picture. In the mid-1950's, for example, the Reader's Digest published what purported to be an exposé of an incredibly scandalous American assistance program in Iran. The article would leave a fallacious impression, never corrected by subsequent facts. Ten years later, the damned Karaj dam project was a major source of power and water for the burgeoning city of Tehran and the road which allegedly would lead to nowhere was serving as a major artery from the Iranian capital to the Caspian Sea.

As skepticism about our fixing up the world grew, American inquisitiveness became tinged with insistence. Programs whose original motivations were largely humanitarian and selfless tended to develop "strings" as they became increasingly judged in terms of our enlightened national self-interest. Like the geologist who was found trying to shoulder a huge boulder up the side of a mountain so that it would conform to his theories, Washington upon occasion sought through the inducement of aid to secure the adoption of measures better left to local determination. Our beneficiaries tended to be proud people, doubting the omniscience of outsiders with respect to their internal political affairs. Upon my arrival in Tehran in 1965, Shah Mohammed Reza Pahlevi was still chagrined over an episode several years earlier when Washington had indicated specific measures which Iran must take, and had even hinted as to who should be Prime Minister, if a $35 million grant-in-aid were to be authorized. In presenting my credentials, I made clear that, as long as I was American Ambassador in Iran, the question as to who was Prime Minister was Iran's business. Three years later, the Shah was to receive what was for him a gratifying accolade. It was an honorary degree, and it was granted by the same American university whose experts had earlier predicted only gloomy prospects for his leadership and had extended advice in the political domain which had been as erroneous as it had been unwelcome. Relating our assistance to the economic performance of recipient countries was, of course, understandable and justified, but involving ourselves in the internal politics of other countries was another matter.

After the war, Japan was, of course, a primary recipient of American attention. In occupation days, the recovery, reform, and reconstruction programs were subject to General MacArthur's administration. In economic matters, there was much American backseat driving, such as by the Dodge Mission of 1949 which set the yen rate at 360 to the dollar. In security matters, there was a parental American interest in keeping Japan out of Communist clutches. To the extent possible, however, existing governmental machinery was utilized. While some complaints were inevitable, the cooperation between Americans and Japanese was remarkable. No less remarkable was the will power of the Japanese. By the late 1960's, the occupation was past history. Japan's economy was booming and the driving was being done from the front seat with Japanese hands on the wheel. Fears about Japan's security ties with the United States had proved unfounded. Japan was standing on its own feet.

On the whole, the American record of non-interference in the internal political affairs of other nations was worthy of pride. One need merely refer to developments on Okinawa. There the political leadership was freely elected and was exercising power, even though its campaign platform, successfully achieved, featured the removal of the American military administration. So in postwar Japan, governments were chosen by the people. Even some candidates who had been under prosecution for wartime activities within a few years resumed positions of authority.

During my Tokyo sojourn, I held high regard for Prime Minister Sato and his associates in the Liberal Democratic

Party. As a diplomatic officer accredited to the government of Japan, it was my duty to transact business with them, for they represented the government. Who would succeed Sato as Prime Minister was the responsibility of the majority party, the LDP. It was not a problem for the American Embassy. Neither was it our problem how the Japanese political scene might evolve in the 1970's. There was, of course, much speculation, duly reported by the Embassy, such as the possible coagulation of elements of the opposition parties to form a coalition which would serve as an electoral alternative to the LDP. These were all decisions to be made by the Japanese.

Regardless of personalities or parties, my own faith has always been centered in the democratic process. As government of, by, and for the people, it comes closest to meeting the needs of those being governed. It also offers the best hope for harmony among nations. Wherever it can be truly practiced, therefore, the chances are that the greatest good will prevail, no matter how stormy the weather nor into whose hands the tiller is entrusted at any given time. In expressing this confidence, it is recognized, of course, that every nation has its unique characteristics which must be taken into account in its adaptation to democratic procedures.

Compatible with this confidence in democracy, always welcome were the contacts which my Embassy associates and I enjoyed with a broad spectrum of Japanese political thought. While we might not always agree, it was helpful to exchange views on matters of interest between our two countries, not only with the various elements of the Liberal Democratic Party but also with representatives of the opposition parties and other observers of the Japanese scene.

In my memory, there had been occasions in other countries where the American government had become excessively identified with the government in power and was considered hostile to the opposition. This was a disservice to all. It tended to widen the chasm between those in power and those outside, whereas constructive dialogue with various parties could encourage an atmosphere conducive to the reconciliation of differences via democratic processes rather than violent confrontation. It was with this rationale that over the years I had always considered as one of the three basic rules of diplomacy, "Keep an in with the outs." The second rule was, "Never let yourself be put in a corner." The third, "Never get between a dog and a lamp post," or, in other words cooperate with the inevitable.

The people with whom the American diplomatic establishment must transact most of its business do not vote in American elections. This circumstance explains, at least in part, the chronic vulnerability of the State Department and the American Foreign Service to public criticism. Having no farm subsidies, veterans' payments, or social security benefits to distribute, our foreign-affairs representatives can become convenient whipping boys for unpleasant developments, abroad or at home. The failure of a textile mill in the Carolinas could be attributed to diplomatic incompetence in Japan.

One frequently heard criticism was that those dealing with our relationships with a particular country were lacking in expertise. To remedy this inadequacy, particularly in light of our expanding international interests, the State Department had soon after the war launched a major "language and area" specialization program. Offered special incentives, young Foreign Service Officers were detached from regular duties to undergo special training programs of up to two years' duration. They studied intensively the language and cultures of non-Western societies such as Japan, the Soviet Union, and the Arab countries. It was an outstanding program, producing many fine area-specialist officers. Our Embassy in Tokyo was a major beneficiary. But the program was not without some weaknesses. One was hesitation on the part of some talented officers to interrupt for two years their fast-moving careers and implicitly narrow their career options. There was only one country, for example, where a Japan-specialist could exercise his expertise. There were also instances where officers, having completed their training, found offers for service outside the government too attractive to resist.

Perhaps the most difficult task for any "expert" is the maintenance of perspective. In becoming familiar with the culture of another people, their problems, and their sensitivities, it is easy to succumb to the dictum of Socrates, "To know all is to forgive all." A conscious effort must, therefore, be made to avoid vicarious involvement. Known variously in the State Department as "parochialism," "advocacy diplomacy," "client relationship," or "localitis," this weakness is not the exclusive province of the "experts." It is a natural temptation for anyone trying to assure healthy relations with the country of his assignment (including vocally anti-"advocacy diplomacy" political appointees). It was a temptation which we sought to resist in Tokyo, although not always successfully. A telegram sent during my absence wrongly predicted the downfall of the Sato government within a matter of days, following the failure of the Japanese-American proposals on Chinese representation at the United Nations General Assembly in the fall of 1971.

The problem with "localitis" is not only that it distorts what would otherwise be an objective assessment of the local scene, but it, at the same time, gives inadequate weight to other considerations, notably the home country's interests. The recognition of other peoples' sensitivities does not require the wearing of their native garb, literally or figuratively. In returning from a businessmen's convention in the United States, a delegation from the American Chamber of Commerce in Japan reported having heard an eloquent address on the need for Americans to understand

Japan and its sensitivities. Apparently, the entire audience was visibly moved. However, as the listeners were adjourning, they began asking whether it was not equally important for the Japanese to understand America, its sensitivities, and its problems.

Quite obviously, "localitis" about Japan was not a problem at the White House. Heavily business-oriented, and understandably alarmed by our economic plight, the administration believed the time had come to be tough, regardless of sensitivities and sympathies. One administration official described our associates in the East Asian bureau of the State Department as a "bunch of neurotics." It was not surprising, therefore, that as the top echelons of the administration focused intensively on our economic problems, the views of the State Department were not accorded appropriate consideration. Neither was it surprising that the handling of important economic issues with Japan was often conducted outside State Department channels.

As Ambassador, I found myself caught in a crossfire. At the close of my Tokyo tour, I wrote the President, "Those with a keen sense of political trends in Japan have been concerned that Japan's postwar orientation, so favorable to us, might be in jeopardy. Those who so understandably have been preoccupied with sustaining a healthy United States economy, without which Japan's economic exhilarations cannot last, have favored tough stances. My own tendency has been to steer the course between Scylla and Charybdis. Tough we should and must be. Also essential is the maintenance of a political regime in Japan cooperating fruitfully with America." What I was trying to say had been taught to me by another of our great diplomatists, Ambassador Raymond Hare, my chief in Beirut eighteen years earlier. A most important quality of a diplomat, he counseled, is to maintain a proper balance between sympathy and cynicism. An excess of either is unwise. In the long run, neither "bleeding heart" telegrams nor incessant table-thumping will produce the most effective results. A productive partnership is more apt to stem from mutual trust and mutual respect.

During my blitz transit of Washington, en route from Tehran to Tokyo, Dr. Henry Kissinger was among the officials with whom I discussed my forthcoming assignment. Aside from his brilliance, which was household knowledge, I was impressed by his frank and easygoing manner. With no sense of gamesmanship, I am sure, he suggested that from time to time I write to give him a more personal impression of the Tokyo scene than was gleaned from normal Embassy communications. At the time, it did not strike me as an unreasonable request.

As a career Foreign Service Officer, my standard operating procedure was to address all reports from abroad to the State Department. Having served in Washington, I was aware that copies of important communications automatically went to the White House. At the end of 1970, when I had drafted and sent to the State Department my customary personal review of the past year's developments in Japan and my prognosis for the year to come, I recalled Dr. Kissinger's request and took the occasion to write him a letter. The purpose was to call his attention to the two year-end telegrams. Added were a few personal observations such as my hope that, pursuant to the recommendation in my telegrams for top-level consultations, the President might one day visit Japan, perhaps after the Okinawa and textile issues were out of the way. Nothing in the letter was designed to short-circuit the State Department. Later, I learned that a copy of the letter had surreptitiously been brought to the attention of the Secretary of State. His reaction, I was told, was one of no little irritation and it became a factor in a suggested game of musical chairs involving our Far Eastern diplomats, but the proposed reshuffle was not approved by the White House.

No man can serve two masters. Other Ambassadors were caught in a similar crossfire, particularly career officers who lacked the freedom to communicate with the White House which political appointees enjoyed. It was an awkward state of affairs. Foreign governments had quickly sensed that the White House was the focal point of power. For Japan, this was particularly obvious with respect to its most critical problem, China. When the President's visit to Peking was announced, our Embassy in Tokyo was handicapped. The only adequate compensation in Tokyo would be a stopover by the President or his Assistant for National Security Affairs, but since the recommendation had to go through State Department channels, it was not couched quite so bluntly. The assignment was given to the Assistant Secretary of State for East Asian Affairs, who, not having participated in the Peking discussions at topmost levels, was in Japanese eyes not an adequate substitute for the President or Kissinger. Later, a strong recommendation was made that the Emperor be invited to the United States and that this be announced at the Sato-Nixon summit at San Clemente. It was difficult to escape the impression that the proposal would have been more effective if it could have been addressed privately to the National Security Assistant, rather than the State Department.

This bit of history is recounted with heaviness of heart. In many ways Secretary Rogers and Dr. Kissinger complemented each other, the former an amiable and superb negotiator dealing with the great bulk of our foreign-affairs operations, the latter a shrewd manipulator of ideas and people, particularly on the more crucial (and glamorous) international political issues. Such division of labor was obviously the way the President wished to exercise his Constitutional responsibility, and the total product, notably the breakthroughs with China and the Soviet Union, was impressive. It could be contended, however, that a more unified direction of our foreign-affairs establishment might have bolstered such successes, particularly with regard to relations with our friends and allies. That this theory was not without validity seemed confirmed subsequently when Dr. Kissinger became Secretary of State, retaining his position as the Assistant to the President for National Security Affairs and committing himself to "institutionalizing" our foreign policy apparatus.

Aside from the State Department and the National Security Council, there was a third force in Washington with which the Embassy in Tokyo needed to reckon. It was the economic hierarchy. Dr. Kissinger seemed to have only a passing interest in economic matters. Despite brave efforts, the State Department was often on the outside looking in. Commerce Secretary Stans was highly influential, particularly in advocating tougher international policies. He was also pressing for a greater role for his Department in the staffing of our Embassies, including the appointment of businessmen to Ambassadorial assignments. Most of the decision-making, however, resided in the White House, but it was not always clear whose voice was more powerful, Assistant to the President Peter Flanigan, OMB Director George Shultz, or CIEP Director Peter Peterson. The Chairman of the Council of Economic Advisors Paul McCracken and the Special Trade Representative Carl Gilbert were playing significant roles. However, they were also in a situation sometimes reminiscent of Leo Durocher's "Nice guys finish last." Treasury Secretary, subsequently Ambassador-at-Large, David Kennedy was also actively engaged. When John Connally took over at the Treasury Department, he was a new power-hitter in a new ball game.

All these top officials were grappling with unprecedented problems in the economic field. Their fast-moving preoccupations left little opportunity for providing guidance to those of us toiling in far-flung vineyards like Tokyo. Thus we played it by ear, trying to pick up the tune from official pronouncements, daily telephone contact with our State Department associates, press reports, and visitors from Washington, particularly the key decision-makers who sooner or later found it prudent to visit Tokyo. The common refrain, which came through loud and clear, was that the times required America to be "tough."

According to the U.S. Constitution, the responsibility for the conduct of foreign affairs rests squarely with the President. How he chooses to discharge that responsibility has, of course, depended on his personal predilections.

A plain-speaking son of Missouri, President Harry Truman had even in foreign affairs an instinct for the jugular. When the Russians intimidated Iran, and later Greece and Turkey, there was prompt American response. Even though our forces were tensely engaged in Korea, he did not hesitate to dismiss a super-hero for insubordination toward his Commander-in-Chief. When the State Department, concerned by the prospect of Soviet gains, the denial of oil, and deep-seated animosities, opposed the creation of Israel, he within minutes recognized the new state and let the State Department know that the President determines American foreign policy. In what was to become a most unusual personal alliance, the small-town ex-haberdasher from provincial mid-America won the admiration and fealty of an urbane Ivy Leaguer who, despite vulgar attacks during his incumbency, became one of our most creative Secretaries of State. With mutual respect and affection, Truman and Acheson worked as a team. The State Department and the Foreign Service had a feeling of being involved, even though it meant sharing some of the unfair McCarthy-era criticisms.

Reflecting his many years of reliance on military staff work, President Eisenhower delegated foreign affairs responsibilities almost entirely to his Secretary of State. A *Washington Post* cartoon once showed a rocket labeled "for-

eign policy" doing somersaults in the sky, with a worried
Eisenhower in the background asking a lever-pulling John
Foster Dulles whether he was sure he had the missile under
control. Secretary Dulles, a lifelong devotee of foreign affairs, was described as carrying the State Department in
his hat. I recall on one occasion our Office of South Asian
Affairs having invested many man-hours preparing materials in anticipation of a visit by Prime Minister Mohammed
Daud of Afghanistan, only to have the Secretary say, "Let's
put all this ritual aside. What are we going to tell the Prime
Minister?" During no administration after the war was the
State Department more fully responsible for foreign affairs, but the sense of exhilaration was qualified by the
limited room under the Secretary's hat for imported wisdom. Structurally, and in conformity with the President's
military background, much emphasis was placed on such
interagency groups as the National Security Council (NSC)
for "policy" and the Operations Coordination Board (OCB)
for the implementation of policy. These organizations gave
other Washington bureaucracies the illusion of more significant participation in foreign-policy formulation than
was actually the case. The voluminous paperwork was a
headache for the State Department, and the lengthy committee meetings with their wrangling over minor language
were tiresome. But neither the NSC nor the OCB inter-
fered with Secretary Dulles's personal conduct of foreign
affairs, featuring his relentless pact-building anti-Communist crusade. It was the Secretary's basic belief that the
State Department should not be encumbered with "operations" such as foreign aid programs, information, and cultural activities.

The Kennedy administration brought the vigor of
youth. Here was a President intensely interested in foreign affairs, even to the extent of personally telephoning
desk officers in the State Department. Having appointed a
number of well-known Americans to subordinate positions

in the Department, the President, thanks to advice from former Secretary Acheson, decided on Dean Rusk as Secretary of State. For those of us who knew Rusk it was a welcome appointment, for he was a solid professional with an impressive record of past experience in international affairs. During ensuing years, the subordinate celebrities one by one moved elsewhere, but, like the marble from his native state of Georgia, Rusk presided resolutely over our foreign affairs establishment throughout the eight years of the Kennedy and Johnson administrations. Teamed with him, as successive Undersecretaries, were men with strong qualifications of their own: Chester Bowles, George Ball, and former Attorney General Nicholas Katzenbach.

The Kennedy years were replete with excitement. Abolishing much of the formal machinery, including the OCB, and rubbing out the distinction between "policy" and "operations," Kennedy instituted a loose, open, and dynamic style. He was the first to install a significant foreign affairs unit in the White House, but McGeorge Bundy's shop was limited in size and served primarily to ensure that the various bureaucratic circuits were connected, among themselves and with the President. The word went forth for the State Department to "take charge," including the giving of foreign policy direction to other Washington agencies. With so many live wires in the White House, however, and with what Secretary Rusk described as too much "layering" (which he reduced) in the State Department, the fulfillment of the "take charge" mandate sometimes fell short. Nevertheless, the personnel of the State Department and the Foreign Service enjoyed the satisfaction of being involved, including in numerous ad hoc "task forces" with State Department chairmen. The fact was that President Kennedy, along with his "can-do" philosophy and eagerness to overcome government inertia, had an insatiable appetite for the opinions of others. While letting each of them feel that his contribution of wisdom was undeniable (note Arthur

Schlesinger's *A Thousand Days*), the President on the key issues would make his own decision.

President Johnson, in my judgment, was a leader whose instincts were sound. An earthy Texan who had worked his way up by his bootstraps, Johnson had the unique ability to sense the feelings of his compatriots, which made him a master of domestic politics. He was less comfortable with foreign affairs. In that sphere, he had admired the work of his predecessor and sought to carry it forward, relying heavily on the advice and support of Kennedy's key foreign-policy advisors. An attempt was made to inject more formality, coordination, and long-range planning into the structure for formulating foreign policy by establishing State-centered "Interdepartmental Regional Groups" (IRG's) and a "Senior Interdepartmental Group" (SIG). However, the key decisions were made at the Tuesday luncheons of the "awesome foursome," which included the President, Secretary Rusk, Defense Secretary Robert McNamara, and the National Security Assistant Walt Rostow, who succeeded McGeorge Bundy. The President tended to defer to the presumably better qualified judgment of his luncheon partners. Well do I remember a visit to the Oval Office when President Johnson listened attentively to my rationale of why it was important for us to permit Iran to purchase a modest amount of military equipment (a small fraction of what was subsequently approved by the succeeding administration). To be honest, I noted that Secretary McNamara was opposed to such expenditures by developing nations. With warm sincerity, the President concluded the conversation saying he felt I had made a good case and he hoped I could persuade our government to go along with it. His sympathy was clear, and, fortunately, Secretary McNamara eventually was persuaded.

Like Kennedy, President Nixon was intensely interested in foreign affairs. During his eight years out of office, he had through his travels acquired an acquaintance with foreign problems and leaders unmatched by any of his White House predecessors. Unlike Kennedy, President Nixon preferred to work through a small handful of intermediaries and to make decisions in private after much personal cogitation. Such concentration required a tightening up of the Presidential schedule. When assigned as Ambassador to Lebanon, I had enjoyed a lengthy exchange of views with President Kennedy about the whole Middle East. During my Tehran assignment, President Johnson had allowed time for beneficial discussions upon my returns to Washington. It was disappointing, therefore, not to have had opportunity to confer personally with the President during the much more important Tokyo mission, although on its conclusion he was kind enough to write, "I have always found your [telegraphed] views and recommendations perceptive, and I have always weighed them carefully in my decisions on our policy toward Asia." Presidential consultations provide a great boost to an Ambassador's credentials in his dealing with the leaders in the country to which he is accredited. With this in mind, I was grateful for quotable words picked up during brief informal exchanges with the President during Sato's official visits to Washington, when the President was emplaning at Anchorage after having greeted the Emperor, and at the departure ceremonies for Sato at San Clemente.

With Presidential burdens becoming ever more crushing, it was perhaps inevitable that personal consultations between the President and his Ambassadors, whose numbers had soared to several score above 100, would be among those customs which would become casualties. Meanwhile, President Nixon's conversations with foreign leaders were normally on a tête-à-tête basis, with only the Assistant to the President for National Security Affairs in attendance. The exclusion of others, such as the Secretary of State or the Ambassador to the country concerned, was no doubt prompted by what I have sometimes called "Meyer's law": the efficiency of a negotiation is inversely proportional to the number of participants. Another factor, quite probably, was that the capability of inquisitive newsmen to ferret out and publish highly confidential information tends to increase at a geometric rate with each additional listener to a conversation. It was probably for reasons such as these that under the Nixon administration the tendency increased to bypass established channels and entrust highly important missions to special secret emissaries. Such shifts from orthodox procedures may have had advantages, but they often had unintended drawbacks, not the least of which was to reflect a lack of trust and, thus, cripple the effectiveness of those officials, including the Secretary of State, who were expected to carry out the broad stream of governmental business day after day.

Structurally, the President and his astute National Security Assistant sought to inject more orderliness into the foreign affairs organization. Reviving the distinction between policy and operations, the National Security Council was reinvigorated, and its staff of youthful professionals grew to unprecedented size. Its work was tailored so that under the direction of Dr. Kissinger, as head of the "Senior Review Group" (SRG), materials on specific foreign-policy issues would be prepared in a manner to provide the President, not with agreed recommendations as in Eisenhower's days, but with well reasoned "options." The President's choice of "policy" would then govern the conduct of our foreign affairs. The system had many advantages. Instead of what some Nixonians considered the "chaotic" improvisations of the Kennedy administration, all foreign policy steps would be linked to a grand design. Foreign policy would be determined not by bureaucratic politics but by sound judgment at the top, based on exposure to various views. Since the materials would be prepared by Interdepartmental Groups, usually in the form of

"National Security Study Memoranda," all concerned agencies of the government would know in advance their roles under the option chosen. Finally, the critical problem of whether the State Department could give direction to other government agencies in foreign-affairs matters was resolved in that this responsibility would be assumed by the White House, i.e., the President or his Assistant for National Security Affairs acting in his behalf. In late 1969, when we were wrapping up the communiqué that would be issued by the President and Prime Minister Sato with regard to the reversion of Okinawa, Dr. Kissinger made it clear that none of us connected with the State Department should attempt to persuade the reluctant Defense Department. This would be handled, he said, by the White House.

Even for Dr. Kissinger, with his seemingly limitless capacities, there were only twenty-four hours in the day. With the President, he was heavily engaged in arranging "peace with honor" in Vietnam, and in negotiations with the Chinese and the Soviets. Often he was traveling abroad, which somewhat blurred the distinction between his "conceptual" role and an "operational" one for the Secretary of State. In handling crises such as Cambodia and Indo-Pakistani hostilities, a "Washington Special Action Group" was convened, and there were several other committees under Kissinger's direction. His focal position in the coordinated management of the President's foreign policy left little room for the delegation of his authority. Memoranda regarding specific countries or special issues were flowing in a steady stream from the State Department to the NSC headquarters in the White House. Despite appeals for brevity, the presentation of "options" tended to lengthen the paperwork. Authors and agencies were anxious that decisions not be made without all the facts. Occasionally, a single course of action seemed obvious but what in effect were straw-man options were included. Inevitably, papers dealing with the most urgent and most critical issues received priority White House attention. On less critical matters, the State Department would usually take action on its own, particularly if past NSC decisions provided clues as to White House wishes. There were, however, numerous occasions where State-to-NSC memoranda, requiring White House decision and dealing with issues of current importance in our relations with other countries, would remain unanswered for several weeks, due to higher-priority White House preoccupations. The absence of a decision could risk long-range damage. It was not always true what Senator Allen Ellender used to say about Embassies, "What needs to be done, must be done by the Ambassador. What the Ambassador does not need to do, does not need doing."

State Department people sometimes get the impression that the belaboring of their institution rivals baseball as America's national pastime. Known both affectionately and slurringly as "Foggy Bottom," the Department was described by President Kennedy as a "bowl of jelly." Others called it a "fudge factory." In his successful 1968 campaign, Richard Nixon scored points by declaring that, if elected, he would do what had never before been adequately accomplished: he would "clean house" at the State Department. To one of my Congressional friends, he indicated that, except for officers numbering less than could be counted on the fingers of one hand, State Department-Foreign Service personnel whom he had encountered during his travels were not as competent as they should be.

Having few constituents in the American electorate, the State Department traditionally serve as a convenient target for politicians, for pundits, for millions of Americans who bear a deep-seated suspicion of their government, and for Washington bureaucracies who are delighted to see discontent centered on an agency other than their own. The supreme practitioner in the art of baiting the State Department was, of course, Senator Joseph McCarthy.

Not entirely unrelated to the McCarthy aberration regarding loyalty to the nation has been the continuing question of the loyalty of State Department personnel to the administration in power. A common criticism, voiced by most postwar administrations, was that the Department was insubordinate, resisting change and failing to carry out the decisions of the President. At the same time, the Department was faulted for lack of creativity and failure to "take charge." Such criticisms contained elements of inconsistency, inevitability, and unfairness. When a new regime came to power in Washington, it quite naturally wished to make spectacular moves, such as encouragement in 1953 to the East German uprisings which were aborted. Conscientious officers could not be expected on Inauguration Day to change advice which was based on their experience and best judgment. If there was hesitancy to "take the lead," it was because Department officers believed, no less stoutly than the White House, that leadership responsibility was Constitutionally on the President's shoulders. Having through the Secretary of State submitted their advice and recommendations, they had no choice but to abide by the President's decisions, whether the concern was the Communist menace, the Middle East, Vietnam, China, or our economic problems with Japan. All of this was not to say that Americans were not living in a world of change. As conditions altered, previously considered approaches might have greater chance for success, and brand new ideas should be explored. It was precisely to assure that policy thinking did not get into a rut that Department and Foreign Service personnel were reshuffled to other positions every two or three years. It allowed fresh minds to look at new, as well as old, problems and to venture new ideas in the light of current overall policies, and the wishes of the administration's leadership.

Having thus risen to the defense of my Alma Mater, it is necessary to acknowledge that the State Department did have its shortcomings. With its 5,000 employees in Washington and 3,400 abroad, it was a colossus too often lacking in efficient responsiveness. Its paperwork was too often verbose, inarticulate, and uninspiring. Its replies could get bogged down for days simply securing the necessary clearances. Substantively, the clearance process all too often resulted in the lowest common denominator. The tendency did exist to seek safety in established policies. Some officers lacked the courage of their convictions or the ability to project them convincingly to others. There were cliques, whose members supported partisan prejudices and scratched each other's backs. But the vast majority of Department and Foreign Service officers were truly dedicated. Seldom were they able to get away when the clock showed 5:30, and the higher they were in the hierarchy the later they got home.

The enormous volume of responsibilities handled by the Department was unknown to and unappreciated by outsiders. Also not properly understood was its encyclopedic understanding of international developments. I remember one of Kennedy's New Frontiersmen at Secretary Rusk's morning staff meeting avowing his intentions to rebuff the next telephone request from the White House demanding an urgent answer to a problem. "There is a lot of wisdom in that bureau of mine," he said, "and, whatever the issue, it is a mistake not to tap it fully." Years earlier, Afghan elder statesman Shah Mahmoud had observed that experienced leaders surefootedly wind their way up the mountain, while the inexperienced and impatient attempt a direct and risky ascent. The problem was to meld experience with creativity to produce a foreign policy that was both wise and vigorous.

It has long been my belief that a book could be written about American foreign policy entitled, "The Horeshoe Nail." Its theme would be that in many cases America's diplomatic misfortunes have not been due to erroneous major policy decisions but were the result of minor mistakes which triggered the unleashing of powerful forces difficult to control. Repercussions from the mistreatment of a diplomat's servants in a remote corner of China could critically affect American relations with the Chinese mainland for a quarter of a century. The turn of a phrase by an Ambassador could spark a public outburst by a foreign leader which would impel the termination of American assistance which would in turn precipitate irrational actions leading to violence which no one intended or wanted. Our involvement in Vietnam was incremental, with opportunities all along the line for better judgment. Such a review would show, I am sure, that in terms of sound advice the State Department's batting average was higher than that of those critics who were understandably impatient for dramatic action and quick solutions. It would also show that due appreciation was seldom accorded those who avoided the mistakes and prevented explosions.

In the postwar years, more than a dozen surveys were taken with a view to "reorganizing" the State Department to make it more "responsive" to the needs of modern diplomacy. From time to time, reforms of varying magnitudes were introduced, but a satisfactory solution remained elusive. At the outset of the 1970's, extensive studies were produced by the American Foreign Service Association and by a battery of thirteen Departmental task forces appointed by Deputy Under Secretary of State for Administration William Macomber. Many of the resulting proposals were usefully adopted, particularly those of an administrative nature. The active role of the White House, however, tended to serve as a brake on the hopes of those who envisaged an organization wherein the State Department would become, as had been recommended by the Hoover Commission twenty years earlier, "the focal point for coordination of foreign affairs activities throughout the government."

Quite rightly, endeavors to adjust the foreign policy machinery for optimum performance would have to continue. However, as Secretary Rusk had once stated, "The real organization of government at higher echelons is not what you find in textbooks or organization charts. It is how confidence flows down from the President." It was in this area, as we saw it from the other end of the line in Tokyo, where the State Department and the Foreign Service had much distance to go. The so-called "Nixon shocks" were fitting reminders.

Parenthetically, it should be noted that the situation described above changed immeasurably in 1973 when Dr. Kissinger assumed the position of Secretary of State and brought his White House role with him. He publicly acknowledged the "difficulties" of the recent past and pledged a greater "institutionalization of foreign policy," with the "entire Foreign Service" being "brought more closely into the operation." For State Department and Foreign Service personnel, these were welcome words that would, hopefully, come true.

In accordance with tradition, my credentials from the President to the Emperor of Japan included the impressive title, "Ambassador Extraordinary and Plenipotentiary." In practice, it was an inaccurate appellation. As to the adjective "extraordinary," what Ohio State coach Francis Schmidt had told his footballers about Michigan players' "putting their pants on one leg at a time" applied equally to Ambassadors. As to authority, my powers were not always "pleni." There were occasions when our government's business affecting Japan was transacted with the Embassy on the sidelines. Also, due in part to faulty State Department connections in the White House switchboard, precise policies being pursued were not always getting through to the President's representatives abroad. My personal appeal to Secretary Rogers in March 1971, that, instead of "operating in the dark," the Embassy be allowed to play a "more useful role" in preventing misunderstanding and confusion on such issues as textiles received a polite reply expressing doubt that the Embassy's role could have been augmented and giving assurance that in no way did this reflect a lack of confidence in the Embassy's competence.

Inadequate instruction of our Embassies abroad was not an invention of the Nixon administration. From experience both in Washington and in the field, I had long since learned that Washington backstoppers, frustrated at getting meaningful instructions cleared through the bureaucratic labyrinth, would breathe a sigh of relief when an Ambassador would proceed on his own to do what was in the nation's interest. In those days, officers in the field could surmise the trend of Washington thinking via informal correspondence with their State Department counterparts. In the much tauter Nixon ship, the State Department crew was often as poorly informed as those of us in far-off ports. Nonetheless, by studying the official and unofficial clues available to us, the general thrust of the administration's policy was discernible, even though our tea leaves failed to forecast the China and economic "shocks." It may be noted that Ambassadorial initiatives in Tokyo required greater care than at previous posts, because there were more high-level quarterbacks. More important, the more difficult problems had multilateral implications; they were, therefore, less amenable to localized treatment.

To suggest that, with regard to such issues as textiles, yen revaluation, and China, the Embassy in Tokyo might have played a more useful role was not to claim superior intelligence for our personnel or to defend what some critics have labeled as the Foreign Service's "subculture." Nor was it a protest against the dispatch of special emissaries from Washington. Because of the nature of certain problems, properly conducted special missions could and did achieve results well beyond the capabilities of the Embassy. In my end-of-tour letter to the President, I referred to such visitors: "Our Tokyo mission has enjoyed cooperating with them, backstopping their endeavors, and sending in to Washington a continuous flow of pertinent information." The Embassy's only interest was to assure optimal results. The emissaries would come and go, but we were on the scene and in daily contact with Japanese officialdom. In a country where decisions were made by consensus, it was especially important to confer with more than just one or two leaders. If reasonably clued-in as to what our government was trying to achieve, we could help the cause along. We could not do so, if, as frequently happened, it would be from our Japanese friends that we would learn of American negotiating positions or of a visit by an American emissary. Moreover, such exclusion from cognizance of what our own government was doing could not but damage our credentials for carrying out the broad responsibilities of the Tokyo mission. More insidiously, excessive secrecy could breed anti-secrecy, such as subsequent indications that Pentagon officials in Washington were resorting to improper means to secure information to which they felt entitled from the National Security Council. Meanwhile, apparent distrust could invite counterdistrust. If government was to be responsive and effective, nothing was more critical, as Rusk had pointed out, than the flow of confidence from the higher echelons.

The hole of the doughnut usually gets more attention than the doughnut as a whole. Dismayed by the "Nixon shocks," our colleagues in the American press corps in Tokyo, and we at the Embassy, let concerns about inadequate coordination with Washington in a few matters overshadow what was overall a highly creditable diplomatic performance. Thanks to exemplary Tokyo-based negotiations, the Okinawa issue was resolved in a manner highly beneficial to both countries. The security issue in 1970 did not explode and disrupt our relationship as had been freely predicted. Frictions were further reduced through the mutually agreed realignment of American military facilities in Japan. Even in the economic field, the Embassy's contributions were noteworthy, e.g., important assistance in securing the reduction of import-quota restrictions from 120 to 33 as over against only a half-dozen or so removed during the preceding five or six years. Regarding the China and economic "shocks," the Embassy was caught by as much surprise as were the Japanese, but the immediate rallying of our efforts to cushion the shocks was not without value.

Aside from the three semi-facetious rules of diplomacy previously mentioned, my lifelong creed had been, "Accentuate the positive; don't accept the negative." In its essence, diplomacy for me meant sitting down with the representative of another country, trying to place yourself in his shoes and him in yours to visualize what was and what was not possible, figuring out that limited area where mutual interests merged, and building on that area of agreement. In those areas where differences existed, the challenge was to persuade the other negotiator why it was in his country's interest to go down one road rather than another, with the former being a mutually acceptable course. Some problems could be solved expeditiously; some would require patience and massaging; some might, if left to time, resolve themselves. Only rarely was it desirable to resort to confrontation, and then, as Dulles had observed, knowing when to go to the brink was the necessary art. Even then, how it was done was as important as what was done.

It did not follow that such principles of diplomacy, so congenial to the Western mind, were equally so for non-Westerners. Years earlier, Ambassador Joseph Grew had sought in vain to convince his American compatriots that one cannot gauge Japanese psychology by "any Western measuring rod." During my Tokyo sojourn I had frank and friendly conversations (this phrase is, regrettably, so frequently used that one fellow diplomat suggested abbreviating it to "FFC" for telegraphic purposes!) with Prime

Minister Sato at least once each month, with the Foreign
Minister about two times per month, and a monthly luncheon with the Vice Minister of Foreign Affairs to discuss
all current problems of mutual interest. Leaders such as
these, of course, had had much experience in international
affairs and they could "put themselves in the other fellow's
shoes." But the more traditional Japanese instinct, which
permeated much of the government, was to fear and resist
foreigners.

Thus, for Western-oriented diplomats, there were added
dimensions in negotiating with the Japanese. Allowances
had to be made for the "consensus" mentality, which often
meant procrastination while a problem was being group-
analyzed, discussed, and homogenized as part of an educational process leading to a more favorable Japanese
disposition. It also meant, incidentally, that summitry with
Japanese leaders could not be expected to produce quick
and effective results as would be the case with leaders in
more authoritarian countries. Concessions came usually in
small increments, but their accumulation could be quite
substantial. Frequently a Japanese spokesman would give
an affirmative response, but it meant only that he understood linguistically. Criticisms by the press and opposition
elements often appeared to be part of the government's
orchestration (not altogether dissimilar from the way
American negotiators hide behind the skirts of hostile press
and Congressional opinion to explain positions which the
American government has decided to take). Tactically,
Japanese negotiators would sometimes set a deadline for
the resolution of a problem which would be leaked to the
press and put the other side under popular pressure to give
ground by that date or face an adversary relationship.

Just because Japanese negotiating behavior was somewhat at variance with our own did not mean that American
negotiators must surrender to it. It did mean, however, that
discretion was often the better part of valor. Of prime

importance was the need to avoid, to the extent possible, losing face. There were various useful methods, such as working through lower-echelon negotiating teams, relying on the importance of the Japanese sense of obligation, or resolving problems via multilateral action, as eventually occurred with the yen revaluation. One thing was certain: once agreement was reached, the Japanese would live up to their commitments as meticulously as they had bargained.

By and large, the staff at the Tokyo Embassy understood the realities, both in Japan and in their own country. Early each morning our key officers would forgather to review Japanese and international developments during the preceding twenty-four hours, note what the Japanese press was saying, discuss important telegrams from Washington and elsewhere, and determine what should be done and by whom. Present at these operations meetings were: the Deputy Chief of Mission, the chiefs of the economic and political sections, the political-military advisor, the administrative counselor, the representatives of the United States Information Agency and the Central Intelligence Agency, my ears and voice in Japan James Wickel, the Commander or Deputy Commander of United States Forces in Japan when they were in town, any visiting firemen from Washington, my staff aide to take minimal but action-oriented notes, and, finally, on a rotating basis, junior officers of the Embassy to give them an impression of how Embassy business was conducted. It was a "command post" operation after which the section chiefs were expected to take such actions as had been decided and to keep their respective staffs in tune. At a larger meeting, once each week, current Embassy problems and policies would be discussed with the heads of all American government agencies represented in Tokyo, and they, in turn, would contribute by discussing their activities and plans.

Operating an Embassy, particularly at an important capital like Tokyo, required, of course, considerable infrastructure, e.g., managing three apartment buildings and other housing, as well as the Chancery and a seven-story annex in the old Manchurian Railway Building. Coping with such matters was a hardworking administrative section, with its large complement of Japanese employees. Keeping the Ambassador efficiently programmed for both the day shift at the office and the night shift on the social merry-go-round, and screening the flow of paper work, was my Personal Assistant Florence Neverman. Having put up with the idiosyncrasies of this particular Ambassador from his first Chief of Mission assignment in Beirut a decade previously, she was the key to the functioning of the "front office."

Chester Bowles once said that, thanks to science, we can send a message halfway around the world in a fraction of a second, but the most important distance is the last two feet. The crucial element is personal communication. This means listening as well as speaking. It means overcoming linguistic and cultural barriers, which in Japan were formidable. It means qualities such as sincerity, integrity, and what Foreign Minister Aichi called "mutual trust."

In Japan, as elsewhere, diplomacy was not confined to conversation in the Foreign Ministry. For democracies such as Japan and the United States, foreign policy is dependent on the degree of support received from society as a whole. Thus, if the productive relationship between the two countries was to continue, extensive communication was essential at various levels: government and non-government, opinion molders, intellectuals, cultural communities, and the ordinary citizenry. It was what former Ambassador Reischauer had called "dialogue," with the subject matter broader than merely the points of issue between our two governments. At no level, of course, was the "dialogue" and "mutual trust" more important than between the leaders of the two countries.

Public anxieties in Japan were difficult to still, but President Nixon's three summit meetings with Prime Minister Sato (and subsequently with Prime Minister Tanaka) did much to reassure the top echelons of the Japanese government of the continuing value attached by Washington to the Japanese-American partnership, despite the painful adjustments being made in that relationship. In addition, the meeting of the President and the Emperor at Anchorage, coming just after the two "shocks," had a salutary impact. However, my hopes for a Presidential visit to Tokyo did not materialize, because, as Sato mentioned in one of our early talks, the time was not "ripe." First, the "anti-treaty struggle" and the Okinawa reversion agreement had to be gotten out of the way, and subsequently the China and economic issues clouded the atmosphere. The Japanese were determined to have no repetition of the humiliating 1960 experience when hostile political manifestations forced the cancellation of a Presidential visit. Knowing how much the Japanese wished to make amends for the 1960 episode, we took the occasion to recommend, as a step toward paving the way for a future Presidential visit, that David and Julie Eisenhower be the special representatives for "America Day" at Expo 70 in Osaka. It was to David's grandfather the Japanese felt an obligation, and in welcoming Julie the Japanese would honor a flesh-and-blood representative of the current American President. The visit was a smashing success. No demonstrators reared their heads. David's Eisenhower grin plus his ability to project friendliness in extemporaneous remarks, and Julie's natural winsomeness, captivated the Japanese and, incidentally, left not a few Tokyo Americans prophesying that this young and attractive couple had a bright future on the American domestic political scene.

As Sam Jameson, Japanese-speaking reporter for *The Chicago Tribune* and subsequently *The Los Angeles Times*, pointed out, my predecessors had had trouble securing

Washington's attention to Japan. My problems, however, were the reverse. The upsurge of American interest and concern was reflected in the flow of VIPs from all sectors of the American government. At one time or another, we welcomed for conferences with their Japanese counterparts all but two of our Cabinet Secretaries, the chiefs of our military services, well over 100 Senators and Congressmen, a bevy of Under Secretaries, Assistant Secretaries, and other high-ranking bureaucrats.

Never did we consider this flow of distinguished Americans a burden. Each visitor represented an opportunity for broadening and deeping the dialogue between Japan and the United States. Our elected officials, trained to keep their ears to the ground in their own constituencies, had a special knack for understanding the problems of other people and establishing communication. In this connection, the annual conference of Japanese and American governors, about eight attending from each side and meeting in the two countries alternately, was an especially productive institution developed during the Reischauer era.

With regard to Congressional travel, it was the conviction of our Embassy in Tokyo that as many of our legislators as possible should learn about Japan firsthand, away from the pressures and preoccupations of Washington. Even with the retrenchment reflected in the Nixon Doctrine, the United States remained inextricably involved in international affairs. How our elected representatives could be expected to cast valid judgments without personal familiarity with the problems was difficult to fathom. For those of us engaged in assuring adjustments in our international relationships consistent with the realities of the times, visiting Congressional representatives could leave helpful imprints on Japanese thinking while improving their own knowledge.

In according hospitality to visiting officials, it was the Japanese who had cause to complain about lack of reciprocity. Cabinet-level Americans seldom came to Tokyo without a useful exchange of views with the Prime Minister. They tended to expect it, as did prominent American Senators, newspaper publishers, and businessmen. In Washington, American officials, due to other preoccupations, were not able to reciprocate so generously. In one instance, a Japanese cabinet minister made a public issue of his abortive effort to see the President. Diet members, both from the LDP and the opposition, were usually welcomed on Capitol Hill by Senators Fulbright, Scott, and others, but there were occasions when appointments with American officials at an adequate level in the Executive Branch required repeated appeals from the Embassy. The point was not crucial, but it did suggest that if Americans meant what they said about partnership of equals, the treatment of visiting officials should be viewed with better balance.

At American diplomatic missions, informational and cultural programs are generally under the supervision of the United States Information Agency. In Washington, no USIA post was considered to be of greater importance than that in Tokyo. Its lively activities included a cultural center, a library, press activities, contacts with youth groups, encouragement of visits by leaders to and from the United States, and a variety of other endeavors designed to develop better understanding between the Japanese and American people. Outside Tokyo, there were "cultural centers" in a number of the prefectural capitals.

A special USIA exertion was directing the participation of the United States in Expo 70 at Osaka. Years earlier, in Afghanistan, I had learned that for American taxpayers such international expositions are dubious propositions. Through tourism, world publicity, and the mesmerizing of the local populace, the host country benefits considerably more than do the participants. For some exhibitors, including the United States, the chief motivation seems to be not wishing to offend the host country by non-participation. While such occasions provided opportunities for some countries, particularly the "socialist" countries, to demonstrate "progress" in such fields as the production of motor vehicles, everyone already knew of America's technological prowess. At Expo 70, due to a Congressional budget slash, USIA and its collaborators settled for a spacious hole in the ground covered by a heavy canvas-like material supported by air pressure. Some jocularly called it a huge "corn plaster." Pursuant to the deft management of special Ambassador Howard Chernoff and his teammates, the contents, including a moon rock, a lunar module, and Babe Ruth's uniform, attracted visitors queuing up in long lines. The Soviet pavilion, a dramatic architectural accomplishment with the hammer and sickle reaching high into the sky, was at least equally crowd-attracting. However, there were reports, probably apocryphal, that an investigation was instituted in Moscow as to why the proletariat needed to fork out more than twice as much for a demonstration of prestige no more effective than that of the American "imperialists."

Altogether, Expo 70 was probably the most spectacular of any such exposition ever staged. Its President was an incredibly energetic octogenarian Taizo Ishizaka, who was assisted by former Ambassador Toru Haguiwara as Commissioner-General. More than 64,000,000 people passed through the turnstiles, great numbers of them in Japanese tour groups, each member with special identifying apparel, trudging intently and indefatigably behind the banner-carrying group leader. For all Japanese, Expo 70 was a justifiable source of pride and exhilaration. At the same time, it undoubtedly furthered its stated cause, "Progress and harmony for mankind." It was good, nonetheless, that international agreement was reached to space out such extravaganzas, thus avoiding a depreciation of their value and easing the burden of the proletariat and other taxpayers of the participating nations.

Tokyo being a major world news capital, there was no reason for USIA to try to compete with the commercial wireservices such as the Associated Press, the United Press International, Reuters, or Kyodo. However, in view of the tremendous influence of the Japanese news media (the three leading dailies—*Asahi, Mainichi,* and *Yomiuri*—had 15,-000,000 subscribers nationwide), we sought to improve what we considered to be an unfair portrayal of the United States. In early 1971, USIA inaugurated a series of "background briefings" by senior Embassy officers, the ground rules being that quotation would be allowed but to nonattributable sources. Useful information was conveyed, but the tendency of the reporters was to prove to one another their immunity to foreign influence by writing unfriendly press comment or distortions. In a front-page article, a *Yomiuri* columnist suggested that if the Embassy wished to increase its effectiveness, it would "have to stop using simple American logic in explaining various events to the reporters."

More valuable were the informal biweekly meetings with small influential groups at the Embassy residence. Instituted shortly after my arrival, and arranged by Press Attaché Frank Donovan, they included in turn the top editorial echelons of each of the newspapers, as well as groups of reporters and commentators. These were stimulating "bull sessions" lasting two hours or more in a relaxed atmosphere at cocktail time. There were no agenda nor specific sales pitches. A frequent question posed to my guests was, "If you were American Ambassador, what would you be doing that is not being done or not be doing that is being done?" The frankness of the guests was heartwarming and helpful, and resulted in return engagements both at the residence or at the newspaper editorial offices.

No one was expected to write any articles. My belief was that if flagrant falsehoods could be forestalled through personal rapport, or unfriendly comments mitigated by a few degrees, it was well worth the effort.

The seminars with Japanese scholars were equally stimulating. These were arranged first by James Morley, and then by James Hoyt, serving as Special Assistant to the Ambassador for maintaining dialogue with the academic community. This was a position which had thoughtfully been created by Ambassador Reischauer. Japan's intellectual community was impressive. However, those of its members who focused on international affairs, particularly specialists on Japanese-American relations, ran the risk of stigmatization by compatriots with xenophobic instincts. Nonetheless, they had thought-provoking contributions to make. Prior to President Nixon's visit to China, for example, Japanese intellectuals provided valuable insights concerning Japanese sensitivities.

True "people-to-people" diplomacy, involving Japanese and Americans not on the government payroll, had burgeoned in the early 1960's when projects for resuming the "broken dialogue" included periodic joint conferences by experts who could talk the language of medicine, natural resources, science, and cultural cooperation. Such colloquia continued actively into the 1970's, augmented by our mutual interests in subjects such as environmental quality, John Volpe's "Experimental Safety Vehicle" project, Charles Lindbergh's campaign for saving blue whales, and of course the reconciliation of differences between the business communities of the two countries.

A welcome development was the establishment in late 1971 of "The Japan Foundation." Its initial resources were in the neighborhood of $30 million in legislated funds, but the ultimate objective was ten times that amount, including substantial contributions from the private sector. In purpose, this project resembled America's "Fulbright Program," which for more than two decades had productively promoted international cultural exchanges. Early activities of the Japan Foundation included support for Japanese studies in universities in foreign countries. Foreign Minister Fukuda, author of the concept, envisaged "mind-to-mind" contact which would "foster a deeper and correct understanding among more and more people abroad" of Japan's "earnest desire to create a peace-loving and cultural state, without military preparations." Fukuda added, "Only in a prosperous and harmonious world can we find a truly worthwhile existence, and this is in the best interests of the Japanese nation."

In the scientific field, no subject more entranced the Japanese than astronautics. It was a great day for Japanese-American relations when Neil Armstrong, Mike Collins, and Buzz Aldrin set foot in Tokyo less than four months after the "small step" on the moon. Although some 5,000 police were mobilized for contingencies, "anti-security treaty" demonstrations were temporarily forgotten. Instead, these Apollo 11 heroes were showered with an estimated six tons of ticker tape during a parade through the Ginza. The Emperor, Japanese officialdom, and the delighted populace were fascinated by what the astronauts had to say, including their firsthand report of not having observed on the moon the three rabbbits which, according to Japanese folklore, pound rice into rice cakes. The latter bit of banter had been suggested by Sen Nishiyama, the USIA's interpreter who was known throughout Japan as "Mr. Apollo" for having been the key translator for the national television network during the lunar landing.

Aside from Japanese fascination with American space exploits and admiration of spacemen, Japan was eager to increase its own participation in the space age. A program of cooperation was, therefore, developed between our National Aeronautics and Space Agency and Japanese space authorities. With the most modest of budgets, Japanese technology was making progress. There were the usual disappointments, as America had suffered, but successful small-scale launches were made. Astronautic costs being astronomic, NASA's Tom Paine and Wernher von Braun discussed projects with the Japanese which would dovetail with advancing space technology and would relieve the Japanese of the horrendous and duplicative costs of developing their own giant launch vehicles. My own hope, which did not materialize, was for a joint project in our bicentennial year of 1976 in which the Japanese would construct one of a number of modules to be hitched as freight cars to an orbiting American spaceship and which would conduct experiments in some of the limitless scientific areas not encompassed in other planned space projects.

Understanding could also be developed through athletics. Golf, for example, had become prestigious in Japan, and visits by American greats such as Jack Nicklaus and Billy Casper never failed to command favorable attention. American football was not well known, but Japanese college players would, nonetheless, gallantly compete on occasions when huskier American teams, such as Utah State University, visited Japan. A postwar recreation which became tremendously popular was bowling, with more than 3,500 bowling centers scattered around Japan by 1970. Tennis stars like Stan Smith and Arthur Ashe were always an attraction. At the Sapporo Winter Olympics, America was represented by the largest team of any participating nation, all fine young competitors of whom we could be proud.

The unique sports language for Japanese and Americans was baseball. When I made my initial call on former Prime Minister Kishi in July 1969, I quickly sensed that his mind was preoccupied with the annual Japan-wide high school baseball championship game. Due to an incredible 18-inning performance by the Misawa pitcher, no decision had been reached the previous day and the game was carried over to the afternoon when Kishi had given me the appointment. My suggestion that we dispense with matters of lesser consequence brought a grin to Kishi's face, and the two of us proceeded to view the game on the TV set in his adjacent office. The Matsuyama team won, continuing southern Japan's supremacy of many years and causing disappointment in the northern half of Japan, including many American Air Force personnel at Misawa who had become enthusiastic supporters of the phenomenal young pitcher and his teammates.

Professional baseball was big time in Japan. The top team and perennial winner of the "Japan Series" (more modestly named than the American "World Series") was the Tokyo club, the Yomiuri Giants. Somewhat reminiscent of the "Ruth and Gehrig wrecking company" days of the New York Yankees, the Tokyo Giants had a home run hitter (39 in 1971) named Sadahara Oh and a slugger named Shigeo Nagashima who in 1971 batted .320. These baseball idols drew salaries comparable with those of American stars at that time, about $120,000 per annum. Most of the other teams in Japan's two major leagues imported American players, usually a maximum of two, but the Giants' roster was entirely Japanese. Their home park, with its 40,000 capacity, was usually filled. The successes of the Yomiuri team were in no small measure due to owner Taro Shoriki, whose father founded the Giant empire, and Vice President Yosoji Kobayashi. In addition to keeping the winning spark alive, they employed impressive management techniques. There was no haggling with the players over salaries, nor were there holdouts. According to Kobayashi, each player's performance (batting average, errors, winning base hits, and so on) was fed into a computer. From the computer emerged the salary for the following year. There could be no argument. It is a system which managers of American baseball (or football or other sports) might well consider.

Over the years, even before the war, American baseballers had made visits to Japan, including the great Babe Ruth. In recent years, the Los Angeles Dodgers and St. Louis Cardinals had made off-season tours to Japan, as did the San Francisco Giants and the Baltimore Orioles during my tenure. It had been hoped that the Orioles would come as "World Series" winners in 1971, but hopes for a super-World Series were not only dashed by the Pittsburgh Pirates but we gained the impression that Brooks Robinson, Frank Robinson, Boog Powell, Jim Palmer and company took out their frustrations on the Japanese, winning ten and tying two of the fourteen games played. Major League Commissioner Bowie Kuhn and American League President Joe Cronin were on hand, actively considering the prospect for a true super-World Series in the foreseeable future. Japanese capabilities were better than reflected in the record against the Orioles, but there were handicaps, primarily in the players' physical size (which, incidentally, was increasing, thanks to an improved diet since the war).

Regardless of physical handicaps or language barriers, the mutual interest of Japanese and Americans in baseball was a generator of goodwill for players and spectators. Whether on the playing field or on social occasions such as at an Embassy reception, the fraternization of the Robinsons and the Nagashimas and the Ohs, and the accompanying public interest, served as welcome diversion from our political and economic difficulties and made a salutary contribution to a general improvement of the atmosphere. Attendance at a game in July 1969 between the Tokyo Giants and their chief rivals, Osaka's Hanshin Tigers (whose lineup included the inveterate crowd-pleaser Willie Kirkland), had prompted Dr. Norman Vincent Peale, the advocate of "The Power of Positive Thinking," to dedicate one of his nationally syndicated columns to the common

Japanese-American attachment to baseball and to conclude, "Enjoy the fellowship of sports fans of whatever country and the world seems a pretty good place after all."

One can hit a foul ball in diplomacy as well as in baseball. After New York's "amazing Mets" scored their miraculous World Series triumph in 1969, delirium had erupted in Shea stadium. Among those infected was an old friend from Capital University days, Neil Stein, who proceeded to send to me a tiny piece of "lucky sod" with the hope that it might be helpful to some Japanese team. Without delay, I forwarded this thoughtful acquisition to Shoriki and Kobayashi along with my wishes that the transplantation of these few tufts of Shea stadium into the turf of the Korakuen ball park would bring luck to Tokyo's Yomiuri Giants (as perennial champions, they were really not in desperate need!). This gesture was, of course, reported in the sports pages of *Yomiuri Shimbun*. Unfortunately, I had not reckoned with the fact that the Japanese Ministry of Agriculture was just as fiendish as the United States Department of Agriculture about the importation of any plant life. My diplomatic immunity precluded any thoughts of summoning me to court, but the "lucky sod" was summarily confiscated and destroyed. As Bobbie Burns would say, "The best laid schemes of mice and men gang aft a-gley."

It was my good fortune to enjoy a common bond with another sector of Japanese society completely removed from our bilateral governmental problems. It was amateur radio, which has been my lifelong hobby. With more than 200,000 operators, Japan was a close second to the United States in the exercise of this avocation. Due to Japanese law which prohibited radio transmission by foreigners, obtaining a license was not easy. However, thanks to Japanese resourcefulness, authorization was arranged for me to operate as a member of a "club" with majority Japanese membership. Unfortunately, time shortage permitted only minimal operation of the station whose assigned call was

JH1YDR. I enjoyed a twice per week early-morning schedule with W3ZNH, operated by Jim Douglas, a Washington friend; a daily ten-minute breakfast chat with fellow amateur Bill Porter, HL9AA, our Ambassador in Korea; the occasional post-midnight flicking on of the switch to chat with King Hussein, JY1, and other Mideastern friends; plus a few minutes, when time could be scrounged, to make contact with Japanese amateurs who seemed genuinely pleased for my interest in a hobby, the values of which, including the development of friendships for Japan, few non-radio amateurs could appreciate.

One Sunday afternoon in downtown Tokyo, a Toyota pulled alongside the Cadillac bearing the flag of the American Ambassador. The Toyota's passengers were complete strangers, but they were beaming. By the time we had reached the second traffic light they had pulled from their pockets and were flashing "QSL" cards to identify themselves as amateurs. Emperor Hirohito, during my farewell call, made mention of this avocation, evincing great interest in it and appreciation for its potentialities in the development of international understanding. My only regret was that, although the Foreign Ministry and the Ministry of Posts and Telegraphs had conjured up "club" arrangements for me and others after my departure, it was not possible to secure Japanese government approval for an agreement extending full operating privileges on a reciprocal basis for the amateurs of our two countries. Thanks to Senator Barry Goldwater (K7UGA), such an exchange of amateur privileges had been made possible with some 41 countries. There was no doubt Japan's 200,000 amateurs wished such arrangements, for even the "club" breakthrough, representing the first operating authorization ever granted a civilian foreigner, was described by one of them as being "like the opening of this country to the outer world."

The list of opportunities for cementing relationships between the Japanese and American people was virtually endless. Common ties in college training existed. Nihon

Kokan consultant David Takahara, for example, arranged periodic gatherings of the alumni of Ohio State University, e.g., on the university's centennial anniversary, on the occasion of alumnus Haruki Mori being appointed Vice Minister of Foreign Affairs, and a "first ever" for a non-Japanese institution when a dozen or so Japanese and American emigrés from the Columbus campus joined in singing the Ohio State "fight song" and "Alma Mater" at a school-song festival held annually at Tokyo's Budokan Hall (our sour notes were in abundance, but the spirit was there). Other people-to-people opportunities included the visit to Tokyo of Mike Masaoka and others of the Japanese American Citizens League, a highly influential contingent, some 700 strong, of Americans of Japanese ancestry. There were also the monthly "prayer breakfasts," where intriguingly the political sector was represented by more "socialists" than members of the ruling party. Finally, there were virtually limitless opportunities for mixing the steady stream of distinguished American visitors with Japanese having mutual interests. It was our practice to seek a hole in our social schedule, at least once per week, when American visitors, not otherwise accorded hospitality, could be brought together in "clusters." This required ceaseless coordination between the Embassy's "front office" and the staff at the residence. For arranging these affairs, and the extensive program of activities at the residence, my wife and I were indebted to two talented organizers, Jane Williams and her successor Pat Wazer. They had their office in the residence and were assisted, almost on a full-time basis, by the administrative section's jack-of-all-trades Joseph Kozlowski. Among Kozlowski's accomplishments was the installation in collaboration with the TEAC company of a sound system for the entire representational area. Aside from providing a capability for background music and an occasional "singalong," the sound system afforded public speaking facilities which would have warmed the cockles of the heart of a former tenant, General Douglas MacArthur.

The Embassy residence in Tokyo had witnessed much history. It was constructed, along with the chancery, after Japan's great earthquake of 1923, and both buildings were as ruggedly built as they were elegant. The local architect, representing a New York firm, was Antonin Raymond, who in his early years had traveled from his native Europe to the United States to work with Frank Lloyd Wright. Wright, of course, became the architect for Tokyo's famed Imperial Hotel (replaced after the war by a much larger and more modern structure). According to Raymond, the present Embassy residence was not only designed to take advantage of winter sunlight, but the orientation of its front entrance, at an angle in a far corner of the premises, was inspired by a local belief that the destruction of the previous Japanese-owned residence during the 1923 earthquake was due to its front door not being oriented in accordance with Japanese traditions. Under construction when the Great Depression occurred, the new residence, not surprisingly, was branded "Hoover's Folly." Its value in the 1970's would be many times the original investment.

In Ambassador Grew's days, the new residential edifice was ideal for entertaining the elite-centered Japanese society. One of the more memorable occasions was an evening in February 1936 when Grew hosted a dinner, after which those invited were treated to the Nelson Eddy–Jeanette MacDonald film hit, "Naughty Marietta." On the following morning, a group of young army activists staged an uprising in which one of Grew's guests of a few hours earlier, Viscount Makoto Saito, the Lord Keeper of the Privy Seal and ex-Prime Minister, was among those killed. After Pearl Harbor, Grew and his Embassy associates were restricted to the Embassy premises for a half year before being repatriated in an exchange of diplomats. To while

away the hours, there was much bridge and poker playing.
One Embassy officer, later to become Ambassador, Charles
Bohlen, liked to recall the pitch-and-putt golf course which
was improvised within the compound . . . somewhat to the
detriment of Embassy window panes. After the war, the
Embassy residence became the home of General Douglas
MacArthur. In its great salon, he would make history by
meeting with Japan's Emperor. In the "family dining
room," in another historic moment, an aide would hand the
Supreme Commander a ticker story reporting that he was
being fired by President Truman. Subsequently, he would
meet in the library for one hour with General Matthew
Ridgway, who had been ordered from Korea to discuss the
change of command.

Thanks to an initiative by our predecessors, Ambassador
U. Alexis Johnson and his wife Pat, and to assistance from
Roger Pineau of the Smithsonian Institution, arrangements
were made during our Tokyo sojourn to exhibit on the walls
of the Embassy residence some historic works of art. They
were six original watercolors of Commodore Perry's visits
to Japan in 1853-54, done by a nineteen-year-old German
artist named Heine who had succeeded in attaching himself
at a meager salary to the Perry expedition. Five of these
historic treasures were loaned to us from the art collection
of our Ambassador to the Netherlands, William Midden-
dorf; the sixth was the property of Brown University.
There was seldom a social occasion when these paintings
did not become topics of conversation, recalling the origins
and the importance of the Japanese-American relationship.
(In urging trans-Pacific commerce, the letter which Perry
had brought from President Fillmore noted as a favorable
factor that California gold production had reached $60 mil-
lion. In 1971, that sum represented only one-half of one
percent of the total volume of Japanese-American trade.)

One of our pet projects in Japan, as at previous posts,
was the cultivation of especially close friendships with our

diplomatic colleagues from Latin America. Most of them had little communication with their home offices; so in the interest of Western Hemisphere neighborliness we tried to be helpful with information and camaraderie. Of all the functions at our Embassy, none were more satisfying than those evenings when, as during Billy Graham's Tokyo visit, we would invite to that historic residence one hundred or more ambulatory Vietnam patients from our military hospitals. One GI danced with casts on both feet, and there were occasional blood stains from unhealed wounds, but most of these fine young Americans made their reluctant departures expressing appreciation for memories which they would carry with them for the rest of their lives.

Parenthetically, it should be noted that when only Americans were involved in hospitality at the residence, the costs, according to State Department regulations, came out of the Ambassador's own pocket, the only consolation being that they were deductible in income tax computations. It was always amusing that members of Congress who voted to slash the item in the State Department budget which they publicly decried as "whiskey money" never hesitated to send letters to Ambassadors requesting that hospitality be extended to visiting constituents. The Foreign Service offers many wonderful rewards, but the accumulation of monetary wealth is not one of them.

One of the Foreign Service's most agreeable rewards is getting out of the capital city and getting to know the people throughout the country of assignment. Just as a foreigner cannot truly understand America by visiting only New York, Los Angeles, and Washington, so in Japan it was important to travel out into Japan's picturesque and fascinating countryside. Such journeys, averaging about three or more days per month, were always refreshing. Uninhibited by the problems which captured attention in Tokyo, the solid citizens out in the prefectures never failed to manifest sincere friendship for America and Americans. On one occasion after another, the Japanese and American flags would be seen side by side, in the form of large banners at major social functions and in miniature on tea tables in offices.

The grass-roots friendliness toward America was not surprising. As a people who set high value on proficiency, most Japanese admired American accomplishments, whether it was the steam-propelled fleet of Commodore Perry or the landings on the moon. They were appreciative for the help received from American experts, teachers, and missionaries during the century since the Meiji Restoration when Japan was determined to "catch up" with the modernized Western world. They were similarly appreciative for the conciliatory attitude and the helpfulness of Americans after World War II.

Symbolic of amity was the Japan-America Society (JAS), which had active units in many of the prefectural centers, as well as in Tokyo. With the welcome mat always out for American visitors, these societies provided opportunities for fellowship and discussion. Similarly dedicated to the promotion of better understanding were more than thirty Japanese-American "Sister City" relationships. Yokohama and San Diego, for example, were in continuing contact, with exchanges of visits, information, and tokens of friendship. On my first of three visits to Hokkaido, traveling from the airport to the mid-island city of Asahikawa, I was impressed how much the landscape resembled the farmland of mid-America: red barns, silos, cattle, and feedgrain crops. When visiting with the Socialist Mayor, Kozo Igarashi, I was reminded that Asahikawa's "sister city" was Bloomington, Illinois, only twenty-eight miles from my home town of Lincoln. That evening at the JAS banquet, we engaged in a delightful debate whether the corn of Hokkaido, stalks of which our efficient Consul Nick Heflin arranged to have available, grew taller than the corn of central Illinois. A resulting photo, which included a charming young lady who had just returned from a year of study at Illinois Wesleyan, was surefire copy for both the Asahikawa newspaper and the Bloomington *Pantograph.*

That the landscape of Hokkaido seemed familiar was not entirely accidental. During Japan's "catching up" period, numerous Americans had assisted in Hokkaido's development in such fields as agriculture, education, railway construction, and even in the planning for the capital city of Sapporo (unlike Tokyo, Sapporo's streets are straight and at right angles). These projects, particularly during President Grant's administration (his former Secretary of Agriculture Horace Capron was a team leader), were requested and financed by the Japanese. Among the motivations was a desire to frustrate Russian territorial ambitions. One advisor, Edwin Dun, who was a major force in Hokkaido's agricultural development, was from 1893 to 1897 American minister, married a Japanese, spent most of his adult life in Japan, and is honored with a monument not far from the site of the Sapporo Winter Olympics. Another monument, on the campus of Hokkaido University, is dedicated to New Englander William Clarke, who in 1876 helped to develop the then Sapporo Agricultural College, designed Sapporo's landmark clock tower with its still-tolling American-made timepiece, advocated preservation of the city's beautiful elms, and is to this date remembered for his admonition to Japanese youth, "Boys, be ambitious."

From the small kelp-producing village of Wakkanai, at the northern tip of Hokkaido, it is possible on a clear day to see Soviet-controlled Sakhalin Island. On Hokkaido's south coast is Hakodate, one of the two ports opened pursuant to the treaty reached with Commodore Perry. Two of his sailors lie buried in a nearby cemetery. Not far from Hakodate, an underwater railway tunnel to the main island of Honshu will, when completed, be the longest in the world.

Some twelve hundred miles southwest of Wakkanai is Kagoshima on Kyushu, the large island at the southern end of the Japanese archipelago. In Kyushu, like Hokkaido, there would be unforgettable rememberances: the friendliness of the principal city of Fukuoka; the excellent community relations between the good people of Sasebo with their extraordinary Mayor Ichizo Tsuji and our Navy people led by Captain Claude Shaw; the resilience of Nagasaki, that ancient Japanese window to the world and more recently A-bomb victim; the active volcano Sakurajima, which the Governor of Kagoshima insisted was not operated by a button at his desk; the Kagoshima high school youngsters who braved Washington's sweltering heat during their annual summer visits to the United States; the lovable youngsters at the Beppu orphanage for whom an American "walking major" had raised funds by hiking all the way from Tokyo; the five-citied industrial complex of Kitakyushu; the incomparable beauty of jumbled tree-covered mountains, rugged coastlines, and the myriad of islands which characterize Japan in general but the Kyushu region in particular; and the day-long voyage, in the company of Grumman Vice President "Corky" Meyer and his wife (delightful cousins), threading our way from Kobe to Beppu through the islands of the picturesque Inland Sea.

In the western portion of the main island of Honshu, our visits were highlighted by: the frequent savoring of Expo 70; the inspiration always forthcoming in visits to the palaces and pavilions in the old Imperial capital of Kyoto, and at Nara; the helicopter overview of the industry-studded coast from Kyushu to the Marine base at Iwakuni, passing over Prime Minister Sato's home prefecture of Yamaguchi; the indelible Hiroshima visits; pitching a stone successfully on the lucky ledge of the torii (gateway) at Miyajima ("Shrine Island"); discussions with the governors and mayors of the flourishing port of Kobe and Japan's commercial metropolis, Osaka, where citizens greet each other with the words, "Are you making any money?"; and the American community at Kobe, whose annual Washington Birthday Ball was a social highlight which we never missed and whose businessmen like Phil Campanella were carrying on the great traditions of their forebears.

Although budgetary stringencies required the closure of our Consulate at Nagoya, we were indebted to Governor Mihine Kuwahara of Aichi prefecture, and Governor Hatori Tanaka of Mie prefecture and many other fine people in west-central Honshu for: learning that $1.6 billion in products of the region left Nagoya ports annually for the United States; inspiration at Ise, the most important of all Japanese shrines; observing the impressiveness of Toyota, MHI, the ultra-modern NKK shipyard at Tsu, the petro-chemical and the pearl industries; participation in the inauguration of the Kansai Electric Power Company's American-built nuclear power plant on the Tsuruga peninsula on the Japan Sea side of Honshu Island; and dining on succulent Matsuzaka beef, which can be cut with a fork and rivals that of Kobe in tenderness, as well as in price.

Three events would always be remembered in the Tohoku region of northern Honshu, and with them generosities of Aomori prefecture's Governor Shunkichi Takeuchi, the *Too Nippo* newspaper for which he was a reporter in his youth, the Mayors of Shariki and Misawa, Colonel Ed Aune of the air base at Misawa, and many others. First, there was the Nebuta Festival at Aomori city in early August 1970, when the six-foot American Ambassador donned the undersized carnival costumery. It was a sight to behold. What a privilege it was to march at the head of a mile-long parade of ogreish floats, clutching one hand of an endearing little youngster whose other hand was held by his grandfather, Governor Takeuchi, all of us clad in Nebuta regalia. The previous day, Governor Takeuchi had participated in dedicating a monument at Shariki, a village on the Japan Sea coast of Aomori prefecture, at the upper tip of Honshu

Island. Constructed by the villagers, the monument memorialized the efforts of the community to rescue and provide succor to the crew of an American sailing vessel, named *Cheseborough*, which ran aground near Shariki in 1889. Nineteen crew members lost their lives, but the four survivors received careful attention from the villagers (in pre-Perry days, shipwrecked foreign sailors had not been welcome in Japan). The third Tohoku event was the dedication on November 4, 1971, near Misawa of another monument, this one honoring two American aviators, Clyde Pangbourn and Hugh Herndon. Constructed by the local citizenry at a site overlooking the Pacific Ocean, it commemorated the first trans-Pacific flight. Precisely forty years earlier, the good people of Misawa had helped prepare the coastal takeoff area, and they had been thrilled by the news that, although the plane "Miss Veedol" had made a crash landing, Pangbourn and Herndon had made it safely to Wenatchee, Washington. They were particularly pleased because Wenatchee, like Tohoku, was a famous apple-growing area. To dramatize this fortieth anniversary, Colonel Aune had arranged for the Navy's famed "Blue Angels" to stage at Misawa one of their breathtaking performances of aerial acrobatics.

Closer to Tokyo, there were two annual occasions which testified to the deep roots which characterized the Japanese-American relationship. One was the "Black Ship Festival" at Shimoda, when in conjunction with the United States Navy, the officials of the small town on the Izu peninsula, which was one of the two ports opened to Commodore Perry, commemorated the first landing there of the Americans from Perry's ships in 1854. The other occasion was the annual ceremony on July 14 at Kurihama, marking the anniversary of Commodore Perry's having first set foot on Japanese soil (in 1971 it was the 118th). The Mayor of Yokosuka, Masayoshi Nagano, a Socialist, was the sponsor for these ceremonies (Kurihama was only a few miles south of Yokosuka). His participation, as with his treatment of the large Seventh Fleet Yokosuka base, reflected his ability to place statesmanship above partisan politics. At Kurihama, appropriate remarks would be made by Japanese and American officials, wreathes would be placed at the monument marking Perry's landing, and doves would be uncaged to demonstrate the dedication of both our countries to a world of peace.

All of these memories and many more became like a photomontage, leaving the reassuring impression that while the painful adjustments of the early 1970's may have caused tremors and no doubt some erosion on the surface, there remained in the Japanese nation a core of goodwill, so long as both the Japanese and American people could retain a feeling of trust in each other. At stake were deep sentiments more consequential than official protestations. After observing an evening in Hiroshima, when, following a dinner with the city's leaders, congeniality prevailed and spontaneous renditions were heard—an industrial executive intoning a favorite Japanese tune, a top official with surprisingly good voice singing "My Old Kentucky Home," and the American guests singing the so-called "Okinawa Theme Song"—Resha Hartley, who with her *Wall Street Journal* husband accompanied us on this safari, would write in *The Japan Times*, "After all the rhetoric, the group relaxed and didn't talk anymore about being friends. They were friends."

No one who has not had the experience could appreciate those occasions when the Japanese would release their normally well-controlled emotions to sing "Auld Lang Syne" in the Japanese language. Our first such experience was at Asahikawa, at a delightful informal dance-reception organized by JAS leader Dr. Motoichi Moriyama. As we were leaving, the group of 100 or more, predominantly the younger generation, clasped hands and broke forth in a continuing chorus of the Japanese version of, "Should old acquaintance be forgot?" There would be other occasions, only slightly less sentimental because they were not the first, e.g., the closure of Expo 70 with thousands of Japanese singing in the Festival Plaza, or the finale of the Winter Olympics.

For me personally, no memory would be more lasting than a farewell luncheon sponsored by the Japan-America Society of Sapporo. Its President, whose age was above three score and ten, was Mitsugi Sato. Sato-san had been an agriculture student at Ohio State University in 1919 in the days of famed footballer Chic Harley. Upon his return to Hokkaido, he had, with typical Japanese ingenuity and hard work, built his Snow Brand milk products company into the largest such organization in Japan. On my previous visits, Sato-san had joined with me and Dr. Juro Wada, an Ohio State alumnus who had performed Japan's first heart transplant, in the singing of the OSU Alma Mater. Closing our Sapporo JAS farewell luncheon, the venerable Sato-san asked that I stand and join him in singing those words from college days which conclude:

> "Summer's heat or winter's cold,
> The seasons pass, the years will roll;
> Time and change will surely show
> How firm thy friendship, Ohio."

It may have been sentimental, but of such ties between peoples can a true generation of peace be built.

Chapter **8**

Two Great Powers
in Search of Their Roles

BEARING IN MIND the caveat that any prophecy might be invalidated by dramatic developments elsewhere in the world, the last pages of the postwar chapter of the Japanese-American relationship could well prove to be the prologue for the post-postwar chapter. It seemed to me that from the strains and pains of the 1969–1972 period both nations emerged sadder and, perhaps, wiser. They had come to realize that changes were taking place in each other, and in the world. By extrapolating their findings, and taking them into account, both countries would be better prepared to cope with common challenges they would be facing in the 1970's. Impressions gleaned during my Tokyo sojourn suggested that future trends might be along the following lines.

The rising tide of nationalist sentiment in Japan,

sparked by the "economic miracle" and resurgent self-confidence, would be reflected during the 1970's in more self-assertive Japanese policies. A step-up of independent initiatives could be expected. In its international relationships, Japan would seek diversification so as not to be excessively dependent on any single country.

Having held the reins of political power on the Japanese domestic scene for most of the postwar period, the Yoshida-LDP-establishment government with its success formula of institutionalized democracy, concentration on economic growth, and reliance on the United States, would face increasing challenge. The three most likely prospects would be: a rejuvenation of the LDP and its preemption of urgent issues such as social welfare; an LDP coalition with one of the less hostile opposition parties; or the structural emergence of a left-of-center alternative to the LDP which might include the Democratic Socialist Party, Komeito, some LDP defectors, and the right wing of the Japan Socialist Party.

Japanese emotional commitment to parliamentary democracy would need deeper roots. It still tended to be a hothouse plant, a sort of "guided democracy" which had been sheltered by an "above-party" elite during the Meiji era, by the American occupation, and by the postwar Japanese establishment. The political system which was likely to evolve would still be influenced by traditional instincts for consensus, social harmony, and a desire to avoid conflict. At the same time, most Japanese would recognize that an effective representative government would provide the best insurance against excessive authoritarianism which had in the 1930's led to disaster. Of critical importance would be a healthy Diet, one which would command the respect of the populace. (During the Khrushchev shoe-pounding episode at the United Nations General Assembly in 1960, Ambassador Charles Bohlen reminded me that it was the discreditation of parliamentary institutions by making them look foolish which had been the standard Communist procedure in destroying such institutions in Eastern Europe prior to the installation of totalitarian regimes.)

While most Japanese would realize the indispensability of Japan's ties with the United States and would seek no disruption, Japan would, at the same time, wish to make clear in the 1970's that it was not an appendage of the United States, nor its military pawn. It would expect to be treated as an equal and would not be as responsive as previously to the desires of its erstwhile "older brother." For the Japanese, there would be the additional psychological problem of envisaging two nations perched on the same rung of the ladder, treating each other on a basis of mutual interests and reciprocity.

For Americans, the challenge would be whether we meant what we said about welcoming other nations standing on their own feet, assuming responsibilities, and making their own decisions. These were noble words, but Washington must brace itself for Japanese initiatives, such as vis-à-vis Hanoi, Peking, and Middle East oil, which might not be completely in tune with Henry Kissinger's operations. In reconciling our own interests with those of Japan, deft diplomacy would be required, and tendencies, sometimes noted in the past, toward such extremes as either doting or bullying would need to be controlled. It would be wise to approach our bilateral problems, to the extent possible, in a multilateral framework. Within the broader international context, fewer Japanese sensitivities would be aroused and the prospects for positive results would be improved.

With virtually no resources except human talent, and thus vitally dependent on imports and exports, Japan would not in the 1970's relax its purposeful and dynamic economic endeavors. In Japanese eyes, it would be a matter of survival.

Due to internal and external factors, Japanese economic growth was not likely to duplicate the rates recorded in the 1960's, 11% in real terms and 15% or more at current prices. The downward adjustment was bound to be painful for a nation whose prosperity had depended so much on the accelerating motorcycle. Nonetheless, satisfactory growth was likely to continue. Political stability would be much influenced by the state of the economy.

A major factor in Japan's reduced economic growth would be the diversion of resources, both government and private, to the betterment of the quality of life. Other factors would include: wage and other labor demands, inflation, a decline in market growth, occasional worrisome investment slowdowns, and some mellowing of Japan's unmatched work ethic.

No factor would be more critical than Japan's vulnerability to the acquisition of raw materials at reasonable costs from foreign sources. Virtually totally dependent on imported petroleum for its extensive petrochemical industries, as well as for fuel, Japan would eagerly seek to diversify its energy sources, both geographically and away from petroleum, which was becoming an Achilles heel. The energy challenge, particularly nuclear-power development, would afford impressive opportunities for Japanese cooperation with the United States and other developed nations. Although in the early 1970's America was supplying several hundreds of millions of dollars worth of enriched uranium, Japan would become increasingly concerned about the reliability of the supply (an anxiety not mitigated by America's 1973 embargo on soybeans, upon which Japan had developed a dependence to the extent of several hundred million dollars annually). With the likelihood that world demand would exceed all expectations, it would be in the long-term interests of both Japan and America to institute joint uranium-enrichment projects, with and without the participation of other nations. Downstream energy problems such as the development of new and more efficient automobile engines offered similar opportunities for collaboration. Japanese ingenuity when confronted by necessity should not be underestimated.

Due to the revaluation of the yen and other factors, Japan's wide competitive advantage in international trade would narrow. Nevertheless, Japanese exports would continue to grow, but at reduced rates. These circumstances would only redouble Japanese resolve. Thus, commercial frictions with the United States, while reduced by the painful adjustments initiated in 1971, were likely to continue. The Japanese would recognize there was no ready substitute for the enormous American market, that Japan was more dependent than the United States on the high volume of bilateral trade, and that from a rational standpoint full reciprocity in trade and investment made sense. Being pragmatic, they would, therefore, make concessions but only minimally and when necessary.

Japan would continue to convey to the world the message of success through hard work. For Americans, even though imitation of Japanese procedures in most instances might not be practicable, there were lessons to be learned, such as a non-adversary relationship between business and government, coordinated government-industry planning to anticipate future market trends, the involvement of mid-management in decision making (which was proving successful in Sony's San Diego plant and Mitsubishi's aircraft assembly factory in west Texas), a sense of participation by all employees in the company's welfare, the need for expeditious settlement of labor disputes, more aggressive interest in developing foreign markets, and the value of an honest day's work.

Barring unforeseen developments, Japan would continue to feel no imminent military threat. Aside from the comfort induced by centuries of immunity from conquest by its neighbors, the fear of Communist aggression, which had influenced Japan's original assent to the alliance with the United States, had receded. China's development of nuclear weaponry was disturbing, but there would be the continued belief in Japan that Peking was absorbed by preoccupations other than thoughts of aggression against Japanese territory. Moreover, the Cold War seemed to be over. A welcome spirit of detente was in the air.

There would, however, continue to be danger spots in the region having "proxy war" potential. The withdrawal of American forces had reduced the ramifications of the Indo-China conflict, but stability in that area seemed remote. Nearer to Japan, and much more worrisome for the Japanese, would be a resumption of hostilities in Korea, traditionally considered a "dagger" at Japan's heart if it fell into hostile hands. More troublesome politically would be Japan's predicament should Peking decide to undertake aggressive action in the Taiwan area. Having in effect recognized Peking's claim to Taiwan, Japan would be confronted with an awkward dilemma if its American ally, pursuant to its defense treaty with Taipei, took counteraction.

Japanese anti-militarism was likely to continue to run deep. Internally, there would remain a revulsion against the possible resurgence of military domination of government policy. Looking outward, the Japanese would continue to be acutely aware that a major military buildup would alarm and alienate their inherently suspicious East Asian neighbors, who were already sensitive to Japan's burgeoning economic influence. In any case, on the Japanese domestic political scene, the chief pressures on the government's modest defense policies would stem from the Leftist political forces, pressing for less rather than greater military investment.

Accordingly, there was every reason to believe that the

size of Japan's Self Defense Forces would continue to be limited to the projected budget, namely, within 1% of GNP. Considering Japan's rapid economic growth, this would still be a sizable sum, representing a doubling of expenditures during the five-year Fourth Defense Buildup Plan. The emphasis would be on more modern equipment, with the goal being the capability to defend the Japanese islands against attacks confined to the deployment of conventional weaponry. There being little chance for changing the anti-military Article IX of the Constitution, competing effectively in the labor market, or passing conscription legislation, the probability was that the SDF force levels would remain under 300,000.

While Japan's conservative leadership would continue to rely on the security treaty with the United States, and in particular on the American "nuclear umbrella," there was likely to be a continued paring down of the American military presence in Japan: because of long-standing Japanese sensitivities, because of American retrenchment under the Nixon Doctrine, and because of indications of relaxed tensions in the region. Joint use and emergency reentry at some of the relinquished facilities would no doubt be arranged. Combat utilization would depend on a joint determination that such usage was necessary for the security of both countries. Under those circumstances, the treaty would be less contentious than previously. For many Japanese, it would be more like an insurance policy, having deterrent effect and serving as a cornerstone for a broader relationship focused less on military objectives. The treaty's dissolution would probably not occur in the 1970's unless government leadership became subjected to more acute pressures from the Left or the Right than seemed likely if events took a normal course.

In the absence of a radical change in Far Eastern conditions, Japan could not be expected to become affiliated with any regional military pacts, nor could it be expected to assume, as some suspected, regional military responsibilities which America was relinquishing pursuant to the Nixon Doctrine. Japan would seek to make its contribution to Far Eastern stability via economic assistance, matching its 1% of GNP in military expenditures with 1% of GNP for foreign aid. Despite frequent conjectures about far-ranging Japanese naval patrols, in the strategic Malacca Straits area for example, the likelihood was that Japan would trust in negotiation rather than confrontation when problems arose and, if necessary, would send its merchant ships over longer circuitous routes. Concentrating on its own defense production, it was probable that Japan would be prepared cautiously to export defense-related items, particularly non-lethal equipment such as helicopters. For the time being, Japan would be likely, as it had pledged, to confine its role in UN-sponsored peacekeeping to the donation of funds and supplies, but it was hoped that a day would come when Japanese sensitivities would be surmounted and modest contingents contributed, if needed, to help keep the peace in regions other than East Asia.

Believing that Japan's superpower economic status would inevitably require a comparable military dimension if Japan were to play her destined role in world affairs, there would be vigorous young nationalists like Diet members Wataru Hiraizumi and Shintaro Ishihara who would advocate a strong and independent military establishment, not excluding a nuclear capability. Such views would appeal to the powerful sense of Japanese pride, as well as to the appetites of Japan's growing military-industrial complex, but my own judgment would be that anti-militarist sentiments would continue to prevail through the 1970's, unless there were an unexpected radical right-wing swing in Japanese domestic politics or unless Japanese rearmament were triggered by external developments which would dramatically aggravate the Japanese sense of insecurity and isolation. Such developments would include: aggressive moves by the Soviet Union or the People's Republic of China which would constitute a clear threat to Japan, moves by other nations which would imperil Japan's economic survival, the disruption of the nuclear-power balance which had tended to dampen Great Power bellicosity, or serious doubts as to the credibility of American intentions with respect to commitments under the alliance.

Even those Washington officials who might wish the assumption by the Japanese of more extensive regional security responsibilities would recognize that Japan had to make its own decisions. The policy of a prudent low military posture obviously reflected, in the early 1970's, the will of the great majority of Japanese. At the same time, by the continued upgrading of its modest forces (eighth in the world from a budget standpoint), Japan was developing an adequate capability for conventional self-defense. That in itself was an achievement and fully consonant with the Nixon Doctrine concept that other nations capable of doing so should be basically responsible for their own welfare.

Having with astonishing success achieved its immediate postwar objective of standing on its own feet, Japan in the 1970's would be groping for its role on the world stage. Its sheer economic strength would leave it no choice but to assume greater responsibilities. With a new post-postwar generation arising, the nation seemed ready and eager to gain due recognition and to display leadership internationally, but there would be hesitancy and uncertainty concerning the nature of Japan's role and its goals.

The "grand experiment" which Prime Minister Sato envisaged was for Japan to play its role as a non-military major power. The accent would be heavily on economic relationships, a field in which Japan was undeniably a world leader. In political matters, Japan would be prepared to undertake greater responsibilities, but with caution and not to the point of alarming its suspicious neighbors and potential adversaries.

The likelihood would be that Japan would keep a watchful eye on the behavior of the three other major powers with interests in East Asia and the Pacific, hoping for a further relaxation of tensions and for a sufficient equilibrium to assure peace. Toward these objectives, Japan would tailor its own relationships with those powers. Japan's ties with the United States would remain indispensable, but not as predominant as in the postwar period. The development of productive relations with the Soviet Union would be tempered by political and emotional inhibitions, but economic opportunities, as in Siberia, would be helpful. Trade and political ties between Japan and the People's Republic of China might fall short of expectations, but they should be useful in the cause of relaxing Far Eastern tensions, as well as being psychologically attractive to the Japanese as a potential alternative to excessive dependence on the United States. While not unmindful of the unaltered ideological ambitions of the Communist powers, it was entirely possible that the Japanese would see value in negotiating with both Peking and Moscow treaties of non-aggression, non-use of force, and peaceful coexistence.

Regionally, Japan's role was bound to be one of economic involvement but also one of great delicacy. There was no prospect that Japan could exercise dominant political leadership and even its economic relationships must take into more careful account the fear of its East Asian neighbors of a new attempt at Japanese hegemony. Thus, while Japan would have an important political role to play in East Asian affairs, it was likely to be, as in the 1970 Djakarta conference, in close concert with other key nations in the area such as Indonesia and Australia. Above all, Japan would wish to avoid provocation of China.

Particularly because of the precariousness of its economy, Japan would try to globalize its relationships. Industrious Japanese representatives would be operating not just in East Asia and the United States, but in Europe, the Middle East, Latin America, and Africa. The natural Japanese instinct would be for bilateral commercial relationships, but multilateral arrangements would have increasing appeal, particularly with respect to "economic cooperation." Thus, in addition to Japanese participation in established organizations such as the Asian Development Bank, GATT, and the Organization for Economic Cooperation and Development, the future might witness increased cooperation by the nations of the Pacific Basin, e.g., Japan, Canada, Australia, and the United States, as well as greater collaboration among the three great non-Communist trading communities, i.e., Japan, Europe, and the United States. On the global scene, Japan would have a genuine interest in a more effective United Nations, and would wish a seat on the Security Council. This would be a logical step, worthy of enthusiastic support by all nations including the United States.

Some foreign observers, as well as a few Japanese, would argue that the absence of a military capability commensurate with Japan's economic power status was unrealistic. They would contend that, as frequently had occurred since Meiji days, Japan's ostrich-like policies were bound to change pursuant to external stimuli, such as Chinese, Soviet, or American moves having destabilizing effects on the Far Eastern scene. It just might be, however, that the "grand experiment" might prove successful, with Japan relying on mutually beneficial economic ties, and in political matters on negotiation rather than confrontation. Moreover, it was conceivable that Japan's giant neighbors would recognize the value of avoiding destabilizing moves which might provoke a major Japanese military buildup. There could be no doubt that, if incited, Japan could technologically become a major military power in record time. If so, it would not be the first time in history that the powerful force of Japanism had undergone a drastic alteration in direction in response to external developments. Perhaps it was the specter of the possible resurgence of Japanese militarism which explained why Soviet and Chinese Communist propaganda against the American security treaty with Japan seemed during the 1970 "anti-treaty struggle" to be less shrill than it might have been.

Internally, Japan might follow up its "economic miracle" with an equivalent miracle in the improvement of the "quality of life." Externally, the "grand experiment" might miraculously succeed. However, there would remain what former Under Secretary of State George Ball described as the "baffling problem of how, in modern technological and affluent societies, we can find meaning and purpose in life beyond the mere production and acquisition of material goods and the power and status they carry with them." In Japan and the United States, Ball noted, tradition and religion had "in past ages given to human striving an essential transcendental spirit." As student restiveness in both our countries reminded us, finding "meaning and purpose" would be the ultimate challenge for Japanese leadership in the 1970's, even as it would be for American leadership.

From time immemorial, the construction of a world order allowing all men to live in peace has been as elusive as securing "meaning and purpose" in life. After World War II, any illusions about a Pax Americana were quickly shattered with the emergence of a bipolar world. With the Cuban missile crisis and the Sino-Soviet rift, bipolarism was demolished. Although smaller nations with minimal resources could throw their weight around at the United Nations and elsewhere, effective power was considered to rest with three, then four, and subsequently five major world centers. Ultimately, a safer description was "multipolar" world. Whatever the nomenclature, Tokyo and Washington would play essential roles in any emerging system.

He who throws a pebble can change the center of gravity of the earth. All nations, indeed every human pebble, can affect the course of history. Thus, rather than trying to reduce the world to a specified number of poles, my own view has been that the political universe is not unlike the celestial universe. The gravitational attraction between any two bodies, as Newton discovered, is directly proportional to their mass and inversely proportional to the square of the distance between them. Defining mass for political entities is, of course, not easy. It must be a composite of economic, military, political, demographic, moral, and other forces. It would also include the capability of exercising creative responsibility in the quest for the international equilibrium which is essential if collisions are to be avoided.

If the universe simile has any merit, Japan could expect in the 1970's, as in the past, to be subject to potent influences from each of its massive Communist neighbors upon which it would be exercising influences of its own. Between Japan and the United States, there would also be considerable gravitational attraction, with both possessing weight in world affairs. However, because of geographic distance and its exponential effect, extra effort would be required by both nations if the Japanese-American relationship were to be operable in preserving Asian-Pacific equilibrium. Such equilibrium would be critical to a prosperous Japan, as it would be to peace in the entire area.

In working together for a peaceful world, Japan and the United States would need to deal with each other with great understanding. There would no doubt be apparent conflicts of national interest and there would be the usual difficulties and sensitivities stemming from disparate cultural heritages. Between two such achievement-oriented societies there would always be problems. However, profiting from the experiences of the recent past, including the mistakes, accommodations in the 1970's should be negotiable.

For Japan, the key challenge might well be adequate

recognition of its inescapable responsibilities in world affairs. Not unrelated would be the traditional task of overcoming inward-lookingness to acknowledge that other nations also had problems which must be taken into account if satisfactory solutions to international issues were to be found. Finding those answers was clearly in Japan's long-range interest, for no nation was more dependent on profitable relations with the outside world. A crucial question would be whether political leadership in Tokyo, accustomed to the time-consuming consensus decision-making system, would be able to participate in international decision-making as expeditiously and as cooperatively as necessary.

For America, improved performance would also be required. In the enterprise of courting our adversaries to reduce world tensions, we should not take our friends and allies for granted. Their governments, which, no less than ours, depend on public support, could be undermined by unilateral and arbitrary American actions, deemed by the electorates to be incompatible with their national interests. Thus, in dealing with other nations, as well as in domestic affairs, American leadership could well take a leaf from the Japanese book on consensus-building. Tendencies toward excessive secrecy, isolated thought, insulation, and surprise, as well as shock tactics, would need reexamination. Without yielding basic American interests, a greater amount of openness and dialogue would assure more fruitful relations with those abroad who had given us their trust, as well as with the Congress, the Executive Branch as a whole, the press, and the American citizenry. In a democratic society, Congressional and public opinion, as well as the endeavors of dedicated, experienced, proficient and loyal public servants, might be tedious, but it does not follow that government would be more successful if conducted primarily through a few highly efficient intermediaries serving as a sort of palace guard. Aside from risks of undue influence by unprincipled elbow-pushers, the noisiest nearby voices, "plumbers" and other secret operatives, heavy campaign contributors and other special interest groups, insulated policy-making would tend to alienate the broad consensus of support which would be needed to achieve optimal results.

In the handling of America's international relationships, much could be said for a meaningful restoration of institutionalized diplomacy, which would mean a central role for the State Department and our Embassies. That channel, as Sato had urged, would provide a "single window." Classic negotiations, such as those employed with respect to the reversion of Okinawa, could still produce effective results, with less rancor and damage than the unorthodox textile negotiations. In international economic affairs, the centrality of the State Department should also be maintained, despite the legitimate interests and involvement of a variety of Washington agencies. During my thirty years in the Foreign Service, the coordinated conduct of our international economic relationships was never as successful as during that period when it was adroitly managed by the ranking Under Secretary of State, C. Douglas Dillon. In the accelerating world, special emissaries on economic and other matters would be necessary, but it should be axiomatic that American Ambassadors attend all conversations with the head of government of the country to which they are accredited. Quite understandably a President might prefer a tête-à-tête, but there would be no reason why at its conclusion his Secretary of State, National Security Assistant, and Ambassador, as well as their counterparts, might not be brought in for a few minutes' resumé of the discussion. In any case, Embassy and State Department officials should be kept apprised, on a "need to know" basis, of all conversations and developments involving United States government representatives and those of foreign countries. The importance of this principle was emphasized as far back as Ambassador Grew's days in Tokyo. In a postmortem analysis of pre-Pearl Harbor developments, Grew complained that he had not been kept informed of Washington's "thoughts and intentions." His own reports, he wrote, had been "like throwing pebbles into a lake at night; we were not permitted to see even the ripples." In a July 1941 telegram he had appealed to Washington, "Unless a motor is hitting on all cylinders, it cannot function effectively." That appeal, so tragically unheeded then, would be equally valid in the 1970's.

Despite the possibilities that minor unpleasantnesses might occur, inevitably distorted by the news media in both countries, an exchange of visits between the Emperor and the President was by the early 1970's overdue. The substantive accomplishments might be modest, but the goodwill could be incalculable. Meanwhile, summit meetings between the President and Japanese Prime Ministers should be continued, but Washington should realize that quick and dramatic results were not as likely to be achieved with the leadership of democratic and consensus-oriented Japan as with the leaders of totalitarian societies such as China and the Soviet Union. In addition to top-level consultations, both Tokyo and Washington would need to strengthen the broad array of consultative forums already existing. The annual joint cabinet meeting (ECONCOM) could well be supported by an active and ongoing task force, designed to identify current and upcoming economic problems and possible solutions. In the security field, the value of the Consultative Committee and the Security Sub-Committee could be reinforced through more frequent meetings, through interim informational exchanges concerning current developments, and, as Japan's Defense Agency Director General Nakasone had proposed, via intimate conversations at least once each year between the American Secretary of Defense and his Japanese counterpart.

The news media of both Japan and the United States could play a more helpful role. While Japanese newspaper readers found daily reports on the front pages about developments in the United States, Americans learned only intermittently about developments in Japan. In preparing this report, examination of the three-year file of *The New York Times* confirmed not only the relative paucity of Japanese news coverage, but the tendency toward the offbeat and the sensational, such as extensive coverage of Yukio Mishima's hara-kiri with the impression that all of Japan was returning to a medieval mentality. In the press, in the academic field, in the broad spectrum of dialogue between the American and the Japanese people there was much room for improvement.

During the 1969–1972 period, despite successes like the reversion of Okinawa, the failure of the "anti-treaty struggle," and the spectacular American moon landings, America's image in Japan was buffeted. The agonizing frustrations in Vietnam, coupled with troubles on the American home front such as Kent State, racial tensions, economic reverses, and political self-flagellation, caused many Japanese, including our best friends, to be concerned that America was "over the hill." The China and economic shocks did nothing to shore up trust in the United States. The Nixon Doctrine was welcomed but at the same time raised suspicions that America might be retreating to some sort of neo-isolationism. Questions were being asked as to America's reliability. For example, would there be a nuclear response by the United States, risking its own cities, if a hostile power should unleash a medium-range missile nuclear assault on Japan's highly vulnerable metropolitan complexes? What was at stake in such questions was not only America's competence but its good name. Both had been pivotal in the orientation of Japan's postwar policies.

The fact was that just as Japan was searching for its new role in the 1970's so was the United States. The challenge for Americans would be to convince our friends such as the Japanese: 1) that American military and economic strength would remain second to none; 2) that, rather than retreating to isolationism, the United States would without question assume its appropriate responsibilities in world affairs; 3) that in a world with unprecedented capabilities for self-annihilation, the United States shared with Japan and all nations a vested interest in reduced tensions, depolarization, and negotiation rather than confrontation; 4) that a new international equilibrium conducive to peace was attainable; 5) that in the new equilibrium, economic power, such as that of Japan, could play a critical role; and 6) that in resolving bilateral problems and working together for a peaceful world, the United States would be firm but also worthy of Japan's trust.

In searching for their respective roles, both Japan and the United States would find neither safety nor complete satisfaction in either military or economic strength. Such strengths were not to be ignored, but more important would be those forces which George Ball had identified as giving "meaning and purpose" to human endeavor.

In Japan, as at every post at which I served, no American name was more revered than that of a lanky Illinois railsplitter who had been born in a log cabin, who had avowed, "I will study and prepare myself and some day my chance will come," who perused borrowed law books by candlelight, who experienced many hardships but by dint of hard work rose steadily up the ladder, and into whose care his nation's fate was entrusted in its darkest hour. His idea of democracy was, "As I would not be a slave, so I would not be a master." With George Washington, he believed that honesty is always the best policy. In being "tough," he yielded to no one, but his firmness in striving for the right was qualified by "as God gives us to see the right" and was enriched by "malice toward none and charity for all." Through all vicissitudes, he maintained humility and a legendary sense of humor. Succeeding generations would be inspired by his faith in the imperishability of "government of the people, by the people and for the people." He was convinced that his own country's "grand experiment" would give hope that burdens would one day be lifted from the shoulders of all mankind.

These Lincolnesque qualities are the wellsprings of America's greatness. After thirty years in our nation's service, they still offer, in my judgment, the best hope for recapturing "meaning and purpose," as well as mutual trust, in our relations with Japan, and with all the masses and pebbles on our planet.

Acknowledgments

"If we could first know where we are, and whither we are tending, we could better judge what to do and how to do it." With that Lincolnian precept as motivation, this account of the 1969–1972 period in Japanese-American relations was written. It is my hope that the endeavor will contribute to improved performance by those on both sides of the Pacific to whom responsibility for the relationship is entrusted. This objective includes assuring an appropriate role for our Embassy in Tokyo and those elsewhere. It is also my hope that a contribution will be made toward awakening greater public interest in the gravity and delicacy of America's relationship with Asia's foremost power. The partnership cannot be taken for granted.

Since the account is a report on operations and perspectives rather than an analysis of foreign policy doctrine, such value as may accrue from its telling (as against its shortcomings) must be shared with all those who participated in the drama.

[375

On the Japanese side, the list would, of course, be headed by Foreign Minister Kiichi Aichi, his successor Takeo Fukuda, and their superiors, the Emperor and Prime Minister Sato. Included would be friends and associates throughout the Japanese government, especially in the "Gaimusho" (Foreign Ministry), and those in the business, journalistic, intellectual, recreational and other non-governmental communities. In checking Japanese names and other data for the manuscript, I am in debt particularly to Teruo Kosugi and Kinji Kawamura.

Among those with whom my Tokyo experiences were shared, and who helped educate this neophyte in Far Eastern affairs, to none am I more deeply indebted than to my colleagues, Japanese and American, at the Embassy. One regret in writing this book was not being able to salute each one by name, an omission inadequately remedied by the appended list of staff-level American teammates (Appendix A). Other valued contributors to my education were American newsmen, businessmen and professors, and my fellow diplomats. The Arabs have a relevant proverb: "A student can be no better than his teacher."

Dean Acheson once remarked that he had never read a memorandum of conversation where the author came out second best. For reducing the percentage of distortion and error, I owe much to a number of friends who stoically but cheerfully agreed to peruse the manuscript while it was being written. Their suggestions invariably rendered the narrative more valid and interesting. Despite his manifold preoccupations, former Ambassador Edwin Reischauer, by coping with the entire manuscript and providing the Foreword, demonstrated once again that he will spare no effort in behalf of our partnership with Japan. I am also grateful to Kei Wakaizumi, Robert Barnett and Donald Shannon, all of whom struggled through the complete text, and to others who assisted on chapters which involved their special interests. The latter group of noble souls included Philip Trezise, Major General Richard Lee, Robert Fearey, Howard Meyers, William Cunninghan, and Francis McNeil. The faithful James Wickel once again permitted me to draw from his storehouse of Japan lore. Needless to say, any errors of fact or of interpretation that remain are my own responsibility.

The brunt of the stresses and strains which accompany authorship falls, of course, on one's family. It was my good fortune to enjoy a domestic environment replete with patience and understanding, plus two exceptional bonuses: sound editorial advice from my wife, Alice, based on her many years of experience on the staffs of Washington newspapers, and the expeditious typing of the manuscript by our daughter, Kathy. A word of appreciation is also due Naima Challita, who as a member of our family has for more than two decades nourished us with the loyalty and resourcefulness which are so characteristic of her native Lebanon.

These acknowledgments would be incomplete if I did not register heartfelt appreciation for being honored with the opportunity to serve my country in its Foreign Service for three decades, culminating in the assignment in Tokyo. To our nation's leadership and to my associates in the Department of State I am eternally in debt. Our country may have its problems, but the ideals for which it stands have never dimmed in luster. I am sure that for no diplomatic representative abroad does the heart swell with pride to the extent that it does for an American Ambassador when, at such occasions on foreign soil as Expo 70 or the Sapporo Winter Olympics, he hears the strains of his country's anthem and sees its emblem unfurling in the sky.

Appendix A

United States Mission to Japan
1969–1972

Front Office. Deputy Chiefs of Mission David Osborn and Richard Sneider, Florence Neverman, James Wickel, Patricia Wazer, Jane Williams, Richard Smith, Stephen Ecton, Carol Moor, Joyce Anderson, Stella Morimoto.

Political Section. Chiefs Richard Ericson and William Sherman, Anthony Arnold, David Brown, Rodney Carlson, George Coale, William Cunningham, John Dayton, Robert Duemling, Thomas Hubbard, Robert Immerman, Joseph Leahy, Herbert Levin, Francis McNeil, Roy Mlynarchik, Robert Ruenitz, Joseph Smith, Gerald Sutton.

Political-Military Affairs Section. Chiefs Scott George and Howard Meyers, Stephen Dawkins, Edward Juchniewicz, James Kelly, Tadao Kobayashi, William Mulligan, Blaine Porter, Harry Slifer, William Wells.

Economic-Commercial Section. Chiefs Herman Barger and Lester Edmond, John Shaw, Oliver Bongard, Peter Lande,

Thomas Stave, James Baker, David Burns, Herbert Cochran, James Delaney, Martha DeWitt, Edward Dubel, George Durgan, Larry Dutton, Michael Goldman, John Gregory, George Knox, John Lloyd, Wyatt Martin, William McRory, Thomas Parker, William Polik, Wilson Riley, Roger Severance, Charles Taber, Bradley Tyrrell, Warren Wagner.

Consular Section. Chiefs Ronald Gaiduk and Thomas Murfin, Florence Adamson, Thomas Cummings, Frances Howell, Lawrence Kujubu, Eric Lindahl, Richard Mann, William Mucci, Alfred Neal, Kiyonao Okami, Don Picard, Norman Singer, Olga Zhivkovitch, Richard Zorn.

Administrative Section. Chiefs Robert Peck and Daniel Williamson, Charles Falkner, Kathryn Groot, Robert Wenk, Robert Bell, Joseph Bezjian, Richard Bodkin, Hypolite Breard, Norman Cansler, Martha Carter, James Cavanaugh, Marvin Chindgren, Robert Davis, Sherman Euler, Donald Field, John Fincher, William Grevencamp, John Grigassy, William Holda, Herbert Klee, Joseph Kozlowski, Charles LeMasters, Robert Littell, William Murphy, Mary Peterson, John Ratliff, Robert Sandberg, Harriet Seiberling, Gary Smith, Helen Spurrier, Mary Van Horn, Bernard Woerz, Ira Wolf, Ida Wright, two nursing gems Mary McGraw and Arlyne Heerlein, and the always faithful Marine Guard detachment.

USIA. Chiefs Edward Roberts and Alan Carter, David Hitchcock, Dr. James Morley, Dr. James Hoyt, Francis Donovan, Dennis Askey, Myron Baskin, Bryan Battey, Melvin Cariaga, Robert Chancellor, Donn Chown, Nicholas Conduras, James Crane, Karl Dixon, Edward Findlay, Thomas Finnerty, Clifton Forster, Robert Fulton, Henry Gosho, Michael Haller, Donald Hausrath, Richard Hughes, Robert Kays, William Keogh, Ray Komai, Duane King, William Lenderking, Stuart Lillico, Theodore Liu, George Louden, Michael Love, John McDonald, Paul Modic, Richard Moore, Walter Nichols, Sen Nishiyama, Warren Obluck, Roy Payne, Douglas Pike, Phillip Powell, Dorothy Robins, Harlan Rosacker, Sanders Rosenblum, Jonathan Silverman, Norris Smith, Hart Sprager, Norman Tolman, Shirow Uyeno, Kurt Wenzel, Harold Wright.

Defense Attachés. Chiefs Captain Lawrence Kurtz and Captain Wilton Atkinson, Col. Richard Leech, Col. Robert Fromm, Col. Fred Swafford, Lt. Col. Andrew Roach, Lt. Col. Henry Wall, Lt. Col. James Link, Commander Alan Bath.

Other Attachés and Agency Representatives. Agriculture: Elmer Hallowell, Theodore Freeman, Alvin Gourley, Alan Hemphill, Leon Mears, Gordon Nicks and Wilferd Phillipson. Atomic Bomb Casualty Commission: Dr. George Darling (Hiroshima) and Dr. Isamu Nagai (Nagasaki). Atomic Energy Commission: Gerard Helfrich and Eli Goodman. Bonneville Power Administration: Peter Iijima. Bureau of Narcotics and Dangerous Drugs: Michael Picini, Russ Aruslan and Wallace Tanaka. Customs: Steve Minas, Jerry Kane, George Morita, Kenneth Stine, Drexel Watson and Thomas Yasueda. Federal Aviation Administration: William Cunningham, John Calon, Charles Hershelman, George Nakamura, Gus Simonton. Federal Bureau of Investigation: Harold Child. Foreign Broadcast Information Service: John Thorn, Stephen McLean, David Shank, Larry Williams. Fisheries: Clinton Atkinson. Geographic Attaché: John Bradley. Immigration and Naturalization Service: Dorris Yarbrough. Internal Revenue Service: Richard Reynolds and Ronald Shaffer. Labor Attaché: Howard Robinson, Herbert Ihrig and Louis Silverberg. Library of Congress: Hisao Matsumoto. Maritime Administration: Martin Stevenson. Mutual Defense Assistance: Col. Richard Stoddard, Lt. Col. Edmund Hartenberger, Lt. Col. John Lindley, Lt. Col. John Willis, Lt. Cmdr. Charles Gertner. National Science Foundation: Henry Birnbaum and Arthur Findeis. Bureau of Reclamation: Charles Kempter. Science Attaché: Robert Hiatt, Robert Webber, William Littlewood. U.S. Trade Center: Edward Simmons and Paul Leinenbach. U.S. Travel Service: Fritz Schmidt. U.S. Dept of Treasury: Schubert Dyche and Wilbur Monroe.

Consulates. Osaka-Kobe: Chiefs William Sherman and Jerome Holloway, Norman Achilles, Rodney Armstrong, Albert Ball, Charles Bass, Maurice Brooks, Edward Beidleman, Rust Deming, Betsy Fitzgerald, Robert Gately, Doyle Gentry, Dorothy George, Sidney Hamolsky, John Malott, Muneo Sakaue, Harris Woods. Sapporo: Chiefs Martin Heflin and Sunao Sakamoto, Robert Flershem, Jon Gibney, Robert Leete, Robert Petersen. Fukuoka: Chiefs Gerald Sutton and James Ashida, Robin Berrington, Karl Richardson, Paul Wisgerhof. Nagoya: Albert Noonan, Peter Pease.

Okinawa. Robert Fearey (Civil Administrator), Eddie Schodt (Advisory Commission), John Knowles (Political Advisor). Consular officers: Clyde Snider, Robert Peterson, William Nikolin, Frank Hagen.

Okinawa Negotiating Team. Chief Richard Sneider, Howard Meyers, Charles Schmitz, Larry Dutton, Dalton Killion. Military Representatives: Vice Admiral Walter Curtis, Col. John Walters, Col. Griffin Moody, Capt. Franklyn Barker, Lt. John Fitzgerald.

U.S. Forces Japan. Commanders (USAF): Lieut. Gen. Thomas McGehee and Lieut. Gen. Gordon Graham. Deputy Commanders (Army): Maj. Gen. Wesley Franklin and Maj. Gen. Richard Lee. Army Command: Maj. Gen. John Goshorn, Brig. Gen. Hugh Richeson, and Brig. Gen. Ross Condit. Navy Command: Rear Admiral Daniel Smith and Rear Admiral Julian Burke.

Index